John Henry Newman, William John Copeland

Sermons Bearing on Subjects of the Day

John Henry Newman, William John Copeland

Sermons Bearing on Subjects of the Day

ISBN/EAN: 9783744743327

Printed in Europe, USA, Canada, Australia, Japan

Cover: Foto ©Lupo / pixelio.de

More available books at **www.hansebooks.com**

CARDINAL NEWMAN'S WORKS.

SERMONS.

PAROCHIAL and PLAIN SERMONS. Edited by the Rev. W. J. COPELAND, B.D., late Rector of Farnham, Essex. 8 vols. Cabinet Edition. Crown 8vo, 5s. each. Popular Edition. 8 vols. Crown 8vo. 3s. 6d. each.

SELECTION, adapted to the SEASONS of the ECCLESIASTICAL YEAR, from the 'Parochial and Plain Sermons.' Edited by the Rev. W. J. COPELAND, B.D., late Rector of Farnham, Essex. Crown 8vo. 5s.

FIFTEEN SERMONS PREACHED before the UNIVERSITY of OXFORD, between A.D. 1826 and 1843. Crown 8vo. 5s.

SERMONS BEARING upon SUBJECTS of the DAY. Edited by the Rev. W. J. COPELAND, B.D., late Rector of Farnham, Essex. Crown 8vo. 5s.

DISCOURSES ADDRESSED to MIXED CONGREGATIONS. Crown 8vo. 6s.

SERMONS PREACHED on VARIOUS OCCASIONS. Crown 8vo. 6s.

TREATISES.

LECTURES on the DOCTRINE of JUSTIFICATION. Crown 8vo. 5s.

An ESSAY on the DEVELOPMENT of CHRISTIAN DOCTRINE. Cabinet Edition. Crown 8vo. 6s. Cheap Edition. Crown 8vo. 3s. 6d.

The IDEA of a UNIVERSITY DEFINED and ILLUSTRATED. Crown 8vo. 7s.

An ESSAY in AID of a GRAMMAR of ASSENT. Cabinet Edition. Crown 8vo. 7s. 6d. Cheap Edition. Crown 8vo. 3s. 6d.

POLEMICAL.

The VIA MEDIA of the ANGLICAN CHURCH. Illustrated in Lectures, Letters, and Tracts, written between 1830 and 1841. With Notes. 2 vols. Crown 8vo. 6s. each. Vol. I. Prophetical Office of the Church. Vol. II. Occasional Letters and Tracts.

CERTAIN DIFFICULTIES FELT by ANGLICANS in CATHOLIC TEACHING CONSIDERED. (2 vols.) Vol. I. Twelve Lectures. Crown 8vo. 7s. 6d. Vol. II. Letters to Dr. Pusey concerning the Blessed Virgin, and to the Duke of Norfolk in Defence of the Pope and Council. Crown 8vo. 5s. 6d.

PRESENT POSITION of CATHOLICS in ENGLAND. Crown 8vo. 7s. 6d.

APOLOGIA PRO VITA SUA. Cabinet Edition. Crown 8vo. 6s. Cheap Edition. Crown 8vo. 3s. 6d.

LONDON : LONGMANS, GREEN, & CO.

ESSAYS.

ESSAYS on BIBLICAL and on ECCLESIASTICAL MIRACLES.
Cabinet Edition. Crown 8vo. 6s. Cheap Edition. Crown 8vo. 3s. 6d.

DISCUSSIONS and ARGUMENTS on VARIOUS SUBJECTS.
Cabinet Edition. Crown 8vo. 6s. Cheap Edition. Crown 8vo. 3s. 6d.

CONTENTS.—1. How to accomplish it. 2. The Antichrist of the Fathers.
3. Scripture and the Creed. 4. Tamworth Reading Room. 5. Who's to Blame?
6. An Argument for Christianity.

ESSAYS CRITICAL and HISTORICAL. Cabinet Edition. 2
vols. Crown 8vo. 12s. Cheap Edition. 2 vols. Crown 8vo. 7s.

CONTENTS.—1. Poetry. 2. Rationalism. 3. Apostolical Tradition. 4. De la
Mennais. 5. Palmer on Faith and Unity. 6. St. Ignatius. 7. Prospects of the
Anglican Church. 8. The Anglo-American Church. 9. Countess of Huntingdon.
10. Catholicity of the Anglican Church. 11. The Antichrist of Protestants. 12.
Milman's Christianity. 13. Reformation of the Eleventh Century. 14. Private
Judgment. 15. Davison. 16. Keble.

HISTORICAL.

HISTORICAL SKETCHES. 3 vols. Crown 8vo. 6s. each.

CONTENTS.—1. The Turks. 2. Cicero. 3. Apollonius. 4. Primitive
Christianity. 5. Church of the Fathers. 6. St. Chrysostom. 7. Theodoret.
8. St. Benedict. 9. Benedictine Schools. 10. Universities. 11. Northmen and
Normans. 12. Medieval Oxford. 13. Convocation of Canterbury.

THEOLOGICAL.

The ARIANS of the FOURTH CENTURY. Cabinet Edition.
Crown 8vo. 6s. Cheap Edition. Crown 8vo. 3s. 6d.

SELECT TREATISES of ST. ATHANASIUS in CONTRO-
VERSY with the ARIANS. Freely Translated. 2 vols. Crown 8vo. 15s.

THEOLOGICAL TRACTS. Crown 8vo. 8s.

CONTENTS.—1. Dissertatiunculæ. 2. On the Text of the Seven Epistles of St.
Ignatius. 3. Doctrinal Causes of Arianism. 4. Apollinarianism. 5. St. Cyril's
Formula. 6. Ordo de Tempore. 7. Douay Version of Scripture.

LITERARY.

VERSES on VARIOUS OCCASIONS. Cabinet Edition. Crown
8vo. 6s. Cheap Edition. Crown 8vo. 3s. 6d.

LOSS and GAIN : The Story of a Convert. Crown 8vo. 6s.

CALLISTA : a Tale of the Third Century. Cabinet Edition.
Crown 8vo. 6s. Cheap Edition. Crown 8vo. 3s. 6d.

The DREAM of GERONTIUS. 16mo. 6d. sewed; 1s. cloth.

LONDON: LONGMANS, GREEN, & CO.

SERMONS

BEARING ON

SUBJECTS OF THE DAY

ST. MARY THE VIRGIN CHURCH.
OXFORD.

SERMONS

BEARING ON

SUBJECTS OF THE DAY

By JOHN HENRY NEWMAN, B.D.

NEW EDITION

LONDON
LONGMANS, GREEN, AND CO.
AND NEW YORK: 15 EAST 16TH STREET
1891

PREFACE.

ON the republication of the present Volume of Sermons in answer to an extensive demand for it, it is well, on behalf both of the Author and of the Editor, to remind the reader of its special characteristic, as separate and distinguished from the volumes republished under the title of " PAROCHIAL AND PLAIN SERMONS."

Of the epithet " PLAIN," indeed, it may be here mentioned, by the way, that the Author always from the first publication of the series so called by its Editors, entertained a doubt whether it had been well chosen, as being, if not in itself inappropriate, yet certainly inapplicable to some of those Sermons which he himself, as well as others contributed to it.

A volume, however, entitled " Sermons on Subjects of the Day," warns the reader by its very title that these Sermons are to be read and understood mainly with reference to their direct or indirect bearing on the occasion and circumstances of their first publication. They have necessarily an historical and controversial aspect, though most of them treat of matters of deep and unfailing interest, and of vast practical importance.

The Advertisement, therefore, and the Notes, which call attention to the peculiarities of this volume, which are pointed out at some length in the Appendix, Note C. of the Author's " History of his Religious Opinions," are retained in this Edition.

In compliance with a wish expressed by various persons for the dates of all the Sermons, two lists of the whole number published, including those in this volume, are appended to it: the one an index of the Sermons in the order in which they stand in the several volumes, with the record of their dates; the other a chronological index of the dates, with references to the Sermons.

It will be seen from this document that some of the Sermons have been re-written—by which word where it occurs it is meant that the *first* Edition of the printed Sermon was " re-written " from the MS. as preached on the day assigned. Thus Vol. III. Sermon I. was printed as it was preached, on July 19, 1829 ; but Sermon II. in the volume was not printed in 1836 as preached on May 9, 1830, but " re-written " for the purpose of printing : others again, in like manner, have been enlarged, or expanded into two, or altered from the original MS. for the first Edition ; and instances may be found, here and there, where a Sermon written for one season has been adapted to another.

In subsequent editions up to the end of 1845, as there are no doubt various differences observable, which are not here specified, most of them only literary, some few doctrinal, it may be here stated, once for all, that the Author was accustomed to correct and retouch the successive editions very carefully; and it may be safely asserted that the variations which are to be found in intermediate editions are such as not to detract from the integrity, but rather to enhance the value of the document here supplied.

In Vol. II. Sermon II., for St. Thomas' Day, there is an addition, and in Sermon XXXI., for St. Simon and St. Jude, an alteration, in the last compared with the first Editions, of sufficient length and importance to be noticed here. And in Vol. II. p. 142, "miraculous" has been substituted, with the Author's approbation, for "immaculate," written by a mistake, which he has also made in a note on the translation of the TREATISES of ST. ATHANASIUS (p. 241). Also, in the present volume (p. 28), the clause "in His own words" has been inserted, to meet a criticism of Mr. Keble's at the time of its first publication.

It may be interesting to the reader to know that the text (Ps. civ. 23) which stands at the head both of the first (itself a recent one) and the last Sermon in this volume, was the text of the Author's first Sermon in 1824, when he went "forth to his work and to his labour," and of his last in 1843, when "the evening" was come.

W. J. COPELAND.

FARNHAM RECTORY, ESSEX,
November 22nd, 1869.

TO

WILLIAM JOHN COPELAND, B.D.

FELLOW OF TRINITY COLLEGE, OXFORD

THE KINDEST OF FRIENDS

WHOSE NATURE IT IS

TO FEEL FOR OTHERS MORE

THAN THEY FEEL FOR THEMSELVES

This Volume

IS AFFECTIONATELY INSCRIBED

ADVERTISEMENT.

THE Sermons which follow were all preached in the Author's late Parish; but in preparing them for publication, a few words or sentences have in several places been added, which will be found to express more of private or personal opinion, than it was expedient to introduce into the instruction delivered in Church to a parochial congregation. Such introduction, however, seems unobjectionable, in the case of compositions which are detached from the sacred place and service to which they once belonged, and submitted to the reason and judgment of the general reader.

LITTLEMORE,
November 25th, 1843.

CONTENTS.

b

Contents.

SERMON XVI.

The Christian Church an Imperial Power.

PAGE

"*And it shall come to pass in the last days, that the mountain of the Lord's house shall be established in the top of the mountains, and shall be exalted above the hills; and all nations shall flow unto it.*"—ISAIAH ii. 2 218

SERMON XVII.

Sanctity the Token of the Christian Empire.

"*With righteousness shall He judge the poor, and reprove with equity for the meek of the earth; and He shall smite the earth with the rod of His mouth, and with the breath of His lips shall He slay the wicked.*"—ISAIAH xi. 4 237

SERMON XVIII.

Condition of the Members of the Christian Empire.

"*Lord, Thou hast heard the desire of the poor; Thou preparest their heart, and Thine ear hearkeneth thereto; to help the fatherless and poor unto their right, that the man of the earth be no more exalted against them.*"—PSALM x. 19, 20 . . 256

SERMON XIX.

The Apostolical Christian.

"*Know ye not, that they which run in a race run all, but one receiveth the prize? so run, that ye may obtain.*"—1 COR-INTHIANS ix. 24 275

SERMON I.

𝔗𝔥𝔢 𝔚𝔬𝔯𝔨 𝔬𝔣 𝔱𝔥𝔢 𝔆𝔥𝔯𝔦𝔰𝔱𝔦𝔞𝔫.

(SEPTUAGESIMA.)

' Man goeth forth unto his work and to his labour until the evening."
—Ps. civ. 23.

THOUGH God created the heavens and the earth in six days, and then rested, yet He rested only to begin a work of another kind; for our Lord says, "My Father worketh hitherto[1]," and He adds, "and I work." And at another time He says, concerning Himself more expressly, "I must work the works of Him that sent Me, while it is day: the night cometh, when no man can work[2]." And when that night came, He said, "I have finished the work which Thou gavest Me to do." "It is finished[3]." And in the text we are told generally of all men, "Man goeth forth unto his work and to his labour until the evening." The Creator wrought till the Sabbath came; the Redeemer wrought till the sun was darkened, and it was night. "The sun ariseth," and "man goeth forth," and works "till the evening;" when "the keepers of the house tremble, and the strong men

---

[1] John v. 17.   [2] John ix. 4.   [3] John xvii. 4; xix. 30.

[S. D.]   B

bow themselves, and those that look out at the windows are darkened, and desire fails, because man goeth to his long home, and the mourners go about the streets ·" when "the silver cord is loosed, and the golden bowl is broken, and the dust returns to the earth as it was, and the spirit returns unto God who gave it[1]." In the evening man returns to God, and his works, whether good or whether evil, "do follow him."

This solemn truth, that we are sent here to do a work, is in various ways set before us in the Service appointed for this day. First, we read, in the beginning of Genesis, of Almighty God's work in the creation of the world, which is the archetype of all works which His creatures are able to do through His grace unto His glory. Then we read of Adam, placed in Paradise, the garden in Eden, "to dress it and to keep it[2]." Soon, alas, did he fall, and become subject to heavier toil, the earth being cursed for his sake, and bringing forth unto him thorns and thistles. God, however, in His mercy, did not desert him; and, accordingly, we read in the Gospel of the householder going out from morning till evening "to hire labourers into His vineyard[3]." He went out early, and then about the third hour, and about the sixth and ninth, nor stopped till the eleventh. Such were His dealings with the race of man till the fulness of time was come, and in the last days, even at the eleventh hour, He sent His Son to gather together labourers for His work from all parts of the earth. And the history of those fresh Gospel labourers is presented to us in to-day's Epistle, in the pattern of St. Paul, who "went a war-

---

[1] Eccles. xii. 3—7.　　　[2] Gen. ii. 15.　　　[3] Matt. xx. 1.

fare¹;" who planted a vineyard; who ploughed, and thrashed, and trod out the corn; for necessity was laid upon him, and it was woe unto him if he preached not the Gospel. Nay, moreover, who kept under his body, and brought it into subjection, lest after he had preached to others, the end should come, and he should be a cast-away.

Thus the Service for this day carries us from the creation of all things to the judgment, and that with this one thought—the work which is put upon us to do. Adam had to dress paradise; fallen man to " eat bread " from the blighted ground " in the sweat of his face ;" the labourers worked in the vineyard, some through the " heat of the day," others in the eventide; and the Apostles and their followers ploughed, and sowed, and planted, in a different field, but still in their Master's service, as it was at the beginning. Thus the lesson put before us to-day contrasts with that of the Epiphany. We have ended the feast of grace, and are now come to the work-days, and therefore we read of man going forth to his work and to his labour from sun-rising unto the evening. Or we may connect these two seasons with Lent, which is to follow; and whereas our Lord, in His Sermon on the Mount, speaks of three great duties of religion, prayer, almsgiving, and fasting—our duties towards God, our neighbour, and ourselves—we may consider the Epiphany to remind us of worship in the temple, Septuagesima of good works, and Lent of self-denial and self-discipline.

Now the lesson set before us to-day needs insisting on,

¹ 1 Cor. ix. 7.

because in these latter times men have arisen, speaking heresy, making much of the free grace of the Gospel, but denying that it enjoined a work, as well as conferred a blessing; or, rather, that it gave grace in order that it might enjoin a work. Christmas comes first, and Septuagesima afterwards: we must have grace before we work, in order to work; but as surely as grace is conferred on us, so surely is a work enjoined. It has been pretended by these teachers that works were only required under the Law, and grace comes instead under the Gospel: but the true account of the matter is this, that the Law enjoined works, and the grace of the Gospel fulfils them; the Law commanded, but gave no power; the Gospel bestows the power. Thus the Gospel is the counterpart of the Law. Christ says, " I am not come to destroy, but to fulfil." The Gospel does not abrogate works, but provides for them. " Man goeth forth unto his work and to his labour " from the morning of the world to its evening. All dispensations are one and the same here. Adam in paradise, Adam fallen, Noah in the morning, Abraham at the third hour, the chosen people at the sixth and ninth, and Christians at the eleventh—all, so far as the duty of work, have one religion.

And thus, says St. Paul, " Do we then make void the law through faith? God forbid. Yea, we establish the law[1]." Again, he tells us, " that as sin hath reigned unto death, even so " grace reigns " *through* righteousness," not without righteousness, " unto eternal life." And again, " The righteousness of the law is *fulfilled* in us, who walk not after the flesh, but after the Spirit."

[1] Rom. iii. 31.

And to the Ephesians, "We are His workmanship, created in Christ Jesus unto good works[1]." And to the Philippians, "Work out your own salvation with fear and trembling; for it is God which worketh in you, both to will and to do, of His good pleasure[2]."

But here an objection may be drawn from the parable of the labourers which requires notice. It may be said that the labourers, who represent the Jews, complain that those who were called in the evening, that is, Christians, had worked but a short time, and in the cool of the day. "They murmured against the good-man of the house, saying, These last have wrought but one hour, and Thou hast made them equal unto us which have borne the burden and heat of the day." Hence it may be argued, that Christians have no irksome or continued toil, but are saved, without their trouble, by grace. Now it is true, we are of those who have been called when the day was drawing to an end; but this neither proves that we have a slight task to do, nor a short time to labour, as a few words will show.

For what is meant by "the burden and heat of the day"? I have explained it already. It means that religion pressed heavily on the Jews as a burden, because they were unequal to it; and it was as the midday heat, overpowering them with its intensity, because they had no protection against it. "The sun," says the Psalmist, "goeth forth from the uttermost part of the heaven, and runneth about unto the end of it again, and there is nothing hid from the heat thereof." And

---

[1] Eph. ii. 10.   [2] Phil. ii. 12, 13.

he continues, " The law of the Lord is an undefiled law, converting the soul; the testimony of the Lord is sure, and giveth wisdom unto the simple [1]." What is so bright and glorious as the sun? yet what so overpowering to the feeble? What so pure and keen as the law of the Lord? yet what so searching and awful to the sinner? " The word of God," says the Apostle, " is quick and powerful, and sharper than any two-edged sword [2];" and therefore it did but probe and wound those who were unprepared for it, and they could but cry out, " O, wretched man that I am, who shall deliver me from the body of this death [3]?" This was the burden and heat of the day: to have a perfect law, and an unregenerate heart; the thunders of Sinai, yet the sovereignty of the flesh; Moses with the tables of stone, and the people setting up the golden calf. At best they could but confess, " The law is spiritual, but I am carnal, sold under sin; for that which I do, I allow not: for what I would, that do I not; but what I hate, that do I." But for us, on the other hand, Christ hath redeemed us from the burden and heat, and the curse of the law, by being made a curse for us; and we henceforth may say, with the Apostle, " What things were gain to me, those I counted loss' for Christ; . . . not as though I had already attained, either were already perfect; but this one thing I do, forgetting those things which are behind, and reaching forth unto those things which are before, I press toward the mark, for the prize of the high calling of God in Christ Jesus [4]."

[1] Ps. xix. 6, 7.   [2] Heb. iv. 12.   [3] Rom. vii. 14—24.   [4] Phil. iii. 7—14.

Do you wish to see how little the Christian is saved from toil by his being saved from "the burden and heat of the day?" consider the Epistle for this Sunday, and the whole chapter of which it is part. It is one of those passages in which St. Paul speaks of himself and his brother labourers in the vineyard; and from this instance you will be able to decide how little Christ has saved those whom He loves from toil and trouble. Christ, we know, is the second Adam, and has restored us to a better paradise. He, for that river which divided into four heads and watered the garden, has given us " a pure river of water of life, clear as crystal, proceeding out of the throne of God and of the Lamb;" and for "every tree of the garden" of which Adam might eat freely, has He given "the tree of life, which beareth twelve manner of fruits, and yieldeth her fruit every month, and the leaves of the tree are for the healing of the nations [1]." Yet compare the state of Adam in the second chapter of Genesis with that of St. Paul in the ninth chapter of his first Epistle to the Corinthians, and it will be plain that our blessedness under the Gospel is not the removal of labour, but the gift of strength; that the original paradise is not yet restored to us with its repose and security, and that our duties still are not those of Adam innocent, but of Adam fallen.

Adam, for instance, was surrounded by his subject brutes, but had no duties towards them; he was lord of the creation, and they ministered to him. God Almighty brought them to him, and he gave them names; and he was free to accept their homage, or to dispense

[1] Rev. xxii. 1, 2.

with it, as pleased him, ranging through the trees of the garden at his will. But what says the blessed Apostle? He makes himself one of those who are even like the brute ox that treadeth out the corn, and only claims that their mouths be not muzzled, but their hire secured to them. He speaks of himself as an Apostle, or one sent unto his brethren; as ministering about holy things; as having necessity laid upon him; and as making himself " servant unto all, that he might gain the more." " And unto the Jews," he says, " I became as a Jew, that I might gain the Jews; to them that are under the law as under the law, that I might gain them that are under the law; to them that are without law, as without law, . . . that I might gain them that are without law. To the weak became I as weak, that I might gain the weak: I am made all things to all men, that I might by all means save some." And Adam, though in a state of quiet and contemplation, was not solitary; for when there was no help meet for him, " the Lord God caused a deep sleep to fall on Adam, and he slept; and He took one of his ribs, and closed up the flesh instead thereof; and the rib which the Lord God had taken from man, made He a woman, and brought her unto the man." But St. Paul tells us that he reversed in his own case this ordinance of God. " Mine answer to them which do examine me is this, Have we not power to eat and to drink? Have we not power to lead about a sister, a wife, as well as other Apostles, and as the brethren of the Lord, and Cephas?" He might have been as Adam, and he would not be. And Adam's task was to dress the garden, no heavy labour in Eden;

to subdue the ground, which needed not much discipline, but obeyed without effort. But what was St. Paul's culture? what was the ground on which he worked? and did he treat it gently, or was he severe with it, to bring it into subjection? Did he indulge in its flowers and fruits, or did he watch against thorns and thistles, and subjugate it in the sweat of his brow? Hear his own account of it: " Every man that striveth for the mastery is temperate in all things: now they do it to obtain a corruptible crown, but we an incorruptible. I therefore so run, not as uncertainly; so fight I, not as one that beateth the air: but I keep under my body, and bring it into subjection: lest that by any means, when I have preached to others, I myself should be a castaway." It cannot be said, then, because we have not to bear the burden and the heat of the day, that therefore we have returned to paradise. It is not that our work is lighter, but our strength is greater.

Nor, secondly, can we argue that our work is shorter from the labourers' complaint, " These have wrought but one hour." For we are called, as is evident, in the world's evening, not in our own. We are called in our own morning, we are called from infancy. By the eleventh hour is not meant that Christians have little to do, but that the time is short; that it is the last time; that there is a " present distress ;" that they have much to do in a little time ; that " the night cometh when no man can work ;" that their Lord is at hand, and that they have to wait for Him. " This I say, brethren," says St. Paul, " the time is short; it remaineth that both they that have wives be as though they had none ;

and they that weep, as though they wept not; and they that rejoice, as though they rejoiced not; and they that buy, as though they possessed not; and they that use this world, as not abusing it, for the fashion of this world passeth away[1]." It was otherwise with the Jews; they had a grant of this world; they entered the vineyard in the morning; they had time before them; they might reckon on the future. They were bid " go their way, eat their bread with joy, and drink their wine with a merry heart, and let their garments be always white, and let their head lack no ointment, and live joyfully with the wife whom they loved all the days of the life of their vanity: . . . for that was their portion in this life, and in their labour which they took under the sun[2]." But it is otherwise with us. Earth and sky are ever failing; Christ is ever coming; Christians are ever lifting up their heads and looking out, and therefore it is the evening. We may not set our hearts on things present; we may not say to our soul, " Thou hast much goods laid up for many years, take thine ease, eat, drink, and be merry[3] :" and therefore it is the evening. We may not think of home, or brethren, or sister, or father, or mother, or wife, or children, or land; and therefore it is the evening[4]. The evening is long and the day was short; for the first shall be last, and the last first. What seems vigorous perishes; what seems ever expiring is carried on; and this last age, though ever-failing, has lasted longer than the ages before it, and Christians have more time for a greater work than if they had been hired in the morning.

[1] 1 Cor. vii. 29—31.   [2] Eccles. ix. 7—9.   [3] Luke xii. 19.   [4] Mark x. 29

O may we ever bear in mind that we are not sent into
this world to stand all the day idle, but to go forth to
our work and to our labour until the evening! *Until*
the evening, not *in* the evening only of life, but serving
God from our youth, and not waiting till our years fail
us. Until the *evening*, not in the day-time only, lest
we begin to run well, but fall away before our course is
ended. Let us " give glory to the Lord our God, before
He cause darkness, and before our feet stumble upon the
dark mountains [1];" and, having turned to Him, let us
see that our goodness be not " as the morning cloud, and
as the early dew which passeth away." The *end* is the
proof of the matter. When the sun shines, this earth
pleases; but let us look towards that eventide and the
cool of the day, when the Lord of the vineyard will walk
amid the trees of His garden, and say unto His steward,
" Call the labourers, and give them their hire, beginning
from the last unto the first." That evening will be the
trial: when the heat, and fever, and noise of the noon-
tide are over, and the light fades, and the prospect sad-
dens, and the shades lengthen, and the busy world is
still, and " the door shall be shut in the streets, and the
daughters of music shall be brought low, and fears shall
be in the way, and the almond-tree shall flourish, and
the grasshopper shall be a burden, and desire shall fail,"
and " the pitcher shall be broken at the fountain, and
the wheel broken at the cistern;" then, when it is
" vanity of vanities, all is vanity," and the Lord shall
come, " who both will bring to light the hidden things
of darkness, and will make manifest the counsels of the

[1] Jer. xiii. 16.

hearts,"—then shall we "discern between the righteous and the wicked, between him that serveth God and him that serveth Him not[1]."

May that day and that hour ever be in our thoughts! When we rise, when we lie down; when we speak, when we are silent; when we act, and when we rest: whether we eat or drink, or whatever we do, may we never forget that "for all these things God will bring us into judgment[2]." For "He cometh quickly, and His reward is with Him, to give every man according as His work shall be[3]."

"Blessed are they that do His commandments, that they may have right to the tree of life, and may enter in through the gates into the city." Blessed will they be then, and only they, who, with the Apostle, have ever had on their lips, and in their hearts, the question, "Lord, what wilt Thou have me to do[4]?" whose soul "hath broken out for the very fervent desire that it hath alway unto His judgments;" who have "made haste and prolonged not the time to keep His commandments[5];" who have not waited to be hired, nor run uncertainly, nor beaten the air, nor taken darkness for light, and light for darkness, nor contented themselves with knowing what is right, nor taken comfort in feeling what is good, nor prided themselves in their privileges, but set themselves vigorously to do God's will.

Let us turn from shadows of all kinds,—shadows of sense, or shadows of argument and disputation, or shadows addressed to our imagination and tastes. Let

---

[1] Mal. iii. 18.   [2] Eccles. xi. 9.   [3] Rev. xxii. 12.
[4] Acts ix. 6.   [5] Ps. cxix. 20. 60.

us attempt, through God's grace, to advance and sanctify the inward man. We cannot be wrong here. Whatever is right, whatever is wrong, in this perplexing world, we must be right in "doing justly, in loving mercy, in walking humbly with our God;" in denying our wills, in ruling our tongues, in softening and sweetening our tempers, in mortifying our lusts; in learning patience, meekness, purity, forgiveness of injuries, and continuance in well-doing.

SERMON II.

Saintliness not forfeited by the Penitent.

(SEXAGESIMA.)

" In nothing am I behind the very chiefest Apostles, though I be nothing."
—2 COR. xii. 11.

SO says St. Paul, after recounting his privileges, his
sufferings, and his services through many chapters,
or rather through his whole Epistle. His Corinthian
converts had learned to undervalue him, and he confesses
that he was by himself as weak and worthless as they
thought him. "I am the least of the Apostles," he
says, "that am not meet to be called an Apostle, because
I persecuted the Church of God." "Not that we are
sufficient of ourselves to think any thing as of ourselves." And in the text he speaks of himself as being
"nothing." Yet though such, viewed in himself, far
other was he in fact, that is, in the grace of God, which
had been shed upon him; or in his own words, "But by
the grace of God I am what I am, and His grace which
was bestowed upon me was not in vain, but I laboured
more abundantly than they all; yet not I, but the grace
of God which was with me." Again, "But our suffi-

ciency is of God." And again, "My grace is sufficient for thee, for My strength is made perfect in weakness." And again, "I suppose I was not a whit behind the very chiefest Apostles[1]." And in the text, "In nothing am I behind the very chiefest Apostles, though I be nothing."

And in both Epistles he enumerates in detail many of the fruits and tokens of this grace which had been given to him, who was once "a blasphemer, and a persecutor, and injurious." "Even unto this present hour," he says, "we both hunger, and thirst, and are naked, and are buffeted, and have no certain dwelling-place; and labour, working with our own hands: being reviled, we bless; being persecuted, we suffer it: being defamed, we intreat: we are made as the filth of the earth, and are the offscouring of all things unto this day." Again, "In all things approving ourselves as the ministers of God, in much patience, in afflictions, in necessities, in distresses, in stripes, in imprisonments, in tumults, in labours, in watchings, in fastings; by pureness, by knowledge, by longsuffering, by kindness, by the Holy Ghost, by love unfeigned, by the word of truth, by the power of God, by the armour of righteousness on the right hand and on the left." And again, "Receive us; we have wronged no man, we have corrupted no man, we have defrauded no man." And again, "In labours more abundant, in stripes above measure, in prisons more frequent, in deaths oft; . . . in weariness and painfulness, in watchings often, in hunger and thirst, in fastings often, in cold and nakedness: . . . . Who is weak,

---

[1] 1 Cor. xv. 9, 10. 2 Cor. iii. 5; xii. 9; xi. 5.

and I am not weak? who is offended, and I burn not?"
And again, "I take pleasure in infirmities, in reproaches,
in necessities, in persecutions, in distresses for Christ's
sake: for when I am weak, then am I strong [1]."

Is it possible to conceive a greater contrast than is
placed before us in the picture of Saul the persecutor of
the Church, and of St. Paul, Apostle, Confessor, and
Martyr? Who so great an enemy of Christ? who so
true a servant? Nor is St. Paul's instance solitary;
stranger cases still have occurred in the times after him.
Not unregenerate sinners only like him, but those who
have sinned after their regeneration; not sinners in
ignorance only, like him, but those who knew what was
right and did it not; not merely the blinded by a false
zeal and an unhumbled heart, like him, but sensual, carnal,
abandoned persons; profligates, who sacrificed to Satan
body as well as soul; these, too, by the wonder-working
grace of God, have from time to time become all that
they were not; as high in the kingdom of heaven as
they were before low plunged in darkness and in the
shadow of death. Such awful instances of Christ's
power meet us every now and then in the course of the
Church's history; so much so, that by a mistake, great
but not unnatural, it has sometimes been laid down as
a sort of maxim, "The greater the sinner, the greater
the saint;" as if to have a full measure of Christ's
cup, a man must first have drunken deeply of the cup
of devils.

Such a doctrine of course is simply wicked and
detestable; but still it derives some speciousness from

[1] 1 Cor. iv. 11—13. 2 Cor. vi. 4—7; vii. 2; xi. 23. 27. 29; xii. 10.

the instances like St. Paul to which I have alluded. Those instances seem to prove something, though not this doctrine; what they prove, it will befit this day, which is a sort of commemoration of St. Paul, briefly to consider.

They prove then this,—that no degree of sin, however extreme (unless indeed it reaches the unpardonable sin, the sin against the Holy Ghost, which of course falls without our subject,—but no degree of sin, which can be repented of), precludes the acquisition of any degree of holiness, however high. No sinner so great, but he may, through God's grace, become a saint ever so great. Great saints may become such, either after being, or without being, great sinners. We cannot argue from what a saint is at his close what he was at his beginning. Look through the lives of the Saints, and you will find that some became such after never turning from God, and others, after turning from Him; and it would be presumptuous to assert that in the catalogue there are not saints as great who have turned from Him and repented, as any of those who have been just persons from their youth up, needing no repentance.

This of course is a very different statement from saying the greater the sinner, the greater the saint. It is only saying that a man may rise as high as he once was low; that great sinners, when they turn to God,—not, in consequence will be greater saints than others, but that they are not hindered from being equal to those others in their saintliness, in spite of their sinning. But even such a statement may seem strong; so now some words shall be added by way of explanation.

[S. D.]

1. First, what is very plain, it is less likely, far less likely, that a great sinner should turn to God and become a great saint. It is unlikely that a gross sinner will listen to the Divine Voice at all; it is much to be feared that he will quench the grace which is pleading with him. Again, even if he follows the call so far as to repent, yet it is less likely still that the habits of sin which he has formed round his soul will so relax their hold of him, as to allow him to lay aside every weight. The probability is, that he has made his will so torpid, and his heart so carnal, and his views so worldly, that, even when his repentance is sincere, he will settle down in an inferior, second-rate sort of religion; he will have no fervour, no keenness, no elevation, no splendour of soul; he will not be able to pray; he will not be able to act on heavenly motives; but corruption will mingle with all he does. Now it stands to reason that the farther a man has gone wrong, the more he has to do to bring himself right; whereas, for the very same reason, he is less disposed than he was once, and less able, to set himself in earnest to the work. The more a man sins the stronger become his soul's enemies, and the weaker he becomes himself: a weight is taken off one end of the balance, and put upon the other; his disadvantage is double.

2. And in this sense I must certainly grant he never can be so great a saint as if he had never sinned; that is, the efforts which he must now make merely to undo what he has done, would, in that case, simply have told towards his advancement in holiness, and would of course have brought him forward to a higher point than they now enable him to reach. In this sense he can

never overtake himself, viewed as he would otherwise
have been. He has lost time in going wrong, he has
lost time and labour in retracing his way: as well
might a man of thirty hope ever to overtake in years a
man of forty, as a repentant sinner, whose feet are
slowly bearing him out of the region of sin, to overtake
what he might have been, had he always, with the same
speed, moved along the narrow way. And of course it
must be ever a matter of deep misery to him that he is
not what he might have been, that he might have done
more than he has done or now can do. But this is true
of all men, even of the innocent and upright. The
greatest saints might have been greater than they are.
We may suppose a point of excellence, and that an
attainable one, higher than the highest that has ever
been actually attained by man. And again, in like
manner, in the abstract, as we see by the parable of the
prodigal son, doubtless those who have ever been with
their Father are higher in God's favour than those who
have left Him. But I am not speaking of possibilities
or abstractions, but of facts. And I say, taking the
points of holiness to which souls which have served God
from their youth up have in fact attained, there is none
so high but, as far as we are given to know or judge, has
been attained by men who have sinned and repented, as
St. Paul's instance shows us.

3. Again, in what I have said, it is of course at once
implied that not so many attain high holiness after
sinning, as after a life of innocence. Of those who have
been saints, we must suppose the greater number are
such as, more or less, have been preserved in holy

obedience from their baptism upwards; the few are
those who, after their baptism, have sinned grievously,
and repented, but still those few may, if St. Paul's instance be in point, rise to be as great saints as the many
who, after their baptism, needed no repentance.

4. Further, it must not be supposed, because sinners
have sincerely repented, that therefore they have no
punishment for their past sins; and this puts a vast
difference between the state of the innocent and the
penitent. In this sense they never can be on a level:
the one, if God so wills, is open to punishment, and the
other is not; for God does not so pardon us, as not
also to punish. When His children go wrong they
are, in St. Paul's words, "judged." He does not abandon them, but He makes their sin "find them out."
And, as we well know, it is His merciful pleasure that
this punishment should at the same time act as a chastisement and correction, so that "when they are judged
they are chastened of the Lord, that they should not be
condemned with the world[1]." But still their visitation
is of the nature of a judgment; and no sinner knows
what kind, what number of judgments, he has incurred
at the hands of the righteous Judge. I say that repentant sinners are in this respect different from innocent
persons; that, it may be, God will bring punishment
upon them for their past sins, as He very often does;
and it may be God's will to make that punishment the
means of their sanctification, as He did in St. Paul's
case. Pain, distress, heaviness, may overwhelm them,
may be their portion, may be necessary for their attaining

[1] 1 Cor. xi. 32.

that holiness to which they aspire. But I am not speaking of the means by which they attain to holiness; I am not speaking of the circumstances or lot in which they are perfecting it, whether pleasant or painful; but of their holiness itself, present and to come: and I say, that the holiness to which at length they do attain, however they attain it, may be as great as that of those whose religious history has been altogether different, who have not sinned as they, nor suffered as they, nor struggled and toiled as they.

And, I will add, that it is our duty to love repentant sinners just as if they had not sinned. Those, who have never fallen as they, are not to suffer the thought of what those others were to rest on their minds, or to treat them in any degree (God forbid!) as if their approach were a pollution to them. If they are reconciled to God, surely they may well be reconciled to their brethren; if Christ condescends to be their meat and drink, surely the holiest of men need not scruple to wash their feet. I am now speaking of the inward feeling of our hearts towards them; for it is often a duty (at least for a time) to put an outward and ceremonial distinction between them and others. First, we cannot be certain, till after a while, that they are really repentant; thus the Apostles were "all afraid" of St. Paul at first, "and believed not that he was a disciple:" and next it may be necessary for their good (particularly when a Church does not enforce the discipline of penance), necessary for their good to put them under disadvantage, and for example sake. Yet all this outward distinction need not interfere with the feeling of our hearts towards them.

As we do not use unrestrained familiarity towards
strangers as well as friends, or to inferiors or superiors,
but only to our intimates, yet still may feel all Christian
love towards them, so we surely may observe certain
rules for a time, or for a permanence, towards those who
have been open sinners, simply as a matter of duty, but
not at all forgetting that in Christian privileges they
are on an equality with ourselves, and may be, or are in
the way to be, even our superiors in the kingdom of
heaven. No one thing is more distinct from another
than is the treating a person with distance or reserve
from looking down upon him. And penitents often have
actually put themselves into some new state or rank
in life, which thus constituted their penance, and saved
their brethren from the task of taking notice of their past
sins, and enabled them to forget that they are penitents.

Now there are various reasons for insisting on this
subject. One reason is thereby to enforce the following
parallel truth; for if it is true that a sinner *may* become
a saint, it is at least as true that an innocent person,
who has never fallen into gross sin, notwithstanding
need not be a saint. It frequently happens that repentant sinners become more holy and pleasing to God
than those who have never fallen. There are a multitude
of persons who go through life in a safe, uninteresting
mediocrity. They have never been exposed to temptation; they are not troubled with violent passions;
they have nothing to try them; they have never attempted great things for the glory of God; they have
never been thrown upon the world; they live at home
in the bosom of their families, or in quiet situations;

and in a certain sense they are innocent and upright.
They have not profaned their baptismal robe in any
remarkable way; they have done nothing to frighten
their conscience; they have ever lived under a sense
of religion, and done their immediate duties respectably.
And, when their life is closed, people cannot help speaking well of them, as harmless, decent, correct persons,
whom it is impossible to blame, impossible not to regret.
Yet, after all, how different their lives are from that
described as a Christian's life in St. Paul's Epistles! I do
not mean different in regard to persecutions, wanderings,
heroic efforts, and all that is striking and what is called
romantic in the Apostle's history; but (if I must con-
dense all I mean in one word) in regard to unselfishness.
All the peculiarity of a Christian consists in his preferring
God and his neighbour to *self*,—in self-denial for the sake
of God and his brethren; according to St. Paul's words
"None of us liveth to himself, and no man dieth to
himself; but whether we live, we live unto the Lord,
and whether we die, we die unto the Lord; whether we
live, therefore, or die, we are the Lord's." But how
many there are who live a life of ease and indolence, as
far as they can—or, at least, who, far from setting the
glory of God before them, as the end of their being,
live for themselves, not to God! And what especially
lulls their consciences in so doing, is the circumstance
that they have never sinned grossly; forgetting that
a mirror is by nothing more commonly dimmed than by
the small and gradual accumulations of daily impurities,
and that souls may silently be overspread and choked
up with mere dust, till they reflect back no portion of

the heavenly truths which should possess them. And thus, while they dream life away, others who started with them, first, being overtaken by pride or passion, fall into sin, and lose their way; and then are shocked and terrified, and manage to regain it, and run forward impetuously, and pass by them; and the last become first, and the first last.

I have also enlarged on this subject for the sake of those (how many they are!) who are conscious to themselves that they have, by wilful sinning, lost the fulness of that blessedness which baptism conveyed to them. Oh, happy they, who have not this consciousness, yet without on that account ceasing to be watchful and fervent in spirit! O my brethren, make much of your virginal state, if you possess it, and be careful not to lose it; lose not the opportunity of that special blessedness, which none but they can have who serve God from their youth up in consistent obedience. What is passed cannot be recalled. Whatever be the heights of holiness to which repentant sinners attain, yet they cannot have this pearl of great price, *not* to *have* sinned. No true penitent forgets or forgives himself: an unforgiving spirit towards himself is the very price of God's forgiving him. Yet still, though sinners never can be to themselves as if they had not sinned, though they cannot so rid them of their past sins, as to be sure that those sins will not, in the words of Scripture, find them out, and bring retribution upon them; yet, as regards the love of God and of their brethren, in this respect, they are, on their repentance, in the condition of just persons who need no repentance. Let this comfort and

encourage all penitents,—they may be high, they may
be highest in the kingdom of heaven; they may be, like
St. Paul, not a whit behind the chiefest. Keen indeed
must be the discipline which brings them to that lofty
seat. Not by languid efforts, not without great and
solemn trials is it reached; not without pain and
humiliation, and much toil, will they make progress
towards it; but it can be gained. This is their great
consolation,—it is in their grasp; they have not forfeited,
they have but delayed, they have but endangered and
made difficult, the prize of their high calling in Christ
Jesus. Let them turn to God with a perfect heart; let
them beg of Him that grace which wrought so powerfully in the blessed Apostle; let them put on the whole
armour of God, that they may be able to withstand in
the evil day, and having done all to stand. Let them
be sure that, if they have but the will for great things,
they have the power. Let them meditate upon the
lives of the Saints in times past, and see how much
a resolute unflinching will did for them. Let them aim
at God's glory; let it be their daily prayer that God
may be glorified in them, whether in their life or in
their death, whether in their punishment or in their
release, in their pain or in their refreshment, in their
toil or in their repose, in their honour or in their dishonour, in their lifting up or in their humiliation. Oh,
hard it is to say this, and to endure to put one's self
into God's hands! Yet He is the faithful God, not
willingly afflicting the sons of men, but for their good;
not chastising us, but as a loving Father; not tempting
us, without making a way to escape; not implanting

the thorn in our flesh, save to temper the abundance of
His revelations. Whatever be our necessary trial, He
will bring us through it—through the deep waters,
through the thick darkness—as He guided and guarded
the blessed Apostle; till we in turn, whatever be our
past sins, shall be able to say, like him, " I have fought
a good fight, I have finished my course, I have kept the
faith; henceforth there is laid up for me a crown of
righteousness, which the Lord, the righteous Judge,
shall give me at that day [1]."

[1] 2 Tim. iv. 7. 8.

SERMON III.

Our Lord's Last Supper and His First.

(QUINQUAGESIMA.)

" And He said unto them, With desire I have desired to eat this pass-
over with you before I suffer."—LUKE xxii. 15.

THERE is something very observable and very touching in the earnestness displayed in these words of
our Lord, and in the acts which preceded them. He had
showed beforehand that great desire, of which He here
speaks. That He had thought much of His last passover
which He was to eat with His disciples, is plain from
the solemnity with which He marked out the place to
them, and the display of supernatural knowledge with
which He accompanied His directions. "He sendeth
forth two of His disciples," "Peter and John," "and
saith unto them, Go ye into the city, and there
shall meet you a man bearing a pitcher of water:
follow him. And wheresoever he shall go in, say ye
to the good-man of the house," "The Master saith,
My time is at hand;" "My time is at hand, I will
keep the passover at thy house with My disciples."

"And he shall show you a large upper room furnished; there make ready." And then, "when the hour was come, He sat down, and the twelve Apostles with Him. And He said unto them, With desire I have desired to eat this passover with you before I suffer. For I say unto you, I will not any more eat thereof, until it be fulfilled in the kingdom of God '."

You may say, indeed, that most important occurrences took place at that feast; and that these He had in view when He gave the command to prepare for it, and when He expressed His satisfaction in celebrating it. Then He washed His disciples' feet, and gave the precept of humility; then He laid down the great note of the Church, brotherly love, impressing it on them most persuasively by His own example; and then He instituted His own heavenly Sacrament, which was to remain on earth, together with that humility and love, unto the end. It is true; but still it is true also, that He chose a festive occasion as the season for these solemn and gracious acts. He closed His earthly ministry, He parted with His disciples, He entered upon His trial, at a feast. The Son of Man had come, in His own words, eating and drinking; and He preserved this peculiarity of His mission unto the end.

There must be something natural, I mean something in accordance with deep principles in our nature, in this action of our Lord's, considering how widely similar observances have prevailed, how congenial they are to us, and that He who thus acted had taken upon Him human nature in its perfection. God has given us " wine that

---

[1] Matt. xxvi. 17—19. Mark xiv. 12—16. Luke xxii. 7—18.

maketh glad the heart of man, and oil to make him a cheerful countenance, and bread to strengthen man's heart[1]." And these good gifts of His, by which our life is strengthened, send the soul forth out of itself in search of sympathy and fellowship; they end not in themselves, nor can be enjoyed in solitude; they create, and convey, and blend with social feelings; they are means and tokens of mutual good-will and kindness; or, to speak more religiously, they are of a sacramental nature. They are intended, by being partaken in common, to open our hearts towards each other in love; and this being the case, we may judge how fearful is the abuse of God's gifts in riot or sensuality, for it is in some sort a profanation of a Divine ordinance, a sacrilege. When then our Lord parted from His disciples in a feast, He took the most tender, affectionate, loving leave of them which could be taken.

Laban, hard man as he was, shows us this in the words in which he expostulates with Jacob, who had stolen away from him. " Wherefore didst thou flee away secretly," he says, " and steal away from me; and didst not tell me, that I might have sent thee away with mirth and with songs, with tabret and with harp; and hast not suffered me to kiss my sons and my daughters? thou hast now done foolishly in so doing?" And when at length son and father-in-law departed from each other, " Jacob offered sacrifice upon the mount, and called his brethren to eat bread; and they did eat bread, and tarried all night in the mount. And early in the morning Laban rose up, and kissed his sons and his daughters,

[1] Ps. civ. 15.

and blessed them. And Laban departed, and returned
unto his place[1]."

And next, I hope it is no refinement to observe that
the very time when the Passover was instituted was a
time of departure. The Israelites indeed did not feast
with those whom they were leaving; for they, . . . though
" they had received them with feastings," then " very
grievously afflicted them[2];" but still it was a solemn
leave-taking on their part of the land of their captivity,
and in the very form of it betokened a journey. "Thus
shall ye eat it: with your loins girded, your shoes on
your feet, and your staff in your hand; and ye shall eat
it in haste[3]."

Another instance, and more apposite, is supplied in the
history of the call of the great Prophet Elisha. Elijah,
when he had left the wilderness, " found Elisha the son
of Shaphat, who was plowing with twelve yoke of oxen
before him, and he with the twelfth: and Elijah
passed by him, and cast his mantle upon him." Elisha
understood that it was a call to follow the persecuted
Prophet in his forlorn course. So he asked his leave to
bid his friends farewell. " And he left the oxen, and ran
after Elijah, and said, Let me, I pray thee, kiss my father
and my mother, and then I will follow thee." God's
calls are not commands, but favours; so the Prophet
said to him, " Go back again; for what have I done to
thee?" but Elisha, though so suddenly visited, had no
intention of shrinking from the summons; he asked
indeed to bid his kindred farewell, but he was not of

---

[1] Gen. xxxi. 27, 28. 54, 55.   [2] Wisd. xix. 16.
[3] Exod. xii. 11.

those whom our Saviour notices, who, having put their hand to the plough, look back, and are unfit for the kingdom of God [1]. He did but wish, before commencing his new life and eventful ministry, to hold a last feast with his friends; and in his mode of doing so, he showed that his mind was made up to leave his former occupations for ever. The materials of his husbandry provided him with an entertainment. "He returned back from him, and took a yoke of oxen, and slew them, and boiled their flesh with the instruments of the oxen, and gave unto the people, and they did eat. Then he arose, and went after Elijah, and ministered unto him [2]."

Again, another instance occurs in the history of St. Matthew. Christ "went forth, and saw a publican named Levi sitting at the receipt of custom, and said unto him, Follow Me. And he left all, rose up, and followed Him. And Levi made Him a great feast in his own house, and there was a great company of publicans, and of others that sat down with them [3]."

Nay, may we not say that our Lord Himself had commenced His ministry, that is, bade farewell to His earthly home, at a feast? for it was at the marriage entertainment at Cana of Galilee that He did His first miracle, and manifested forth His glory. He was in the house of friends, He was surrounded by intimates and followers, and He took a familiar interest in the exigences of the feast. He supplied a principal want which was interfering with their festivity. It was His contribution to it. By supplying it miraculously He showed that He was beginning a new life, the life of a Messen-

[1] Luke ix. 62.   [2] 1 Kings xix. 19—21.   [3] Luke v. 27—29

ger from God, and that that feast was the last scene of the old life. And, moreover, He made use of one remarkable expression, which seems to imply that this change of condition really was in His thoughts, if we may dare so to speak of them, or at all to interpret them. For when His Mother said unto Him, "They have no wine," He answered, "What have I to do with thee¹?" He had had to do with her for thirty years. She had borne Him, she had nursed Him, she had taught Him. And when He had reached twelve years old, at the age when the young may expect to be separated from their parents, He had only become more intimately one with them, for we are told that "He went down with them, and came to Nazareth, and was subject unto them²." Eighteen years had passed away since this occurred. St. Joseph (as it seems) had been taken to his rest. Mary remained; but from Mary, His Mother, He must now part, for the three years of His ministry. He had gently intimated this to her at the very time of His becoming subject to her, intimated that His heavenly Father's work was a higher call than any earthly duty. "Wist ye not," He said, when found in the Temple, "that I must be about My Father's business³?" The time was now come when this was to be fulfilled, and, therefore, when His Mother addressed Him at the marriage feast, He answered, "What have I to do with thee?" What is between Me and thee, My Mother, any longer? "The time is fulfilled, and the Kingdom of God is at hand⁴."

And hence the words which I have quoted were but

¹ John ii. 3, 4.   ² Luke ii. 51.   ³ Luke 49.   ⁴ Mark i. 15.

the introduction to others like them, in which He seemed to put His Mother from His thoughts, as being called to the work of a divine ministry. When He was told that His Mother and His brethren stood without, and sent unto Him, calling Him, He seemed to answer, that henceforth He had no mother and no brethren after the flesh, for He was called on to fulfil His own precept, as fulfilling all righteousness, and to " hate His father and mother, and brethren and sisters, yea, and His own life also[1]." "He answered and said unto him that told Him, Who is My Mother? and who are My brethren? and He stretched forth His hand towards His disciples, and said, Behold My Mother and My brethren. For whosoever shall do the will of My Father which is in heaven" (about whose "business," in His own former words, He was then engaged), "the same is My brother and sister, and Mother[2]."

At another time, when " a certain woman of the company lift up her voice, and said unto Him, Blessed is the womb that bare Thee, and the paps which Thou hast sucked," He answered, " Yea rather, blessed are they that hear the word of God and keep it[3]."

Nor is there any token recorded in the Gospels of His affection for His Mother, till His ministry was brought to an end, and we know well what were the tender words which almost immediately preceded "It is finished." His love revived, that is, He allowed it to appear, as His Father's work was ending. " There stood by the cross of Jesus, His Mother, and His Mother's sister, Mary

---

[1] Luke xiv. 26.   [2] Matt. xii. 48—50.
[3] Luke xi. 27, 28.

the wife of Cleophas, and Mary Magdalene. When
Jesus therefore saw His Mother, and the disciple stand-
ing by whom He loved, He saith unto His Mother,
Woman, behold thy son ! Then saith He to the disciple,
Behold thy Mother ! And from that hour that disciple
took her unto his own home[1]."

He took leave then of His Mother at a feast, as He
afterwards took leave of His disciples at a feast. But
there is perhaps a still closer connexion between the
feast of Cana and His Paschal Supper, and, as we are
already engaged in the subject, it may be allowable to
proceed with it.

It will be observed, then, that though He was bidding farewell to His earthly home in the one, and His
disciples in the other, yet in neither case was He leaving
them for good, but for a season. His Mother He
acknowledged again when He was expiring; His disciples on His resurrection. And He gave both the one
and the other intimations, not only that He was then
separating Himself from them, but also that it was not
a separation for ever.

Observe, He said to His Mother, "What have I to
do with thee? Mine hour is not yet come." Perhaps
this implies that *when* His hour was come, then He
would have to do with her again as before; and such
really seems to be the meaning of the passage. "What
have I to do with thee *now?* I have had, I shall have;
but what have I to do with thee now as before? what
as yet? what *till* My hour is come?" He says here
that His hour is not yet come, but just before His

[1] John xix. 25—27.

passion He said, "The Master saith, My time is at hand;" and again, "Behold, the hour is at hand, and the Son of Man is betrayed into the hands of sinners[1];" and it was *during* His passion that He acknowledged His Mother again. While His work was in progress, He turned from His Mother; but in alluding to an hour that was to come, He gave her to understand that her separation from Him was to end in that hour.

And moreover let this too be observed, that on several occasions, the evil spirit, whom He was about to cast out, used towards our Lord the same phrase which He used towards His Mother. "There was in their synagogue a man with an unclean spirit; and he cried out, saying, Let us alone; what have we to do with Thee, Thou Jesus of Nazareth? art Thou come to destroy us[2]?" It is observable, too, that in another instance the devils alluded to the destined time. "They cried out saying, What have we to do with Thee, Jesus, Thou Son of God? art Thou come hither to torment us *before the time*[3]?" They knew a time was coming when He was to reign, and they to be punished; but they miscalculated it, and thought that because His work was not yet done, their torment was not yet to begin. And as when they said, "What have we to do with Thee, before the time?" they implied that they should have to do with their Judge when the time came, and merely meant to say, "What have we to do with Thee yet?" so when our Lord says to St. Mary, "What have I to do with thee? Mine hour is not yet come;" He too means, "What have I to do with Thee,

[1] Matt. xxvi. 18. 45.   [2] Mark i. 23, 24.   [3] Matt. viii. 29.

as I once had, as yet,—before that hour?" and implies that in that hour He should have to do with His Mother again. And similar to this is His language to St. Mary Magdalene, when He says to her after His resurrection, "Touch Me not, for I am not yet ascended to My Father[1];" implying, as we may reverently infer, that leave would be given to her after His ascension. He withdrew Himself only for a time.

And now let us turn to that other most sacred and sad feast to which the text relates; sad because it was designed to introduce, not His ministry, but His passion, yet in this respect agreeing with the feast in which He began to manifest His glory, that it was a feast of valediction, a sort of sober carnival, before He entered upon His trial. We shall find, as in the former feast, that He intimated both that He was leaving those with whom He had hitherto companied, yet that it was for a time only, not for ever.

To His Mother He had said, "What have I to do with thee?" and now to His Apostles, "Little children, yet a little while I am with you. Ye shall seek Me: and as I said unto the Jews, Whither I go, ye cannot come, so now I say unto you." On this, "Simon Peter said unto Him, Lord, whither goest Thou?" and when our Lord answered him, that whither He went, he could not follow Him then, the zealous and impatient Apostle persisted, "Lord, why cannot I follow Thee now[2]?"

On the other hand, He promised that the separation should be but for a season. As to St. Mary, He had

---

[1] John xx. 17.   [2] John xiii. 33. 36.

said, " Mine hour is not yet come; " so He said to St.
Peter, in the passage just cited, " Whither I go thou
canst not follow Me now, but thou shalt follow Me
afterwards." And as at His first feast, He had seemed
to turn from His Mother's prayer, while He granted it,
because of the time, so to His Apostles He foretold, at
His second feast, what the power of their prayers should
be hereafter, by way of cheering them on His departure.
" Ye now therefore have sorrow, but I will see you
again, and your heart shall rejoice, and your joy no man
taketh from you. In that day ye shall ask Me nothing.
Verily, verily, I say unto you, Whatsoever ye shall ask
the Father in My Name, He will give it you[1]." And
again, " Ye are My friends, if ye do whatsoever I command you. Henceforth I call you not servants, for the
servant knoweth not what his lord doeth; but I have
called you friends, for all things that I have heard of
My Father, I have made known unto you[2]." In the
gifts then promised to the Apostles after the Resurrection, we may learn the present influence and power of
the Mother of God.

Such seems to be the connexion between the feast
with which our Lord began, and that with which He
ended His ministry. Nay, may we not add without
violence, that in the former feast He had in mind and
intended to foreshadow the latter? for what was that
first miracle by which He manifested His glory in the
former, but the strange and awful change of the element
of water into wine? and what did He in the latter, but
change the Paschal Supper and the typical lamb into

---

[1] John xvi. 22, 23.   [2] John xv. 14, 15.

the sacrament of His atoning sacrifice, and the creatures of bread and wine into the verities of His most precious Body and Blood? He began His ministry with a miracle; He ended it with a greater.

These are thoughts wherewith to enter upon that solemn season of the year, when for a time we separate from each other, as far as may be, and from the other blessings which God has given us. Pass a few days, and, like Abraham, we shall have been called to quit things visible and temporal for the contemplation and the hope of God's future presence. Come the fourth day from this, and, like Moses, we shall have gone up into the Mount, to remain there forty days and forty nights in abstinence and prayer. We shall be called, as it were, out of sight; for though our worldly duties will remain and must be done, and our bodily presence is in the world as it was, yet for a season we must be, more or less, cut off from the intercourse, the fellowship, the enjoyment of each other, and be thrown upon the thought of ourselves and of our God. Earth must fade away from our eyes, and we must anticipate that great and solemn truth, which we shall not fully understand until we stand before God in judgment, that to us there are but two beings in the whole world, God and ourselves. The sympathy of others, the pleasant voice, the glad eye, the smiling countenance, the thrilling heart, which at present are our very life, all will be away from us, when Christ comes in judgment. Every one will have to think of himself. Every eye shall see *Him*; every heart will be full of *Him*. He will speak to every one; and every one will be rendering to Him his own account. By self-restraint, by abstinence, by prayer, by meditation, by recollection, by penance, we now anticipate in our measure that dreadful season. By thinking of it beforehand, we hope to mitigate its terrors when it comes. By humbling ourselves now, we hope to escape humiliation then. By owning our faults now, we hope to avert the disclosures of that day. By judging ourselves now, we hope to be spared that judgment which mercy tempers not. We prepare now to meet our God; we retire, as it were, to our sick room, and put our house in order. We " remember our Creator in the days of our youth" and strength, " while the evil days come not, nor the years draw nigh, in which is no pleasure ;" ere " the keepers of the house tremble, and the strong men bow themselves, and the doors are shut in the streets, and the daughters of music are brought low, and desire fails : or ever the silver cord be loosed, or the golden bowl be broken, or the pitcher be broken at the fountain, or the wheel broken at the cistern[1]." We leave the goods of earth before they leave us.

Let us not shrink from this necessary work; let us not suffer indolence or carnal habits to get the better of us. Let us not yield to disgust or impatience; let us not fear as we enter into the cloud. Let us recollect that it is *His* cloud that overshadows us. It is no earthly sorrow or pain, such as worketh death; but it is a bright cloud of godly sorrow, " working repentance to salvation not to be repented of[2]." It is the hand of God which is upon us; " let us humble ourselves therefore under the mighty hand of God, that He may exalt

---

[1] Eccles. xii. 1. 3, 4. 6.   [2] 2 Cor. vii. 10.

us in due time[1]." " Whoso dwelleth under the defence of the Most High, shall abide under the shadow of the Almighty. He shall defend thee under His wings, and thou shalt be safe under His feathers, His faithfulness and truth shall be thy shield and buckler. Thou shalt not be afraid for any terror by night, nor for the arrow that flieth by day; a thousand shall fall beside thee, and ten thousand at thy right hand; but it shall not come nigh thee. . . . For He shall give His angels charge over thee, to keep thee in all thy ways[2]."

[1] 1 Pet. v. 6.   [2] Ps. xci. 1. 4—7. 11.

SERMON IV.

𝔇angers to the ℘enitent.

(LENT.)

"O tarry thou the Lord's leisure; be strong, and He shall comfort thine heart; and put thou thy trust in the Lord."—Ps. xxvii. 16.

NO state is more dreary than that of the repentant sinner, when first he understands where he is, and begins to turn his thoughts towards his Great Master whom he has offended. Of course it is tempered with comfort and hope, as are all acts of duty; and on the retrospect, far from being distressing to dwell upon, it will be even pleasant. But at the time it is a most dreary state. A man finds that he has a great work to do, and does not know how to do it, or even what it is, and his impatience and restlessness are as great as his conscious ignorance; indeed, he is restless because he is ignorant. There is great danger of his taking wrong steps, inasmuch as he is anxious to move, and does not know whither. Let me now make some remarks upon certain faults into which he is likely to fall.

But, observe, I am supposing a really sincere and

earnest mind, not a languid, dreaming, halting, double-minded penitent, who repents a little and not much. Such a one is certainly not in danger of becoming enthusiastic or superstitious; he has not the *power* of being intemperate or wayward in his grief, and has little need of guidance. Nor does what I am saying apply to persons of sound judgment or calm temperament, who though they do truly repent, yet repent with the reason rather than with the feelings. But still there are a number of persons to whom it does apply.

1. I observe, then, that repentant sinners are often impatient to put themselves upon some new line of action, or to adopt some particular rule of life. They feel that what they have done in time past is, as far as this life is concerned, indelible, and places an impassable barrier between themselves and others: happy only if that badge of guilt and shame does not outlast the grave, but is wiped out in the day of account. They feel that they can never be as others are, till the voice of Christ pronounces them acquitted and blessed. And their heart yearns towards humiliation, and burns with a godly indignation against themselves, as if nothing were too bad for them; and they look about for something to do, some state of life to engage in, some task or servile office to undertake. Now it commonly happens that God does not disclose His will to them at once,—and for that will they ought to wait, whereas they are impatient; and when God's will does not clearly appear, they try to persuade themselves that they have ascertained it when they have not. St. Paul should be the pattern of the true penitent here. First he said, " Lord, what wilt

Thou have me to do?" then he was "obedient to the heavenly vision;" he waited three days, till God spoke to him by Ananias; and after that he suffered himself to be led about by Providence hither and thither, as though he had been still blind, without apparent method or purpose, and in no regular calling. It was not till years afterwards that the Holy Spirit said, "Separate Me Barnabas and Saul for the work whereunto I have called them[1]." What a lesson is this for patient waiting on God! "O tarry thou the Lord's leisure;" wait till He speaks. It is impossible but He means to put you on some service; but in His house are many posts, many offices. Be quite sure you are taking the place He would have you take. Since you have gone wrong, and now wish to go right, be sure to ascertain the right; take not only what is good, but what is best. This you cannot do, except by following His call; and for His call you must wait,—whether He will call you forward in your present state of life, or call you to change it. Like the prophet, you must stand upon your watch, and set you on the tower, and watch to see what He will say to you, and what you shall answer when you are reproved: recollecting that "the vision is yet for an appointed time, but at the end it shall speak and not lie; though it tarry, wait for it; because it will surely come, it will not tarry[2]." Never regard how long you have to wait; be it for years, suffer it. Say not time is short, for God can make it long. If He use you not, even till the eleventh hour, He can make that hour a

---

[1] Acts xiii. 2.   [2] Habakkuk ii. 1. 3.

thousand, and can reward you in proportion to the years of your patient waiting.

2. And next I would say to such persons as I have described, Be on your guard, not only against becoming committed to some certain mode of life or object of exertion, but guard against excess in such penitential observances as have an immediate claim upon you, and are private in their exercise. The danger is, that what is really an excess, seems to such persons to be only moderation. When men are in horror and anguish at their past sins, they are anxious to put some burden on themselves, which may relieve their feelings, and remind them of what they have been, what they are. Now nothing is more unadvisable in most cases than to begin with severity. Persons do not know what they can bear, and what they cannot, till they have tried it. They think almost they can live without food, without rest, without the conveniences of life to which they are accustomed. Then when they find they cannot, they despond and are miserable, or fall back, and a reaction ensues. It is a great fault to be ambitious, and men may easily aim at praying more than they can, or meditating more than they can, or having a clearer faith and a deeper humility than at present they can have. All things are done by degrees; all things (through God's grace) may come in time, but not at once. As well might a child think to grow at once into a man, as the incipient penitent become suddenly like St. Paul the aged. Moreover, even if we could possibly have those views of God and of ourselves, which are the simple truth, it would not be good for us to have them,—they

would be too much for us. As Christ hides Himself from us in the Holy Eucharist, so does He hide from us ourselves, in mercy. We are weak,—we are not able to bear great burdens yet; light burdens are heavy to us. Moreover, if penitents are bent on lading themselves heavily, let them know that the greatest of burdens, as well as the most appropriate, is what is lasting, what is continual. A slight penance, if long, is far more trying than a severe one, if short. This stands to reason; for it outlasts their present agitated state of mind. For the same reason, it is more beneficial, for it reminds them of what they afterwards will be likely to forget. A stone in time is hollowed by a continual dropping; and be sure that a very easy rule, if it endures, is a very severe trial. It is not much of a penance to take upon one what is a mere relief to the feelings, and to end it when the feelings cease to require it. True penitence is that which never comes to an end; and true penance is that which lasts as long as penitence. Nor does any one, I suppose, but those who have tried it, know what a peculiar character of severity is given to any observance whatever, by the knowledge that it is never to cease; or even that it is to last for a certain number of years. And independent of the prospect for the future, even monotony itself is often a severe punishment, and requires to be tempered, lest it should unfit us for our duties.

3. What has been last said leads me to another subject, on which some remarks ought to be made. When persons are in acute distress about their sins, they are sometimes tempted to make rash promises, and to take on them professions without counting the cost. They

think their present state of mind will last for ever; it
changes—but their promise remains; they find they
cannot duly fulfil it; then they are in great perplexity,
and even despair.   Perhaps they have been even impru-
dent enough to make their engagement in the shape of a
vow, and this greatly increases their difficulty.   They
do not know whether it is binding or not—they cannot
recollect the mode in which, or the feelings under which,
they took it; or any of the minute circumstances on which
its validity turns.   Now all this on the very first view
of the case shows thus much, how very wrong it is to
make private vows.   We cannot be our own judge in a
matter of this kind.   Yet, if we take on ourselves an
engagement without telling any one else of it, we trust
it in a great measure to our own memory and judgment.
The special publicity and distinctness with which the
marriage vow is made, gives us a pattern how vows
should be undertaken.   The Church should hear them,
and the Church should bless them.   In the early Church
even the highest ecclesiastical authorities were appealed
to as their witnesses and imposers.   But unless in some
sense or form the Church is present, it seems rash to
make vows.   I would rather recommend an observance,
which is safer and more expedient.   Persons who wish
to repent of their past sins, are tempted to make vows
of poverty, or continence, or humble estate, or the like.
Now I do not say that they are wrong in wishing for
themselves this or that kind of life which the Apostles
exercised.   I do not say that it is enthusiastic, or wild,
or fanciful to wish to be like St. Paul, considering that
he expressly wished all men to be as he was.   I do not

say that there is any thing eccentric or reprehensible in grudging oneself those comforts which our Saviour refused; but, as things are, it is best to confine ourselves to the wish and the endeavour, and to spare ourselves the solemn promise. I say this, because I think there is something which persons may do, which will practically come to the same thing, yet without the risk of their acting on their own judgment, unaccompanied by the formal blessing of the Church on their act. I mean, they may make it a point ever to pray God for that gift, or that state which they covet. If they desire to be humble, and of little account in this world, let them not at once make any engagement or profession to that effect, but let them daily pray God that they may never be rich, never be in high place, never in power or authority; let them daily pray God that their dwelling may be ever lowly, their food ordinary, their apparel common, their home solitary; let them pray Him that they may be least and lowest in the world's society; that others may have precedence of them, others speak while they are silent, others take the first seats, and they the last, others receive deference, and they neglect; others have handsome houses, rich furniture, pleasant gardens, gay equipages, great establishments. Will not such a prayer be a sort of recurrent vow, yet without any of that dangerous boldness which a private self-devised resolution implies? Who can go on day by day thus praying, yet not imbibe somewhat of the spirit for which he prays? As the creed is in one sense a prayer, so surely such a prayer may in some sense be considered a profession. Yet even such a prayer let not a man begin at once; let him count the cost before offering it, for this reason, because, assuredly, it is a sort of prayer which Almighty God is very likely to grant.   There are prayers which we have no confidence will be answered; but there are others which, as the experience of all ages assures us, are dangerous ones, because they are so effectual.   Often the word has passed the tongue, and is written in heaven, and in spite of our own change of wish it is accomplished. Among such prayers are prayers for affliction, and for trial; and again, those which I have been describing, for the manner of life of the Apostles and first Christians, or (what may be called by way of distinction) the scriptural life.   Let no one then rashly pray for that scriptural life; lest, before he wish it, he gain his prayer.   Yet still, if after much thought he considers he really and deeply covets it, let him pray for it, and pray for grace to endure it; but this will be enough, he need not take any vow.

4. What was said just now naturally leads to one other remark, viz. that when men are in the first fervour of penitence, they should be careful not to act on their own private judgment, and without proper advice.   Not only in forming lasting engagements, but in all they do, they need a calmer guidance than their own.   They cannot manage themselves; they must be guided by others; the neglect of this simple and natural rule leads to very evil consequences.   We should all of us be saved a great deal of suffering of various kinds, if we could but persuade ourselves, that we are not the best judges, whether of our own condition, or of God's will towards us.   What sensible person undertakes to be his own physician? yet are the diseases of the mind less numerous, less intricate,

less subtle than those of the body? is experience of no
avail in things spiritual as well as in things material?
does induction lose its office, and science its supremacy,
when the soul is concerned? What an inconsistent age
is this! every department of things that are, is pronounced to be capable of science, to rest upon principles,
to require teaching, to exercise the reason, except self-
discipline. Self-discipline is to take its chance; it is *not*
to be learned, but it can be performed by each man for
himself by a sort of natural instinct. And what is more
preposterous still, a person is thus to be his own guide
and instructor at the very time, when by the nature of
the case he is in error and difficulty. How can a person
show himself the way, when by the very hypothesis he
has lost it? how can he at once guide and be guided?
The very seasons I am speaking of are those, when a
man is agitated, excited, harassed, depressed, desponding;
the very time when of course his judgment is not clear,
when he is likely to be led away with fancies, when he
is likely to be swayed by inclination, when the light that
is in him becomes, if not darkness, yet a meteor leading
him the wrong way. But if the blind lead the blind,
shall not both reason and passion, shall not the whole
man, fall into the ditch?

Nor is it to the purpose to say, that we cannot be
guided without the grace of God, and that the grace of
God *will* guide us; and that the grace of God is gained
by private prayer. For still God makes use of means;
we must do our part; we must act, and God will guide
us *while* we act; and the question is, whether taking the
advice of others is not God's way, *through* which He

[S. D.]   E

blesses and enlightens us, and without which our souls
will not prosper.

I state my deep conviction when I say, that nothing
healthy can be expected in the religion of the community, till we learn that we cannot by our private judgment manage ourselves; that management of the heart
is a science which it needs to learn; and that even
though we have paid attention to it, we are least able
to exercise it in our own case, that is, then when we
most need it. We must use in religious matters that
common sense, which does not desert us in matters of
this world, because we take a real interest in them;
and as no one would ever dream of being his own lawyer
or his own physician, however great exposures, whatever
sacrifice of feeling may be the consequence, so we must
take it for granted, if we would serve God comfortably,
that we cannot be our own divines, and our own
casuists.

To conclude, let us excite each other to seek that
good part which shall not be taken away from us. Let
us labour to be really in earnest, and to view things in
the way in which God views them. Then it will be but
a little thing to give up the world; only an easy thing
to reconcile the mind to what at first it shrinks from.
Let us turn our mind heavenward; let us set our
thoughts on things above, and in His own time God
will set our affections there also. All will in time
become natural to us, which at present we do but own
to be good and true. We shall covet what at present
we do but admire. Let the time past suffice us to have
followed our own will; let us desire to form part of that

glorious company of Apostles and Prophets, of whom we read in Scripture. Let us cast in our lot with them, and desire to be gathered together under their feet. Let us beg of God to employ us; let us try to obtain a spirit of perfect self-surrender to Him, and an indifference to one thing above another in this world, so that we may be ready to follow His call whenever it comes to us. Thus shall we best employ ourselves till His voice is heard, patiently preparing for it by meditation, and looking for Him to perfect what we trust His own grace has begun in us.

There are many persons who proceed a little way in religion, and then stop short. God keep us from choking the good seed, which else would come to perfection! Let us exercise ourselves in those good works, which both reverse the evil that is past, and lay up a good foundation for us in the world to come.

SERMON V.

The Three Offices of Christ.

(EASTER.)

"Full of grace are Thy lips, because God hath blessed Thee for ever. Gird Thee with Thy sword upon Thy thigh, O Thou most mighty, according to Thy worship and renown."—Ps. xlv. 3, 4.

OUR Lord is here spoken of in two distinct characters. As a teacher,—" Full of grace are Thy lips;" and as a conqueror,—" Gird Thee with Thy sword upon Thy thigh;" or, in other words, as a Prophet and as a King. His third special office, which is brought before us prominently at this season, is that of a Priest, in that He offered Himself up to God the Father as a propitiation for our sins. These are the three chief views which are vouchsafed to us of His Mediatorial office; and it is often observed that none before Him has, even in type or resemblance, borne all three characters. Melchizedek, for instance, was a priest and a king, but not a prophet. David was prophet and king, but not a priest. Jeremiah was priest and prophet, but not a king. Christ was Prophet, Priest, and King.

He is spoken of as a prophet by Moses, as a prophet

like, but superior, to himself.—"A Prophet shall the
Lord your God raise up unto you of your brethren, like
unto me; Him shall ye hear." And Jacob had already
described Him as a king, when he said, "Unto Him
shall the gathering of the people be." Balaam, too,
speaks of Him as a conqueror and great sovereign.—
"There shall come a Star out of Jacob, and a sceptre shall
rise out of Israel. . . . Out of Jacob shall come He that
shall have dominion." And David speaks of Him as a
priest, but not a priest like Aaron.—"Thou art a Priest
for ever after the order of Melchizedek;" that is, a royal
priest, which Aaron was not. And again, the very first
prophecy of all ran, " He shall bruise thy head (that is,
the serpent's), and thou shalt bruise His heel[1]." He
was to conquer through suffering.

Christ exercised His prophetical office in teaching,
and in foretelling the future;—in His sermon on the
Mount, in His parables, in His prophecy of the destruction of Jerusalem. He performed the priest's service
when He died on the Cross, as a sacrifice; and when He
consecrated the bread and the cup to be a feast upon
that sacrifice; and now that He intercedes for us at the
right hand of God. And He showed Himself as a
conqueror, and a king, in rising from the dead, in ascending into heaven, in sending down the Spirit of grace, in
converting the nations, and in forming His Church to
receive and to rule them.

Further, let it be observed, that these three offices
seem to contain in them and to represent the three

[1] Acts vii. 37. Gen. xlix. 10. Numb. xxiv. 17. 19. Ps. cx. 4.
Gen. iii. 15.

principal conditions of mankind; for one large class of men, or aspect of mankind, is that of sufferers,—such as slaves, the oppressed, the poor, the sick, the bereaved, the troubled in mind; another is, of those who work and toil, who are full of business and engagements, whether for themselves or for others; and a third is that of the studious, learned, and wise. Endurance, active life, thought,—these are the three perhaps principal states in which men find themselves. Christ undertook them all. On one occasion He said, with reference to His baptism in Jordan, "Thus it becometh us to fulfil all righteousness [1]." Every holy rite of the law did He go through for our sakes. And so too did He live through all states of man's life up to a perfect man, infancy, childhood, boyhood, youth, maturity, that He might be a pattern of them all. And so too did He take man's perfect nature on Him, body, and soul, and reason, that He might sanctify it wholly. And therefore in like manner did He unite in Himself, and renew, and give us back in Him, the principal lots or states in which we find ourselves,—suffering, that we might know how to suffer; labouring, that we might know how to labour; and teaching, that we might know how to teach.

Thus, when our Lord came on earth in our nature, He combined together offices and duties most dissimilar. He suffered, yet He triumphed. He thought and spoke, yet He acted. He was humble and despised, yet He was a teacher. He has at once a life of hardship like the shepherds, yet is wise and royal as the eastern sages who came to do honour to His birth.

[1] Matt. iii. 15.

And it will be observed, moreover, that in these offices He also represents to us the Holy Trinity; for in His own proper character He is a priest, and as to His kingdom He has it from the Father, and as to His prophetical office He exercises it by the Spirit. The Father is the King, the Son the Priest, and the Holy Ghost the Prophet.

And further this may be observed, that when Christ had thus given a pattern in Himself of such contrary modes of life, and their contrary excellences, all in one, He did not, on His going away, altogether withdraw the wonderful spectacle; but He left behind Him those who should take His place, a ministerial order, who are His representatives and instruments; and they, though earthen vessels, show forth according to their measure these three characters,—the prophetical, priestly, and regal, combining in themselves qualities and functions which, except under the Gospel, are almost incompatible the one with the other. He consecrated His Apostles to suffer, when He said, "Ye shall drink indeed of My cup, and be baptized with My baptism;" to teach, when He said, "The Comforter, which is the Holy Ghost, He shall teach you all things;" and to rule, when He said to them, "I appoint unto you a kingdom, as My Father hath appointed unto Me; that ye may eat and drink at My table in My kingdom, and sit on thrones, judging the twelve tribes of Israel [1]."

Nay, all His followers in some sense bear all three offices, as Scripture is not slow to declare. In one place it is said, that Christ has "made us kings and priests

[1] Matt. xx. 23. John xiv. 26. Luke xxii. 29, 30.

unto God and His Father;" in another, "Ye have an unction from the Holy One, and ye know all things [1]." Knowledge, power, endurance, are the three privileges of the Christian Church; endurance, as represented in the confessor and monk; wisdom, in the doctor and teacher; power, in the bishop and pastor. And now to illustrate this more at length, by way of showing what I mean.

1. I mean this,—that when we look abroad into the world, and survey the different states and functions of civil society, we see a great deal to admire, but all is imperfect. Each state, or each rank, has its particular excellence, but that excellence is solitary. For instance, —if you take the highest, the kingly office, there is much in it to excite reverence and devotedness. We cannot but look up to power, which God has originally given, so visibly and augustly displayed. All the pomp and circumstance of a court reminds us that the centre of it is one whom God, the Almighty King, maintains. And yet, on second thoughts, is there not this great defect,—that it is all power, and no subjection; all greatness, and no humiliation; all doing, and no suffering? Great sovereigns indeed, like other men, have their own private griefs, and, if they are Christians, have the privileges of Christians, painful as well as pleasant; but I am speaking of kingly power in itself, and showing what a contrast it presents to Christ's sovereignty. Princes are brought up princes; from their birth they receive honours approaching to worship; they will a thing, and it is done; they are on high, and

[1] Rev. i. 6.   1 John ii. 20.

never below. How different the sovereignty of Christ! Born, not in golden chambers, but in a cave of the earth, surrounded with brute cattle, laid in a manger; then bred up as the carpenter's son; when He displayed Himself as the King of Saints, still without a place to lay His head, and dying on the Cross a malefactor's death. He was not a king without being a sufferer too. And so in like manner His followers after Him. He washed His brethren's feet, and He bade them in turn do the like. He told them that, "whosoever would be chief among them, let him be their servant, even as the Son of Man came not to be ministered unto, but to minister, and to give His life a ransom for many[1]." He warned them that they should receive " houses and lands, *with persecutions*[2]." Such is the kingly power of Christ,—reached through humiliation, exercised in mortification.

2. Take another instance. How much is there to admire and revere in the profession of a soldier. He comes more nearly than a king to the pattern of Christ. He not only is strong, but he is weak. He does and he suffers. He succeeds through a risk. Half his time is on the field of battle, and half of it on the bed of pain. And he does this for the sake of others; he defends us by it; we are indebted to him; we gain by his loss; we are at peace by his warfare. And yet there are great drawbacks here also. First, there is the carnal weapon: it is a grievous thing to have to shed blood and to inflict wounds, though it be in self-defence. But again, which is more to our present purpose, after all, the soldier is

---

[1] Matt. xx. 27, 28.   [2] Mark x. 30.

but an instrument directed by another; he is the arm, he is not the head; he must act, whether in a right cause or in a wrong one. His office is wanting in dignity, and accordingly we associate it with the notion of brute force, and with arbitrariness, and imperiousness, and violence, and sternness, and all those qualities which are brought out when mind, and intellect, and sanctity, and charity, are away. But Christ and His ministers are bloodless conquerors. True, He came as one from the battle; and the Prophet cried out on seeing Him, "Who is this that cometh with dyed garments? . . . wherefore art Thou red in Thine apparel, and Thy garments like him that treadeth in the winefat[1]?" But that blood was His own; and if His enemies' blood flowed after His, it was drawn by themselves, by the just judgment of God, not by Him. "He was brought as a lamb to the slaughter, and as a sheep before her shearers is dumb, so He openeth not His mouth[2]."

But there is "a time to keep silence, and a time to speak;" so in season He spoke, and then He was a Prophet. In season He opened His mouth and said, "Blessed are the poor in spirit;" and so with the other beatitudes upon the mount. "In Him are hid all the treasures of wisdom and knowledge;" "Full of grace are His lips, because God hath blessed Him for ever." He not only commands, He persuades. He tempers His awful deeds, He explains His sufferings, by His soothing words. "The Lord hath given unto Him the tongue of the learned, that He may be able to speak a word in season to him that is weary." And when He

---

[1] Isa. lxiii. 1, 2   [2] Isa. liii. 7.   Acts viii. 32.

began to teach, "all men marvelled at the gracious words which proceeded out of His mouth." He taught them "as one having authority." David, himself a prophet and king, a man of sacred song, though a man of blood, had shown beforehand what kind of ruler the promised Christ must be;—"He that ruleth over men must be just, ruling in the fear of God; and He shall be as the light of the morning." And Moses before him, another ruler of God's people; "My doctrine shall drop as the rain, my speech shall distil as the dew; as the small rain upon the tender herb, and as the showers upon the grass [1]." And hence it was said of the Saviour to come, "He shall not strive nor cry, neither shall any hear His voice in the streets; a bruised reed shall He not break, and smoking flax shall He not quench, till He send forth judgment unto victory [2]." Hence such stress is laid in the Prophets on His being a Just God and a Saviour; on "righteousness and peace kissing each other;" on "righteousness being the girdle of His loins, and faithfulness the girdle of His reins [3]." Such is the Divine Prophet of the Church, the Interpreter of secrets, ruling not like conquerors of the earth, but by love; not by fear, not by strength of arm, but by wisdom of heart, convincing, persuading, enlightening, founding an empire upon faith, and ruling by a sovereignty over the conscience. And such, too, has been the rule of His servants after Him. They have been weak personally, without armies, without strongholds, naked, defenceless, yet sovereigns,

---

[1] 2 Sam. xxiii. 3, 4.   Deut. xxxii. 2.   [2] Matt. xii. 18—20.
[3] Isa. xi. 5.

because they were preachers and teachers, because they appealed to the reason and the conscience; and strange to say, though the arm of force seems as if it could do all things, the sovereignty of mind is higher, and the strong and the noble quail before it.

3. Once more. We know that philosophers of this world are men of deep reflection and inventive genius, who propose a doctrine, and by its speciousness gather round them followers, found schools, and in the event do wonderful things. These are the men, who at length change the face of society, reverse laws and opinions, subvert governments, and overthrow kingdoms; or they extend the range of our knowledge, and, as it were, introduce us into new worlds. Well, this is admirable, surely, so vast is the power of mind; but, observe how inferior is this display of intellectual greatness compared with that which is seen in Christ and His saints, inferior because defective. These great philosophers of the world, whose words are so good and so effective, are themselves too often nothing more than words. Who shall warrant for their doing as well as speaking? They are shadows of Christ's prophetical office; but where is the sacerdotal or the regal? where shall we find in them the nobleness of the king, and the self-denial of the priest? On the contrary, for nobleness they are often the " meanest of mankind;" and for self-denial the most selfish and most cowardly. They can sit at ease, and follow their own pleasure, and indulge the flesh, or serve the world, while their reason is so enlightened, and their words are so influential. Of all forms of earthly greatness, surely this is the most

despicable. One sorrows to think that the soldier is by his profession but a material and brute instrument; one owns that great defect in earthly royalty, that it is worshipped without worshipping, that it commands without obeying, and resolves and effects without suffering; but what shall we say to men like Balaam, who profess without doing, who teach the truth yet live in vice, who know, but do not love?

Such is the world: but Christ came to make a new world. He came into the world to regenerate it in Himself, to make a new beginning, to be the beginning of the creation of God, to gather together in one, and recapitulate all things in Himself. The rays of His glory were scattered through the world; one state of life had some of them, another others. The world was like some fair mirror, broken in pieces, and giving back no one uniform image of its Maker. But He came to combine what was dissipated, to recast what was shattered in Himself. He began all excellence, and of His fulness have all we received. When He came, a Child was born, a Son given, and yet He was Wonderful, Counsellor, the Mighty God, the Everlasting Father, the Prince of Peace. Angels heralded a Saviour, a Christ, a Lord; but withal, He was "born in Bethlehem," and was "lying in a manger." Eastern sages brought Him gold, for that He was a King, frankincense as to a God; but on the other hand myrrh also, in token of a coming death and burial. At the last, He "bore witness to the truth" before Pilate as a Prophet, suffered on the cross as our Priest, while He was also "Jesus of Nazareth, the King of the Jews."

And so His Apostles after Him, and in His likeness, were kings, yet without the pomp; soldiers, yet with no blood but their own; teachers, yet withal their own disciples, acting out in their own persons, and by their own labours, their own precepts.

And so, in after-times, those Saints and Fathers to whom we look up, have joined these three offices together. Great doctors they have been, but not mere philosophers or men of letters, but noble-minded rulers of the churches; nor only so, but preachers, missionaries, monastic brethren, confessors, and martyrs. This is the glory of the Church, to speak, to do, and to suffer, with that grace which Christ brought and diffused abroad. And it has run down even to the skirts of her clothing. Not the few and the conspicuous alone, but all her children, high and low, who walk worthy of her and her Divine Lord, will be shadows of Him. All of us are bound, according to our opportunities,—first to learn the truth; and moreover, we must not only know, but we must impart our knowledge. Nor only so, but next we must bear witness to the truth. We must not be afraid of the frowns or anger of the world, or mind its ridicule. If so be, we must be willing to suffer for the truth. This was that new thing that Christ brought into the world, a heavenly doctrine, a system of holy and supernatural truths, which are to be received and transmitted, for He is our Prophet, maintained even unto suffering after His pattern, who is our Priest, and obeyed, for He is our King.

SERMON VI.

faith and Experience.

" The Lord seeth not as man seeth ; for man looketh on the outward appearance, but the Lord looketh on the heart."—1 SAM. xvi. 7.

HE among the sons of Jesse, whom Samuel thought to be the destined king of Israel, was of imposing countenance and stature ; not like David, a youth, ruddy indeed, and handsome, but one whom the Philistines might despise. Samuel and Goliath, a prophet of God and a heathen giant, both judged by what met their eyes. Samuel, when he saw the manly form and face of Eliab, said, " Surely the Lord's anointed is before Him." And God answered him, " Look not on his countenance, or on the height of his stature, because I have refused him, for the Lord seeth not as man seeth; for man looketh on the outward appearance, but the Lord looketh on the heart." And Goliath, when " he looked about and saw David," " disdained him, for he was but a youth, and ruddy, and of a fair countenance." And to him David answered for himself; " The Lord saveth not with sword and spear, for the battle is the Lord's[1]." Even then, as

[1] 1 Sam. xvii. 42. 47.

in the latter days, the weak were strong, and the strong weak; the first last, and the last first; the mighty cast down from their seat, and the humble and meek exalted.

And much more now, when the Most High has hid Himself beneath a servant's form, and after ascending into heaven, sent His Holy Ghost as our invisible Guide and Comforter, now, far more than before, do we require to be warned, not to judge by what we see, but by what God has said. When His word and His outward world are at variance in the information they convey to us, it is our bounden duty to trust the revealed word, and not the visible world. Not that sight is not His gift, but that He has demanded of us as Christians, as a sort of poor return for His love to us, that when these two informants, one natural, the other revealed, oppose each other, we should trust for a little while the latter,—for a little while, till this world of shadows passes away, and we find ourselves in that new world, in which there is no contradiction between sight and hearing, but absolute unity and harmony in all things, for He is the light of it. But till then, it is our very profession, as children of the kingdom, to walk by faith not by sight. And hence many warnings are given us in the New Testament, against our forming absolute judgments of men and things, from what we see; to "judge nothing before the time, till the Lord come, who both will bring to light the hidden things of darkness, and will make manifest the counsels of the hearts; and then shall every man have praise of God." Again, St. Paul says, "Do we look on things after the outward appearance? if any man trust to himself that he is Christ's, let him of himself think this again, that as he is Christ's, even so are we Christ's." And in like manner our Saviour, " Judge not according to the appearance, but judge righteous judgment¹."

Now I propose to consider one part of this large subject; viz. to insist on a point which is very important, the necessity we lie under, if we would be Christians indeed, of drawing our religious notions and views, not from what we see, but from what we do not see and only hear; or rather, the great mistake under which men of the world lie, of judging of religious subjects merely by what the experience of life tells them. We must believe something ; the difference between religious men and others is, that the latter trust this world, the former the world unseen. Both of them have faith, but the one have faith in the surface of things, the other in the word of God. Men of the world take it for granted, that all that seems to be really is. They fancy there is nothing deeper than what presents itself at first view. They cannot bring themselves to think that truth is hidden; that men's characters, words, works, professions, fortunes, doctrines, reasonings, must be carefully and critically examined, before we can find even the traces of truth. They readily allow that in sciences of the world, the appearance is contrary to the truth of things. They quite understand that the great agencies in the material system are invisible, and that what is visible is deceptive. They are not loth to admit that the stars do not move, though they seem to do so; and that subtle fluids and

¹ 1 Cor. iv. 5.   2 Cor. x. 7.   John vii. 24.

[s. d.]   F mysterious influences, which it has required ages to detect, are the causes of the most wonderful revolutions in nature; yet they think it folly to distrust the face of the world in religious matters, or to search amid the perishable shadows of time for the footsteps and the resting-places of the Eternal.

On the other hand, the very ground from which religious men start, is the avowal, that the sights of this world are against them, and that they must believe God in spite of this. This deserves attention, because it is very common for cavillers to bring it, and for Christians to feel it, as an objection to the doctrines of Scripture, that they contradict sight. But whatever be the worth of the objection in the mouth of an unbeliever, it is irrelevant and preposterous when dwelt upon by Christians; seeing that, when we were made Christians, we began as a first step by owning that sight was against us, and resolving, by God's grace, to trust His word more than sight. This is a representation, which, so made, few persons will deny; I proceed to exemplify more fully what I mean by particular instances, which will make it, I fear, more difficult to be received by a good many.

1. For instance: Let us consider a doctrine much debated and much resisted at this day,—the doctrine of Baptismal Regeneration. Scripture tells us expressly that, " except a man be born of water and of the Spirit, he cannot enter the kingdom of God ; " and that God has saved us " by the washing of regeneration ; " and that " Baptism saves us ; " and that we " wash away our sins " by Baptism. No other means have been pointed out to us for attaining regeneration, or the new birth; so that, while

Baptism is said to take us out of a state of nature into a state of grace, if a man is not born again in Baptism, it does not appear how he is to be born again. Such is the true doctrine, which has ever been received in the whole Church. Yet, on the other hand, consider how hard a battle faith has to fight against experience in this matter, and how certain it is that nothing but faith can overcome it.

That Baptism really does change a man's moral state as well as his state in God's sight, that it gives him the means of being a better man than he otherwise would be, and therefore, in the end, occasions his being a much better or a much worse man than he would have been without it; that two souls, one baptized and one not, are not in the same moral condition, but that the baptized, as having been regenerate, is inwardly either better or worse, or both at once,—in some things better, and in some things worse,—than the unbaptized; so that Baptism may be said to be like the effect of the sun's light in place of twilight, removing the sameness or the dulness of the landscape, and bringing it out into all sorts of hues, pleasant or unpleasant, according as we profit by it or not; or like education, which also (though in another way) developes and diversifies the mind;—all this seems to be certain from Scripture. But whether certain or not, these effects do not show themselves perceptible at first, or perhaps at all. Knowing others, as we here know them at best, knowing them but a little, and not any number of them in the same respect, so that we cannot compare them together, we are not able, commonly speaking, to discover the minute points of their characters; and therefore the great diffi-

culties which I am going to state lie in the way of the
Scripture doctrine of Baptismal Regeneration.

I say then, we have these startling appearances :—
Persons brought up without Baptism may show themselves just the same in character, temper, opinions, and
conduct, with those who have been baptized ; or when
these differ from those, this difference may be sufficiently or exactly accounted for by their education.

An unbaptized person may be brought up with baptized persons, and acquire their tone of thought, their
mode of viewing things, and their principles and
opinions, just as if he were baptized. He may suppose
that he has been baptized, and others may think so ;
and on inquiry it may be found out that he has not
been baptized.

On the other hand, a baptized person may acquire the
ways of going on, and the sentiments and modes of
talking of those who despise Baptism, and seem neither
better nor worse than they, but just the same.

An unbaptized person may in after-life be baptized ;
and if quiet and religious before, may remain so afterwards, with no change of any kind in his own consciousness about himself, or in the impression of others
about him.

Or, he may have had a formed character before Baptism, and not a pleasing one ; he may have been rude
and irreverent, or worldly-minded. He may have improved ; he may have had faith sufficiently to bring him
to Baptism, and, as far as we can judge, may have
received it worthily ; yet he may remain, improved
indeed just so much as is implied in his having had

faith to come to Baptism, but apparently in no greater measure.

Or, he may come to Baptism and improve after it, but only in such way as to all appearance he might have improved without having received it when he did; viz. from the intercourse of friends, from reading religious books, from study and thought, or from the trials of life.

Again, he may come to Baptism as a mere form, or from worldly motives, and yet in appearance be no worse than he was before. If he had a mixture of good and evil in him before, the same apparently remains.

And again, whether he has received Baptism or not, he is liable to the same changes of mind, to the same religious influences, nay, may run through the same spiritual course, may be gradually moulded on the same habits,—perhaps be affected in some remarkable way, so remarkable that it may be called a conversion, and what he himself may incorrectly call a regeneration,—which it cannot be, if we judge according to Scripture, and not appearance, since he either has been already regenerated in Baptism, or has not yet been regenerated, being un-baptized. Yet the same religious experience (as it sometimes is called) may befall him, whether he has been baptized or not.

It is indeed most obvious and striking how, in all systems, whether we take our own, or that which principally obtains abroad, or that of any dissenting bodies, we find the same sort of moral character attaching to this or that class of persons; how rank, wealth or power forms men every where alike; how all systems

have their freethinkers; how all have the same parties.
Men are formed every where by the influence of visible things on the same types, and correspond one to
another, as if proving against the Word of God, that
baptism and grace are not the really influential principles
among men, but the world that is seen.

Here then, I say, is experience counter to the word of
God, which says, that except a man be born of water
and the Spirit he is no member of Christ's kingdom.
To which may be added, the nature of the rite of
Baptism itself, its great simplicity, even supposing
immersion is used, and much more in the case of pour-
ing or sprinkling. No outward rite indeed can measure
the great dignity of the gift of regeneration; were the
outward ceremonies ever so laborious they would not be
adequate; a simple rite, on the other hand, is a symbol
of the freeness of the grace given us, which requires
nothing on our part but repentance and faith;—yet, at
the same time, the more simple the outward rite is, and
the greater, on the other hand, the hidden gift, the
greater trial is it to believe that it is given through the
rite. Whether, then, we consider the ceremony of Baptism itself, or the persons who are made subjects of it, in
both respects, sight and the word of God, the doctrine
and the fact, are strangely contrasted. Let us not deny
that it is so; why should we? Let us fairly and
calmly gaze upon the contrariety, upon the difficulty, as
some call it, or rather on the trial,—the trial of Faith,
which alone overcomes the world.

2. This, then, is one trial of Faith. Another, which
has in all ages assailed it, and not the least in our own

age, is the success which attends measures or institutions which are not in accordance with the revealed rule of duty. This was the perplexity of believers in the old time, as we read in the Psalms and Prophets, viz. that the wicked should prosper, while God's servants seemed to fail: and so in Gospel times. Not that the Church has not this peculiar prerogative with it, which no other religious body has, that as it began with Christ's first coming, so it will never fail till He comes again; but that for a time, in the course of single generations, nay, I may say in every age and at all times, it seems to be failing, and its enemies to be prevailing. It is the peculiarity of the warfare between the Church and the world, that the world seems ever gaining on the Church, yet the Church is really ever gaining on the world. Its enemies are ever triumphing over it as vanquished, and its members ever despairing; yet it abides. It abides, and it sees the ruin of its oppressors and enemies. "O how suddenly do they consume, perish, and come to a fearful end!" Kingdoms rise and fall; nations expand and contract; dynasties begin and end; princes are born and die; confederacies are made and unmade, and parties, and companies, and crafts, and guilds, and establishments, and philosophies, and sects, and heresies. They have their day, but the Church is eternal; yet *in* their day they seem of much account. How in early times must the Church have been dismayed, when, from the East, the false religion of Mahomet spread far and near, and Christians were extirpated or converted by it by thousands! Yet even that long-lived delusion is now failing; and though younger than the Church by some centuries, has aged before it. And so in like manner, in spite of the duration of the Christian name hitherto, much there is to try our faith at this moment, who cannot see the future, and therefore cannot see the short duration of what shows proudly and successfully now. We at this day see a number of philosophies, sects, and parties, thriving and extending, and the Church seems poor and helpless, as if its very place were to be insulted, and its very calling to give way. We see men in one department of philosophy rejecting the accounts, for instance, of the Creation or the Deluge, as they stand in the Old Testament; others setting aside the precepts of almsgiving, and the like, as given in the New; others disputing the historical narratives contained in the Old; and others denying those interpretations of the doctrinal portion of Scripture which have ever been received. We see imperfect forms of Christianity made the religion of states and nations, and apparently bringing forth good fruit; nay, apparently flourishing more than many forms which are more perfect and catholic. We see the Church in slavery apparently flourishing more than the Church free. We see sects apparently flourishing more than the Church. We see wrong principles, unsound doctrines, apparently making men what Christians should be, and what the true Gospel can alone really make any one. We find the teachers of what we must call heresy, and the ministers of division, doing what the Church does not, or cannot do; we find dissenting bodies sending missions to the heathen, and apparently succeeding in converting them. I do not speak of the fact, that good men are found among bodies which are not in communion with the Church. This is no difficulty to faith. That God who raised up Elijah and Elisha in Israel, has no where said He will not now also extend His mercies wider than His promises: but I speak of the apparent infringement of His promises in the visible disorders of the Church, and the triumph of other bodies over it. When we dwell on such facts as these, I do think it requires some special faith in those who are exposed to the temptation, to keep close to the ancient ways of the Church Catholic, and to remain untouched by the sophistries and unmoved by the successes, of this world which surrounds us.

3. Another instance in which Experience and Faith are seriously opposed to each other, though the contrast is not exhibited on so open or so wide a field, is to be found in the case of those who deny the doctrine of the Ever-blessed Trinity, or the Incarnation, or the Atonement, or original sin, or eternal punishment. These persons, indeed, are often such in their tempers and lives as to be no difficulty to the Christian. They are men of immoral habits, or at least grossly self-indulgent; or men who for years have never thought any thing of religion, and then just at the last consider that they must take up some profession, and adopt whatever meets their taste; or they are evidently worldly, insincere men, as far as we can judge of others, or overbearing men and unamiable. But this is not always the case. We may meet with persons of unsound faith so adorned with interesting traits of character, as to try us severely. Of course we are not called on to judge any one abso-

lutely; we leave that to God. But I can fancy a case
of the following kind. A man on the one hand strong in
his contempt for the most sacred subjects; not believing
the doctrines of original sin, everlasting punishment,
and the Atonement; having no formed opinion concerning our Lord, whether He was really God or not; never
partaking in Holy Communion, and seldom going to
Church : and I can conceive the same man, not merely
amiable, benevolent, and friendly—this might easily be
allowed—but showing forth (at least to our perceptions)
an integrity in his daily business, an honourable view of
things, a correctness, a delicacy of sentiment, a consider-
ateness and generosity of conduct, and, in a certain sense,
a reliance upon Providence, a feeling of the greatness of
religion and of its awfulness, a knowledge and admiration
of Scripture, and when he comes into trouble, a recur-
rence to it, and a touching application of its words to
himself;—the while his doctrinal views are to all appearance as unsatisfactory as before. And to those who see
this, is it not a trial of Faith, quite as great as the doctrine of Baptismal Regeneration can be, how a person
apparently with open eyes, can deny the power and the
grace of our Saviour, and the great need of His coming
on earth, and yet have so much religious feeling and
principle as he has? Is such a man acting under the
influence of God's grace or not? If not, how is it he
practises so much? and if he is, how is it he does not
believe more?

4. One more instance shall be mentioned, of this opposition between Christian Faith and the Experience of
life. We are expressly told in Scripture that the im-

penitent shall go into fire everlasting. Now this, though
so plainly stated by our Lord Himself, that one would
think no one, believer or not, can deny that He has said
so, nevertheless is a hard thing surely to receive, where
men will not believe, and will go by sight. It is, indeed,
no difficulty for any one to sit at home and believe the
doctrine; it is no trial to his faith if he live among
books, or be blessed with a religious circle of friends, or
happily be under a parent's roof, or, like young Samuel
or aged Anna, live almost in the temple of God: but if
he is thrown upon the world, if he has an opportunity
of coming very near profligate, or hardened, or worldly,
or unbelieving men, or, which is the same thing, if
he has any particular tie connecting him with any
such, then will he feel how hard a saying it is that
any one, even the most wicked of men, can be destined
to eternal punishment. There is no man ever so bad
but to our erring eyes has some redeeming points of
character. There is no man but has some human feelings or other: and those very feelings impress us with a
sort of conviction that he cannot possibly be the destined
companion of evil spirits. Hell is the habitation of no
human affections. Let a man be ever so blood-stained,
so awfully blasphemous, or so profligate, yet at least, at
times, perhaps when in pain or weariness, he shows
something to excite our interest and pity. And if not,
then his very pain seems to plead for him. His capa-
bility of pain, and his showing that he feels it, seem to
connect him with us, and to disconnect him with those
fallen spirits, who have no sympathies, no weaknesses, but
are impenetrable and absolute evil, even though they suffer.

Even the witch of Endor showed some compassion for Saul, and moves us by showing it. We are told, " And the woman came unto Saul, and saw that he was sore troubled, and said unto him, Behold, thine handmaid hath obeyed thy voice, and I have put my life in my hand, and have hearkened unto thy words which thou spakest unto me. Now therefore, I pray thee, hearken thou also unto the voice of thine handmaid, and let me set a morsel of bread before thee, and eat, that thou mayest have strength, when thou goest on thy way. But he refused, and said, I will not eat. But his servants, together with the woman, compelled him; and he hearkened unto their voice [1]." Such was the conduct of one who avowedly dealt with familiar spirits. Oh miserable we then, if we are of the number of those who prefer sight to Faith! Oh, miserable, if when our Saviour, the very Word of God, and the True Witness, speaks plainly one way, we listen to the serpent's voice, saying, " Ye shall not surely die!" We have no right indeed, surely not, to say absolutely that this or that man whom we see and can point at, is destined to future punishment. God forbid! for we can but judge by out-ward appearance, and God alone seeth the hearts of men. But we are expressly told that there are persons so destined; we are told that the finally impenitent, whoever they shall be, are so destined; and whatever the sight of things may tell us, however the weaknesses and way-wardnesses of our hearts may plead against such awful truths, however our feelings, and imaginations, and reason may be assailed, yet " let God be true, and every

[1] 1 Sam. xxviii. 21—23.

man a liar;" let us believe Him, though the whole world rose up and with one voice denied His words. Let us accept the truth, as an act of faith towards God, and as a most solemn warning to ourselves, that "the wicked shall be turned into hell, and all the people that forget God;" that they "shall be punished with everlasting destruction from the presence of the Lord, and the glory of His power, when He shall come to be glorified in His saints, and to be admired in all them that believe, in that day[1]."

To conclude. Let us pray God to teach us: we need His teaching; we are very blind. The Apostles on one occasion said to Christ, when His words tried them, "Increase our faith." Let us come to Him honestly: we cannot help ourselves; we do not know ourselves; we need His grace. Whatever perplexity the world gives us, whether about the doctrine of regenerating Baptism, or about the Church Apostolic, or about the necessity of maintaining the Gospel faith, or about the doctrine of everlasting punishment, (blessed are they who have no such trials, but some have!) let us come to Him with pure and sincere minds; imploring Him to reveal to us what we know not, to incline our hearts when they are stubborn, and to make us love and obey Him honestly while we seek, and not to seek mere barren knowledge, "which perisheth with the using."

---

[1] Ps. ix. 17. 2 Thess. i. 9, 10.

SERMON VII.

Faith and the World.

" Though hand join in hand, the wicked shall not be unpunished: but the seed of the righteous shall be delivered."—PROV. xi. 21.

WHEN we hear speak of the wicked, we are apt to think that men of abandoned lives and unprincipled conduct, cruel, crafty, or profligate men, can alone be meant. This obtains almost universally; we think that evil, in any sufficient sense of the word, is something external to us, and at a distance. Thus in the case of children, when they hear of bad men and wicked men, they have no conception that evil can really be near them. They fancy, with a fearful curiosity, something which they have not seen, something foreign and monstrous, as if brought over the seas, or the production of another sphere; though, in truth, evil, and in its worst and most concentrated shape, is born with them, lives within them, is not subdued except by a supernatural gift from God, and is still in them, even when God's grace has brought it under. And so, when we grow up, whether we are thrown upon the world or not, we commonly do not understand that what Scripture says of sin, of its odiousness and its peril, applies to us. The world itself, **even** though we see it, appears not to be the world ; that is, not the world which Scripture speaks of. **We do not discern,** we do not detect, the **savour of its** sinfulness ; **its ways** are pleasant to us ; and **what** Scripture **says of** wickedness, and of misery as attending **on it, does not,** as we think, apply **to the** world **we** see.

And hence it is, that when we read, as in the text, of the short triumph and the overthrow of wickedness, when we **read** that "though hand join in hand, the **wicked shall not** be unpunished," **we** have **a picture** brought before **us of some overbearing tyranny,** or some perfidious conspiracy, **or some** bold and avowed banding against religion, some event of a generation **or a** century, **and** nothing short of it. And such specimens of evil doubtless are especially intended **by** the sacred writer; still, after all, much more is included in his meaning, much which is ordinary, **much which we** see before our eyes.

Can **it** indeed be otherwise ? Is not the world in itself evil? Is it an accident, **is it** an occasion, is it but an excess, or a crisis, **or a** complication of circumstances, which constitutes its sinfulness ? or, rather, is it not one of our three great spiritual enemies, at all times, and **under** all circumstances and all changes, ungodly, **un-**believing, seducing, and anti-christian ? Surely we must grant **it to be so.** Why else in Baptism **do we vow to** wage **war** against **it ?** Why else does Scripture speak of it in the **terms which we** know **so well,** if **we** will but attend to them ? St. James **says,** that "the friendship of the world is enmity with God [1]," **so that** "whosoever

---

[1] James iv. 4.

will be a friend of the world is the enemy of God." And St. Paul speaks of "walking according to the course of this world, according to the prince of the power of the air, the spirit that now worketh in the children of disobedience [1];" and exhorts us not to be "conformed to this world," but to be "transformed by the renewing of our mind [2];" and he says that Christ "gave Himself for our sins, that He might deliver us from this present evil world [3]." In like manner St. John says, "Love not the world, neither the things that are in the world. If any man love the world, the love of the Father is not in him [4]." Let us be quite sure, then, that that confederacy of evil which Scripture calls the world, that conspiracy against Almighty God of which Satan is the secret instigator, is something wider, and more subtle, and more ordinary, than mere cruelty, or craft, or profligacy; it is that very world in which we are; it is not a certain body or party of men, but it is human society itself. This it is which is our greatest enemy; and this it is of which the text in its fulness speaks, when it says that "though hand join in hand, the wicked shall not be unpunished." It is powerful at present, but in the end it shall be overthrown; and then these its separate members "shall not be unpunished," but "the seed of the righteous shall be delivered."

Now I shall attempt an explanation of what may be supposed to be meant in the text by "hand joining in hand," and of the sense in which it is fulfilled in the course of human affairs in every age. The one peculiar and characteristic sin of the world is this, that whereas

---

[1] Eph. ii. 2.   [2] Rom. xii. 2.   [3] Gal. i. 4.   [4] 1 John ii. 15.

God would have us live for the life to come, the world
would make us live for this life. This, I say, is the
world's sin; it lives for this life, not for the next. It
takes, as the main scope of human exertion, an end which
God forbids; and consequently all that it does becomes
evil, because directed to a wrong end.

This is a thing which seems easy to say, but which
should be steadily considered. In this respect the temptations of the world differ from temptations of the flesh.
The flesh is not rational, nor appeals to reason; but the
world reasons. The works of the flesh are such as St.
Paul describes them,—variance, hatred, murders, adulte-
ries, uncleanness, and drunkenness. Pride, cruelty, wrath,
revenge, obstinacy, sensuality, are works of the flesh.
They are the spontaneous fruit of the unrenewed mind,
as thorns and thistles are the natural growth of the earth.
But the case is different as regards the world. The
world has many sins, but its peculiar offence is that of
daring to reason contrary to God's Word and will. It
puts wrong aims before itself, and acts towards them.
It goes wrong as if on principle, and prefers its own way
of viewing things to God's way. When Eve saw that
the forbidden fruit was good for food, she was tempted
through the flesh; and when the serpent said, "Ye shall
not surely die," he used the temptation proper to the
world—false reason.

Now you will see this by taking a survey of the
world, and seeing how and why it disobeys God. God,
in Scripture, says one thing; the world says another.
God says that we should live for the life to come; the
world says that we should live for this life. How is it

able to say so? what are the arguments it uses? Let
us consider.

Men seem made for this world; this is what prevails
on them to neglect the next world: they think they
have reason for concluding, they think they see, that
this world is the world for which they are to labour,
and to which they are to devote their faculties. And
therefore they persist in denying that they must live for
the next world. It is not that they profess to run
counter to God's Word, but they deny that He has said
that they must live directly for the next world. As the
Israelites did not avowedly cast off the God of Abraham
when they worshipped the golden calf, but professed to
worship Him under that symbol, so men generally,
when they pursue this world as their supreme good, and
as their god, deny that they *are* disowning their Lord
and Maker, but maintain that He wishes them to
worship Him by means of and in this world.

Now these are the sort of considerations which seduce
them to think that this world is all in all :—

1. For instance, there are a number of faculties and
talents which seem only to exist in this world, and to be
impossible in another. Consider the varieties of mental
gifts which are in active exercise on all sides of us, and
you will see what I mean; such as talent for business,
or talent for the useful arts, mechanical talent. Or,
again, consider the talents which go to make up a great
warrior. They seem as if evidently made for this
world, and this world only. If such ability is not to be
used, it may be asked, why is it given? If a person
lives only for the next world, what is the use of it?

Our aim then, they say, must be an aim of this life, our
end of action must be in this world, because our talents
point that way. Talents are not necessary for religion,
talents are not necessary for preparing for the life to
come; yet they are given, therefore they are given for
this life. Thus men argue : I do not say that they
bring out their full meaning in words; but this is the
argument latent in their minds. They say or think that
if religion disowns the wisdom of this world; if it disowns, as its real and true ground, power, and rank, and
might, and knowledge, and ability,—which it does; then,
all these things may disown religion, do not belong to
religion, need not aim at religion. It parts with them,
they part with it. Religion, therefore (they say), is
not for this world. It is a private thing for each man's
own conscience, but not for society, not for acting upon
on a large scale. And this, both because man has
faculties which religion does not deign to make its
instruments; and also because these faculties do not
exist beyond this life, and therefore, if they are to be
employed, must be employed here.

2. Another consideration of the same kind, which is
adapted to influence men of this world in the same
direction, if they give their minds to consider the
matter, is the existence of national character. This
seems to them to be a providential mark of what this
world is intended to be. The character of *one individual* may be accidental, and may arise from his own
caprice or wilfulness; but when a whole multitude are
one and the same, this cannot arise from themselves, it
must arise from their very nature, it must be a token of

the will of God. That character, they say, whatever it is, must be pleasing to God. Now one nation is manly, and another is brave but cruel, and a third sagacious, and a fourth energetic and busy. These then, it is argued, are the qualities of mind for which this life is intended. Where was there ever a religious nation? or, at least, how is it possible, in the nature of things, that nations, differing as they do, and so complete in their differences, should have been intended for one form or creed? Religion, then, is for the next world, not for this. No (thus men seem to proceed), energy and activity, enterprise, adventure, rivalry, and invention,— war, politics, and trade,—these are what men are made for here; not for faith, fear, humiliation, prayer, self-discipline, penance, tenderness of conscience, sanctity. It is very well if individuals feel themselves called this way; but it is a private matter for themselves, not to be urged on others. Or again, if we look at the religion of different men, one developes one set of ideas, another another; one adopts a strict creed, another is free and bold. All religions then are matters of opinion, because they are matters of disposition and habit.

3. I have spoken of nations, because the argument then can be made to look specious; but men generally apply it to the case of individuals. They go into the world, and they find individuals of this or that character, and not religious; and hence they argue that religion is but a theory, because it is not on the face of society. This is what they call seeing life and knowing the world, and it leads them to despise strict principle and religious conduct as narrow-minded. They say that religion is

very well for a domestic circle, but will not do for the world; for they take men as facts, as they might take the materials of the physical world, stones or vegetables; as if they were what they were, and could not be otherwise; and as one cannot change the elements, but must take them for what they are, and use them, so they think we ought to deal with human beings. And as a person would be called a theorist, who cherished certain ideas about the natural world, to which the facts of that world did not answer, so they think a man a mere dreamer, who says that men ought not to be what they confessedly are; who comes to them with a doctrine which is above them, refuses to deal with them as he finds them, and tries to raise them, and change them, and to make them what they are not. As they would think a man a madman who waited for rivers to have done flowing, or mountains to make way before him, so they think it obstinate, impracticable, perverse, and almost insane, to run counter to the natural man, to thwart his wishes, to condemn his opinions, and to insist on his submitting to a rule foreign to him. Great philosophers have said, that in the case of the material creation we overcome nature by yielding to it, and because this is true of matter, the world would have it in the same sense true of mind.

4. Another consideration which the world urges in its warfare against religion, as I have already implied, is, that religion is unnatural. It is objected (what indeed cannot be denied, and is almost a truism) that religion does not bring the elementary and existing nature of man to its highest perfection, but thwarts and impairs

it, and provides for a second and new nature. It is said, and truly, that religion treats the body hardly, and is severe with the soul. How different is the world, which conceives that the first object of life is to treat our inferior nature indulgently, that all methods of living are right which do this, and all wrong which do not! Hence men lay it down, that wealth is the measure of all good, and the end of life; for a state of wealth may be described as a state of ease and comfort to body and mind. They say that every act of civil government is wrong, which does not tend to what they thus consider to be man's happiness; that utility and expedience, or, in other words, whatever tends to produce wealth, is the only rule on which laws should be framed; that what tends to higher objects is not useful or expedient; that higher objects are a mere dream; that the only thing substantial is this life, and the only wisdom, to cherish and enjoy it. And they are so obstinate in this their evil view of things, that they will not let other people take their own view and rest in it; but are bent on making all men (what they call) happy in their way. In their plans of social and domestic economy, their projects of education, their mode of treating the poor, the one object which they think sufficient for happiness is, that men should have the necessaries of life according to their condition. On the other hand, they think that religion in all its duties clashes with this life, and is therefore unnatural. Almsgiving they think the virtue of a barbarous or half-civilized or badly-managed community. Fasting and watching are puerile and contemptible, for such practices interfere with nature, which

prompts us to eat and sleep. **Prayer again is a** mere
indolence. **It is better, they say, to put the** shoulder **to**
the wheel, than **to spend** time **in wishing it to** move.
Again, making **a stand for particular doctrines is**
thought unnecessary **and unmeaning, as if there were**
any excellence or **merit in believing this rather than**
that, or **believing any thing at** all.

These are some of the arguments on **which the world**
relies, in defending the interests of this life against those
of the next. It says, that the constitution of **our body**
and the powers of our mind tend towards an **end short of**
the next life; and therefore **that religion, or** the thought
of the next world, is unnatural. **I answer by admitting**
that religion is in this sense unnatural; but I maintain that
Christ came to bring in **a higher nature into** this world
of men, and that **this** could not **be done except** by interfering with the nature which originally belongs to it.
Where the spiritual **system runs counter to** the natural,
the natural must **give way. God has** graciously willed
to bring us **to** heaven ; **to** practise **a** heavenly life on
earth, **certainly, is a thing** above earth. It is like trying
to execute some high and refined harmony on an insig-
nificant instrument. **In** attempting it, that instrument
would be taxed **beyond** its powers, and would be sacri-
ficed to great ideas beyond itself. And **so, in a certain**
sense, **this** life, and **our** present nature, is sacrificed for
heaven and the new creature ; that while our outward man
perishes, our **inward man may** be renewed day by day.

If, indeed, **men will urge** that religion is against
nature, **as** an objection **to** religion, certainly we must
become infidels at once ; for can any thing be so mar-

vellously and awfully beyond nature, both the nature
of man and the nature of God, as that the Eternal Son
of God should take flesh and be born of a virgin, and
suffer and die on the cross, and rise again? Let us
cease, then, to fear this taunt, that religion makes us lead
an unnatural or rather supernatural life, seeing it has no
force, except it withal persuade us to disown our Saviour,
who for us took on Him another nature not His own,
and was in the economy of grace what by His Divine
generation from the Father He could not be.

5. But to proceed: the strongest argument which the
world uses in its favour, is the actual success of its ex-
periment in cultivating the natural faculties of body and
mind; for success seems a fresh mark of God's will, over
and above the tendencies of nature. This is what influences men most especially to neglect the words of Scripture. Any thing that is used for an end unsuited to it
is likely to fail; but human nature, when used for this
world, does not fail, but does its work well, and therefore
it seems as if it ought so to be used. For instance, we
argue that a certain animal is the work of God; why?
because its parts fit in together and sustain one another.
We bring it as a proof of design, a proof that it is made
by God, and does not come of chance, that its teeth and
its claws are fitted to its nature and habits, and to each
other. Now human society, or this world our enemy,
seems in like manner to bear about it marks of design,
and therefore to come from God. Enter the mixed multitude of men, and see how they go on. Men may or
may not have the fear of God before their eyes, yet they
seem to go on equally well either way. Each has his

own occupation, his own place; he may be an irreligious and immoral man, a scoffer, or covetous, or heartless, or he may be serious and correct in his conduct, yet none of these things interfere much one way or the other with the development of our social state, the formation of communities, the provisions for mutual protection, the interchange of good offices, and the general intercourse of man with man. Punctuality, honesty, business-like despatch, perseverance, sobriety, friendliness, trust in each other, steady co-operation, these are the sort of virtues which seem sufficient for carrying on the great empires of the world; what a man's character is besides, seems nothing to the purpose. Each nation testifies to each, north to south, and east to west, as to what is enough, and what is required, and Christianity is not included in the list of requisites. East and west, north and south, are of different religions,—here there is no agreement; the form of religion may be this or may be that, and the world goes on the same; but the value of such qualities as I have named is acknowledged every where. If these did not constitute the true excellence of our nature, it is argued, they would not be enough to live by. No vital part can be wanting in the world, because, in fact, it has life.

I am obliged to state this in an abstract way, and cannot proceed to instances, because I should become familiar. But let any one betake himself to the world, and go through but one day in it; let him consider the course of occurrences through which he passes, only by taking a journey and passing day or night among strangers, or at an inn; and he will recognize what I mean. He will understand what this argument is, which the very face of society presents; viz. that religion is not needed for this world, and therefore is of no great importance.

Now, let it be observed, what I have already implied, men of the world do not deny the existence and power of God. No; they only hold this—(I do not mean in words, but implicitly)—they hold, I say, not that there is not an Almighty Ruler, whose subjects they are, but they deny in their hearts all that is meant by religion, or religious service; they deny their duty towards God; they deny His personal existence, and their subjection to Him. Yes; and if they are obliged at any time to own the existence of religious duty, then they say, to get rid of the subject, in an insincere way, lightly, heartlessly, sometimes scoffingly, that the best kind of religion is " to do their duty in this world," that this is the true worship of God; in other words, that the pursuit of money, of credit, of power, that the gratification of self, and the worship of self, is doing their duty. This unbelief you see in a variety of shapes. For instance, many persons openly defend the aim at rising in the world, and speak in applause of an honourable ambition; as if the prizes of this world were from heaven, and the steps of this world's ladder were the ascent of Angels which Jacob saw. Others, again, consider that their duty lies simply in this,—in making money for their families. The soldier thinks that fighting for his king is his sufficient religion; and the statesman, even when he is most blameless, that serving his country is religion. God's service, as such, as distinct from the service of this world, is in no sense recognized. Faith, hope, love, devotion, are mere names; some visible idol is taken as the substitute for God.

And will God Almighty thus be defrauded of what is due to Him? Will He allow the seductions of this world's sophistry, against which He has Himself warned us, to excuse us in His sight at the last day? Will it be sufficient to acquit us at His judgment-seat for neglecting His Word, that we have trusted the world? for scoffing at faith, that we have lived by sight? Will it compensate for neglecting the God and Father of our Lord Jesus Christ, that we have been Pantheists? is not this our very calling as Christians, to live by faith? If we do not, it is mere trifling to call ourselves Christians at all. The world promises that, if we trust it, we cannot go wrong. Why? because it is so many—there are so many men in it; they must be right. This is what it seems boldly to say,—"God cannot punish so many." So it is, we know, in human law. The magistrate never can punish a very great number of the community at once; he is obliged to let the multitude of culprits escape him, and he makes examples;—and this is what we cannot help fancying God will do. We do not allow ourselves to take in the idea that He can, and that He has said He will, punish a thousand as easily as one. What the poor and ignorant man, who lives irreligiously, professes, is what all really profess. He, when taxed with neglect of religion, says that "he is as good as his neighbours," he speaks out; he speaks abruptly, but he does but say what multitudes feel who do not say it. They think that this world is too great an evil for God to punish; or rather that therefore it is not an evil, because it is a great one. They cannot compass the idea that God should allow so great an evil to exist, as the world would be, if it is evil; and therefore, since He does allow it, it is not an evil. In vain does Scripture assure them that it is an evil, though God allows it. In vain does the whole Psalter, from beginning to the end, proclaim and protest that the world is against the truth, and that the saints must suffer. In vain do Apostles tell us, that the world lieth in wickedness; in vain does Christ Himself declare, that broad is the way that leadeth to destruction, and many there be that go in thereat. In vain do Prophets tell us, that in the end the saints shall possess the kingdom,—implying they do not possess it now. In vain is the vast judgment of the Deluge; in vain the instant death of the first-born in Egypt, and of the hosts of Sennacherib. No, we will not believe; the words of the Tempter ring in our ears,—" Ye shall not surely die!" and we stake our eternal interests on sight and reason, rather than on the revealed Word of God.

O how miserable in that day, when the dead bones rise from their graves, and the millions who once lived are summoned before their Omnipotent Judge, whose breath is a fiery stream, and whose voice is like the sound of many waters! How vain to call upon the rocks to fall on us; or to attempt to hide ourselves among the trees of the garden, and to make our brother's sin cover our own; when we are in His presence, who is every where at once, and is as fully and entirely our God and Judge, as if there were no other creature but each of us in the whole world! Why will we not learn here, what then

to a certainty we shall discover, that number is not
strength? Never was a greater fallacy than to suppose
that the many must necessarily be stronger than the few;
on the contrary, power is ever concentrated and one, in
order to be power. God is one. The heathen raged,
the people imagined a vain thing; the kings of the earth
and the rulers joined hands and took counsel together;
and Christ was one. Such is the Divine rule. "There
is one Body and one Spirit," and "one hope," and "one
Lord, one faith, one baptism, one God and Father of
all." No; the number of the wicked will be but an
increase of their misery; they will but crowd their
prison.

Let us then leave the world, manifold and various as
it is; let us leave it to follow its own devices, and let us
turn to the living and true God, who has revealed Himself to us in Jesus Christ. Let us be sure that He is
more true than the whole world, though with one voice
all its inhabitants were to speak against Him. And if
we doubt where the truth lies, let us pray to Him to
reveal it to us; let us pray Him to give us humility,
that we may seek aright; honesty, that we may have no
concealed aims; love, that we may desire the truth; and
faith, that we may accept it. So that when the end
comes, and the multitudes who have joined hands in evil
are punished, we may be of those who, in the words of
the text, are "delivered." Let us put off all excuses, all
unfairness and insincerity, all trifling with our consciences, all self-deception, all delay of repentance. Let
us be filled with one wish,—to please God; and if we
have this, I say it confidently, we shall no longer be

deceived by this world, however loud it speaks, and however plausibly it argues, as if God were with it, for we shall " have an unction from the Holy One," and shall " know all things."

SERMON VIII.

The Church and the World.

" *After that ye have known God, or rather are known of God, how turn
ye again to the weak and beggarly elements, whereunto ye desire
again to be in bondage?* "—GAL. iv. 9.

IT is a doctrine frequently used by St. Paul, I need
scarcely say, as by the other sacred writers, that
the New Covenant of the Gospel has superseded the
Jewish Law and all its ordinances; that by Baptism all
who believed, Jews as well as Gentiles, were rescued
through Christ from all elements of this world, and therefore from the Jewish Law, which henceforth had no
power over them.   This he expresses in the text, in
which he rebukes the Galatians for wishing to return to
the bondage of Judaism, after they had known the God
of grace.   Again, he says to the Colossians, "If ye be
dead with Christ from the rudiments of the world, why,
as though living in the world, are ye subject to ordinances?"   Again, to the Romans he says, "Ye are
become dead to the Law by the body of Christ, that ye
should be married to another, even to Him who is
raised from the dead."   Again, "Now we are delivered
from the Law, that being dead wherein we were held :

that we should serve in newness of spirit, and not in the oldness of the letter." And again, "There is verily a disannulling of the commandment going before, for the weakness and unprofitableness thereof. For the Law made nothing perfect, but the bringing in of a better hope did. . . . The Law maketh men high priests which have infirmity; but the word of the oath, which was since the Law, maketh the Son, who is consecrated for evermore [1]." And in token of this, when our Lord gave up the ghost upon the cross, the veil of the Temple was rent in twain; for the sanctity of that Holy Place hitherto had been, but now was no more.

Such is the great doctrine which was of especial interest when St. Paul preached, ere yet the Temple was destroyed by the Romans; viz. that though we must be children of Abraham, if we would be saved, yet it is faith that makes us children; though we must be of Israel to be elect, yet that the election follows the line of the spiritual Israel, the line of Christ, the chosen Seed, and of those who are born of the Spirit of Christ; that though we must belong to the Church of God, yet that that Church is now no longer local or at Jerusalem only, but is to be found and may be propagated in all lands; that though we are under the Law, yet it is the new, or Gospel Law, which we are under, not the Law of the Letter, the Law of Moses; and "in that He saith a new Covenant, He hath made the first old. Now that which decayeth and waxeth old is ready to vanish away [2]." The Law of Moses then has failed and is gone, because Christ has come.

[1] Col. ii. 20. Rom. vii. 4, 6. Heb. vii. 18, 19. 28.   [2] Heb. viii. 13.

Now when this is said, it is sometimes asked, " If all this be so, if the Jewish Law is dead, how could it ever have been alive ? If the Law ever had power, it must have been a power from God, and if from God it must abide. Either it is not from God, or it could not come to an end. Either it never lived, or it never died. How can the appointments of the Law be what St. Paul calls them in the text, 'weak and beggarly elements,' or 'rudiments of the world,' or 'dead ordinances,' if they were divine? and that they were divine the New Testament as well as the Old assures us."

This is a question which I shall now attempt to answer.

The case then seems to be as follows :—Almighty God, in what He has graciously done for man from the beginning, has not acted against the appointments of this world, but through them. He has made those things, which in themselves were weak and unprofitable, good by His blessing; but when He withdrew His blessing, they were weak again. The Jewish polity was an element of earth, made divine by His presence, and while His presence lasted; when He withdrew it, it was again earthly, as it had been at first. Let me explain myself.

I mean this:—When God would raise up a people to be a witness of His name, He did not send on earth a race of Angels, He did not frame a polity such as man had never seen, but He took a polity of earth, and breathed His Spirit into it, that it became a living soul. Of course the Jewish government and nation were in many respects peculiar and unlike the nations around them; but they were peculiar much more in the object aimed at, viz. the worship of the true God, than in the means of promoting it. Unbelievers have been very eager before now to make out that many parts, if not the whole, of the law and customs of Moses are to be found in other nations. Thus, for instance, the rite of circumcision, which God gave to Abraham, is found to have existed among the Egyptians and elsewhere. And this holds good of a great number of the Jewish rites and usages. Accordingly, unbelievers have said with scorn, "This, then, after all, is your singular people; this is what their claim to a divine origin ends in! No part of Judaism is original; it is taken from the Egyptians and their other neighbours: it is not divine." And they have gone on to consider the Jews and to place their history in a mere secular light, and with a good deal of success. They have shown that the nation had its rise and fall like other nations, that the same political principles were in operation, the same events occurred. They have treated of the rise of the monarchy as a natural result of existing causes; and of the revolt of the tribes under Jeroboam, as a natural and justifiable revolution. They have spoken of the wealth of the Jews, and of their trade, and of their wars, and of their agriculture, all in the same worldly way, philosophically, as they have called it, and with no little disdain and superciliousness.

But in all this they have missed what was the real peculiarity of Judaism. Certainly it was, for the most part, moulded on the model to which other Eastern nations were conformed; but it differed from them in this, that, however much it was the same outwardly, there was a different principle within it. An invisible

Divine Agency was at work there, giving it an object distinct from all other polities, and drawing it up towards God. It had an external aspect, and an inward. To men of the world it looked like a polity of this world; but to the pure in heart, and to them whose eyes were opened, it would seem to be, what it really was, a minister of God. To men like Saul and Ahab it was but an earthly kingdom. Probably they saw no kind of difference, they were not sensible of any difference, between the Temple at Jerusalem, and the heathen temple at Gaza or Ascalon, or the house of Rimmon, or of Ashtaroth, the goddess of the Sidonians, except that the latter might please their taste better; as the altar at Damascus approved itself to King Ahaz. They were not aware of any thing in the Holy Land which was not in Syria or Philistia. Miracles were not so common as we are apt to suppose. They looked at Jerusalem, and its priests, and its temple, and its ceremonies, very much as worldly men regard the Church Catholic in this day, as a mere establishment.

Further, such being God's pleasure, the Jewish polity being, like other polities, and in itself, and apart from His presence, but an element of the world, would have a beginning and an end, a rise and a fall. All powers have come to an end, and so did the Jewish; I mean, from the natural progress of events. This is a circumstance which especially deceives the unbeliever. He thinks he sees in its mutability and mortality a mark that the Jewish nation was but like other nations, and that God did not reveal Himself in and through the Jews. He sees that natural causes did work a beginning

and an end to the nation; and having what he calls
accounted for its history, he thinks he need do no more:
whereas, in truth, laws of operation mark the presence,
not the absence, of the Divine Hand, and though the
outward form of Judaism was earthly, God had secretly
inspired it and used it for His purposes.

The case is the same with Christianity also. Unbelievers have been busy in assigning human causes for
its rise,—such as the discipline of the Church, or the
doctrine of a future life; and some of its defenders have
been as eager to show that these cannot be assigned.
It seems, however, to matter little whether we determine
the question this way or that; or, rather, it is more likely
beforehand that human causes *did* effect, as we familiarly
use the word " effect," what is imputed to them.   Unbelievers of this day, who profess to be philosophical,
speak of Christianity as a wonderful fact indeed in the
history of the world, but still as being human.   Now we
need not deny that in one sense it is human; that is, as
far as it is viewed externally.   It is a divine treasure,
but in earthly vessels.   Its history is that of a certain
principle of universal empire, repressed and thwarted by
circumstances; its conquests, indeed, were achieved by
moral instruments, " weapons not carnal," as St. Paul
speaks, but still they were conquests; and it may be
compared to empires of this world, to the conquests of
Nebuchadnezzar, or of the Romans, made with the sword;
or, again, it may be spoken of as a philosophy, and compared to the philosophies of men.   But if it be an empire,
if it be a philosophy, as it had its rise, it will have its
fall.   This is what unbelievers prophesy.   They look out

calmly and confidently for the fall of Christianity at length, because it rose. Since they read of its beginning, they look for its end; since the world preceded it, they think the world will outlive it. Well, and were not Scripture pledged that it should continue to the end, when Christ shall come, I see nothing to startle us, though it were to fall, and other religions to succeed it. God works by human means. As He employs individual men, and inspires them, and yet they die; so, doubtless, He might employ a body or society of men, which at length, after its course of two thousand years, might come to an end. It might be withdrawn, as other gifts of God are withdrawn, when abused. Doubtless Christianity might be such; it might be destined to expire, just as an individual man expires. Nay, it *may* actually be destined so to expire; it may be destined to age, to decay, and at length to die;—but we know that when it dies, at least the world will die with it. The world's duration is measured by it. If the Church dies, the world's time is run. The world shall never exult over the Church. If the Church falls sick, the world shall utter a wail for its own sake; for, like Samson, the Church will bury all with it. But still, so it may be in very truth, that the Christian Church may come to an end, may well come to an end, as the Jewish Church did; that is, so far as it is mortal, so far as its members are mortal.

This peculiarity of God's Providence which has now been noticed, is almost seen in the creation of man himself. Man was made rational, after he was made corporeal. " The Lord God formed man of the dust of the ground, and breathed into his nostrils the breath of life, and man *became* a living soul [1]." Here are two acts on the part of the Creator,—the forming the dust, and the breathing the life; and they are to the point here as illustrating the principle I have been insisting on. Man is confessedly formed on the same mould as other animals; his skeleton is like theirs; he is very like some of them. And unbelievers, in consequence, have been forward to assert that he does not really differ from them; and because he is outwardly like them, and has an organized body, and can be treated by medical art, as if he were but a framework of matter, and is obliged to employ his brain as an instrument of thought, that in consequence, he has not a soul; just as in regard to Judaism they have denied it to have a heavenly spirit in it, because it had an earthly body.

And the case is the same as regards the Sacraments of the Gospel. God does not make for us new and miraculous instruments wherewith to convey His benefits, but He takes, He adopts means already existing. He takes water, which already is the means of natural health and purity, and consecrates it to convey spiritual life. He changes the use of it. Again He selects bread and wine, the chief means and symbols of bodily nourishment,— He takes them, He blesses them; He does not dispense with them, but He uses them. He leaves them in appearance what they were; but He gifts them with a Divine Presence, which before they had not. As He filled the Jewish Temple of wood and stone with glory, on its consecration   as He breathed the breath of life

[1] Gen. ii. 7.

into the dust of the earth, and made it man; so He comes down in power on His chosen symbols, weak though they be in themselves, and makes them what they were not.

Now, from what has been said, this lesson may be learnt,—that things of this world are only valuable so far as God's Presence is in them, so far as He has breathed on them; in themselves they are but dust and vanity; and it is as monstrous and insane, if we thought aright, to be enamoured of any thing earthly, except it be instinct with a light from heaven, as to desire to feed on ashes, or to be chained to a corpse.

This was the fault of the Jews, as regards their Law; and this is why St. Paul calls it "ordinances," "rudiments of the world," "weak and beggarly elements," "carnal," and "unprofitable." They were indeed at all times such, compared with the Christian worship; but they were peculiarly so, when viewed in their then state, when God had left them. The Gospel restored man to the same state, or rather to a higher state than that from which he had fallen. When Adam was in paradise, he had a gift which afterwards he had not,—the gift of the Spirit; he was inhabited by a divine glory, or heavenly power, which he lost on sinning; after sinning, only his natural soul remained to him; and when he died, then that soul went away too. The Gospel then is as far above the Law, even in the best estate of the Law, as the spirit is above the mere soul, as the man of God is above the natural man. Such was the Law at best, being but a step towards restoration in those privileges in which man was first created; framed by God, but not the dwelling-place of God's Holy Spirit; only visited by Him from time to time, and having in it a certain Presence of God which sanctified it, and made it live. But when Christ came with the recovered gift of grace and glory, then that Divine Presence, whatever it was, which once had been in the Law, left it: then it was altogether dead, it was reduced back again to the mere condition of the world from which it had been taken; it relapsed into the deadness and unprofitableness of a fallen and perishable state of being; and for Christians to concern themselves with it, or to profess it, as the Galatians and others did, was as preposterous and as perverse as to join themselves to the world in any other way,—in the service of ambition and the pursuit of wealth. Well then might the Apostle say, in the words of the text, "After ye have known God, how turn ye again to the weak and beggarly elements, whereunto ye desire again to be in bondage?"

And now, too, we are able to see how far the warning of St. Paul against subjection to ordinances applies to us. Granting that this age is in no danger of Judaism,— about which I will not here pronounce,—yet, at any rate, there are dead things besides the Law of Moses, on which we are in danger of setting our hearts. The Law became carnal *when* God left it; but there are things which never were otherwise than carnal, in which God never was at all: and these may be our temptations, as the Jewish Law was a temptation to the Jews. St. John says expressly, "Love not the world, neither the things that are in the world; for *all* that is in the world, the lust of the flesh, and the lust of the eyes, and the pride of life, is not of the Father, but of the world." And again, "The world lieth in wickedness." The world may be in one age somewhat better or somewhat worse than in another, but it is in substance always the same. I mean, that the whole visible course of things, nations, empires, states, polities, professions, trades, society, pursuits of all kinds, are, I do not say directly and formally sinful (of course not), but they "*come* of evil;" they hold of evil, and they are the instruments of evil; they have in them the nature of evil; they are the progeny of sinful Adam, they have in them the infection of Adam's fall; they never would have been as we see them, but for Adam's fall. All of them, every thing in the world is in itself alien from God, and at first sight must be regarded and treated as being so; and though there are (blessed be God) exceptions to the rule through the power of the Gospel, and it is our duty to aim at increasing these, yet they must be proved to be such before we can take them to be such. Satan is the god of this world. God created all things good; but when man fell, an evil spirit possessed them, and they are evil till God touches them again with His Divine Light. In Abraham, He made a new beginning and sanctified a holy household, and that spread into a nation, and that nation became holy to the Lord. And then the mass fell away, and He preserved a remnant; and from it He has spread and diffused abroad a spiritual and regenerate kingdom far and wide, and this has encroached in a blessed way upon the world. But it is only in proportion as things that be are brought into this kingdom, and made sub-

servient to it; it is only as kings and princes, nobles
and rulers, men of business and men of letters, the
craftsman, and the trader, and the labourer, humble
themselves to Christ's Church, and (in the language of
the prophet Isaiah) "bow down to her with their faces
toward the earth, and lick up the dust of her feet[1],"
that the world becomes living and spiritual, and a fit
object of love and a resting-place to the Christian.

Now it is plain how little the mass of men aim at
taking their standard of things, or seeking a blessing
on what they do, from religion. Instead of raising
the world by faith to the level of a regenerate son of
God, they debase themselves to the world and its ordinances. It is plain, as any one will find who gives
himself the trouble to attend to it, that men in general
do not give, or feel, or seek for religious reasons for
what they do. So little is religion even the profession
of the world at present, that men, who do feel its
claims, dare not avow their feelings,—they dare not
recommend measures of whatever sort on religious
grounds. If they defend a measure publicly, or use
persuasion in private, they are obliged to conceal or put
aside the motives which one should hope do govern
them, and they allege others inferior,—nay, worldly reasons,—reasons drawn from policy, or expedience, or
common-sense (as it is called), or prudence. If they
neglect to do this, they are despised as ill-judging and
unreasonable. Nay, they are obliged thus to act, else
they will not succeed in good objects, and (what is more
to the purpose) else they will be casting pearls before

[1] Isa. xlix. 23.

swine. Can we have a clearer proof than this, that the current of things at present, in spite of the boasts of men, is essentially and radically evil,—more evil indeed, because of their boasts?

Or, again, take any of the plans and systems now in fashion,—plans for the well-being of the poor, or of the young, or of the community at large; you will find, so far from their being built on religion, religion is actually in the way, it is an encumbrance. The advocates and promoters of these plans confess that they do not know what to do with religion; their plans work very well but for religion; religion suggests difficulties which cannot be got over. On a subject of this kind one cannot go into detail; but those who look about them will recognize what I mean, and, I think, will acknowledge its truth.

And so again in those efforts which are laudably made for the sake of preserving things as they are, and hindering ruin and destruction coming on the country, men are afraid to take their stand on "the old commandment which ye have heard from the beginning[1]." They are afraid to kindle their fire from the altar of God; they are afraid to acknowledge her through whom only they gain light and strength and salvation, the Mother of Saints.

When we go into the details of life, the same truth, as in every age, comes upon us forcibly and convincingly. I am not going to the question whether this age is better or worse than former ages; this is not to the present purpose. The world always "lieth in

[1] 1 John ii. 7.

wickedness;" but we are accustomed sufficiently to confess the faults of former times, which do not concern us; we do not see what is evil in our own. Therefore, we need to be reminded of it. We need to be reminded that all our daily pursuits and doings need not be proved evil, but are certainly evil without proof, unless they can be proved to be good. Unless that holy and superhuman influence which came forth from Christ when He breathed on the Apostles, which they handed onwards, which has ever since gone through the world like a leaven, renewing it in righteousness,—which came on us first in Baptism, and reclaimed us from the service of Satan,—unless this Divine Gift has been cherished and improved within us, and is spread round about and from us, upon the objects of our aims and exertions, upon our plans and pursuits, our words and our works, surely all these are evil, without being formally proved to be so. If we engage in a trade or profession, if we make money, if we form connexions in life, if we marry and settle, if we educate our children, whatever we do, we have no right to take it for granted that this is not earthly, sensual, and of this world; it will be so without our trouble, unless we take trouble the other way, unless we aim and pray that it may not be so. Left to itself, human nature tends to death, and utter apostasy from God, however plausible it may look externally. What was it men were doing before the flood came? things very different from what men do now? No; they did the same things as we. "They did eat, they drank, they married wives, they were given in marriage, they bought, they sold, they planted,

they builded[1]." Are these things evil? Yes; they are
evil unless they are good; they are evil unless they
have become good; they are evil until Christ sanctifies
them; and then, and not till then, are they good. They
are evil in the case of every one of us, except Christ has
sanctified them in us, unless they have been touched
with the finger of God, and illuminated by the doctrine
and the power of His Son.

In all things, then, we must spiritualize this world;
and if you ask for instances *how* to do this, I give you
the following. When a nation enters Christ's Church,
and takes her yoke upon its shoulder, *then* it formally
joins itself to the cause of God, and separates itself from
the evil world. When the civil magistrate defends the
Christian faith, and sets it up in all honour in high
places, as a beacon to the world, *so far* he gives himself
to God, and sanctifies and spiritualizes that portion of
it over which he has power. When men put aside a
portion of their gains for God's service, *then* they
sanctify those gains. When the head of a household
observes family prayer and other religious offices, and
shows that, like Abraham, he is determined with God's
help to honour Him, *then* he joins himself to the kingdom of God, and rescues his household from its natural
relationship with this unprofitable world. When a man
hallows in his private conduct holy seasons, *this* is
offering up of God's gifts to God, and sanctifying all
seasons by the sacrifice of some. When a man who is
rich, and whose duty calls on him to be hospitable, is

Luke xvii. 27, 28.

careful also to feed the hungry and clothe the naked, *thus* he sanctifies his riches. When he is in the midst of plenty, and observes self-denial; when he builds his house, but builds Churches too; when he plants and sows, but pays tithes; when he buys and sells, but withal gives largely to religion; when he does nothing in the world without being suspicious of the world, being jealous of himself, trying himself, lest he be seduced by the world, making sacrifices to prove his earnestness;— in all these ways he circumcises himself from the world by the circumcision of Christ. This is the circumcision of the heart from the world. This is deliverance from dead ordinances; and though, even if this were done perfectly, it would not be enough, for we have to separate ourselves from the flesh also, yet, at least, it is the victory over a chief and formidable enemy.

My brethren, this is no matter of words: a thing to be listened to carelessly, because we have heard it often before. The death and resurrection of Christ is ever a call upon you to die to time, and to live to eternity. Do not be satisfied with the state in which you find yourselves; do not be satisfied with nature; be satisfied only with grace. Beware of taking up with a low standard of duty, and aiming at nothing but what you can easily fulfil. Pray God to enlighten you with a knowledge of the extent of your duty, to enlighten you with a true view of this world. Beware lest the world seduce you. It will aim at persuading you that itself is rational and sensible, that religion is very well in its way, but that we are born for the world. And you will be seduced

most certainly, unless you watch and pray that you enter
not into temptation. You must either conquer the world,
or the world will conquer you. You must be either
master or slave. Take your part then, and " stand fast
in the liberty wherewith Christ hath made us free [1]."

[1] Gal. v. 1.

SERMON IX.

Indulgence in Religious Privileges,

(ROGATION SUNDAY.)

" These are spots in your feasts of charity, when they feast with you, feeding themselves without fear."—JUDE 12.

THE false brethren, spoken of by St. Jude in this passage, were stained with such heinous guilt, both in life and doctrine, that it may seem to promise little profit to us to take any part of it as a text. · Their sin has passed with the early age, and let it pass from our thoughts. So it may be said, and in one sense both rightly and truly said; for it is true that the enormities which once were, are not now, and it is right surely to turn away from evil and hide it, when it is a thing past, not present. And yet, without recurring to those instances of fearful depravity and corruption, which insinuated themselves even into the Apostolic Church, according to the prophecy that the kingdom of heaven is like a net which gathers of every kind, good and bad, I think we may gain a lesson in matters which concern ourselves from the words in question, which have occurred

in the Service[1], and are not unsuitable to this season of
the year.

The first thought which the text suggests to us, when
it speaks of religious feasting, obviously relates to the
temper of mind in which we are accustomed to come to
the most Holy Sacrament of the Lord's Supper. The
feasts indeed spoken of by St. Jude were of a different
kind; they were an institution which soon came to an
end, in consequence of the abuses to which they led; but
still Holy Communion is especially "a feast of charity,"
and the fault which the Apostle imputes to certain
apostate Christians of his day, may, in its degree (though
God grant but in a very slight degree!), adhere to us.
He says, that they were "spots in the feast," a disfigure-
ment, and a disgrace, because they "feasted with" their
brethren "without fear." They did in no sense recognize
and realize that Holy Presence, before whom even St.
John fell down as dead, till He laid His hand on him
and said, "Fear not[2]." He says to all His servants
"Fear not," *when* they fear; but till then, He says on
the contrary, very emphatically, "Fear." For instance,
"Serve the Lord with fear, and rejoice with trembling[3]."
"Let us have grace, whereby we may serve God acceptably, with reverence and godly fear." "Work out
your own salvation with fear and trembling, for it is God
which worketh in you, both to will and to do of His good
pleasure[4]."

We must come to God with fear. Yet we are told to
"come boldly unto the throne of grace[5]." Are not

[1] May 1.   [2] Rev. i. 17.   [3] Ps. ii. 11.
[4] Heb. xii. 28.   Phil. ii. 12, 13.   [5] Heb. iv. 16.

these precepts incompatible with each other? No, surely, not in themselves, but *we* are very likely to find them incompatible, when we attempt them. We are very likely to find it difficult to fulfil two opposite duties, which are nevertheless both possible, and which *are* duties, *because* they are so opposite, *because* they are so difficult; for no one can suppose that easy matters are our duty, but difficult matters. We are very likely from our Lord's great condescension, from His gracious invitations, so free, so repeated, so unwearied, to forget His Majesty, and to become familiar with Him; and then we "feast without fear." And it stands to reason, the more frequently we accept His invitation, and seek Him in His sacred ordinance, the greater is our danger of this irreverence, unless we be on our guard.

Now in saying this, my brethren, I am not addressing myself to those of us who are in the practice of availing themselves in this church of our Lord's invitation to seek His Presence once a week. I have no reason for saying, I humbly trust I may with truth deny, that they are wanting in "reverence and godly fear;" though, of course, all of us, any one of us, might have far deeper and more solemn thoughts than we have at present, and (it is to be hoped) shall have, as year after year passes away; and though we, as others, are in danger of irreverence, unless we are on our guard. But I am not speaking of ourselves; I am thinking of the Church generally; I am thinking of the age. There is at this moment a growing perception of the beauty of religion, a growing reverence for, and insight into the privileges of the Gospel. Persons begin to understand

far more than they did, that Christianity is not a mere
law, a Jewish yoke, but a new law, a service of freedom, a rule of spirit and truth, which wins us as well
as commands, and influences us while it threatens.
Hitherto, it has seemed as if all sense of the privileges
and pleasures of religion were possessed by those who
had but erroneous views of doctrine, and who, however
well-intentioned and respectable in themselves, came more
or less of an heretical stock; while men of more correct
and more orthodox views seemed to be of a cold and
forbidding school—nay, the less fervent, the less spiritual
for their very exactness: but all this is gone by. A
more primitive, Catholic, devout, ardent spirit, is abroad
among the holders of orthodox truth. The piercing,
and thrilling, and kindling, and enrapturing glories of
the kingdom of Christ are felt in their degree by many.
Men are beginning to understand that influence, which
in the beginning made the philosopher leave his school,
and the soldier beat his spear into a pruning-hook.
They are beginning to understand that the Gospel is
not a mere scheme or doctrine, but a reality and a life;
not a subject for books only, for private use, for individuals, but for public profession, for combined action, for
outward manifestation. Hence there is an increasing
cultivation of all that is external, from a feeling that
external religion is the great development and triumph
of the inward principle. For instance, much curiosity is
directed towards the science of ecclesiastical architecture,
and much appreciation shown of architectural pro-
prieties. Attention, too, is paid to the internal arrange-
ment and embellishment of sacred buildings. Devo-

tional books also of an imaginative cast, religious music,
painting, poetry, and the like are in request. Churches
are more frequently attended on week-days, and continual service is felt to be a privilege, not a task. And
two services are felt to be short of that measure of devotion which the religious mind desires to pay to its God
and Saviour.

Now no one can suspect me of meaning to imply that
such signs of the times are not in themselves hopeful
ones. They are so; but, O my brethren, be jealous of
these things, excellent as they are in themselves, lest
they be not accompanied with godly fear. I grieve to
say, that the spirit of penitence does not keep pace with
the spirit of joy. With all this outward promise of
piety, we are suspicious of that which alone is its inward
soul and life; we are very jealous indeed of personal
strictness and austerity. We are alarmed at any call to
national or personal humiliation and amendment; we
like to be told of the excellence of our institutions, we do
not like to hear of their defects; we like to abandon
ourselves to the satisfactions of religion, we do not like
to hear of its severities. We do not like to hear of our
past sins, and the necessity of undoing them; and thus,
however gay our blossoms may be in this our spring, we
have a fault within which will show itself ere our fruits
are gathered in the autumn. "The sun is no sooner
risen with a burning heat, but it withereth the grass,
and the flower thereof falleth, and the grace of the
fashion of it perisheth." We are cherishing a shallow
religion, a hollow religion, which will not profit us in
the day of trouble. We are taking words for things;

we are led captive by an unreality. This is no new language on my part; I have said it[1] before men took that interest which now they take in the Catholic doctrine: I say so now. I said then, as now, that the age, whatever be its peculiar excellences, has this serious defect, it loves an exclusively cheerful religion. It is determined to make religion bright and sunny and joyous, whatever be the form of it which it adopts. And it will handle the Catholic doctrine in this spirit; it will skim over it; it will draw it out in mere buckets-full; it will substitute its human cistern for the well of truth; it will be afraid of the deep well, the abyss of God's judgments and God's mercies.

Alas! . . . Surely we are pretending allegiance to the Church to no purpose, or rather to our own serious injury, if we select her doctrines and precepts at our pleasure; choose this, reject that; take what is beautiful and attractive, shrink from what is stern and painful. I fear a number of persons, a growing number, in various parts of the country, are likely to abandon themselves to what may be called the luxuries of religion—nay, I will even call them the luxuries of devotion; and the consequence of this it is very distressing to contemplate. They are tending to "feast without fear." For this reason I should even look with jealousy on any considerable revival of weekly Communions. We are not fit for them; I am sure, men in general, such as we are, even religious persons, are not fit for them. We need a much deeper religion, a more consistent creed, a keener faith, a clearer insight into things unseen, a

[1] Parochial Sermons, Vol. i., Sermon 2 k

more real understanding of what sin is, and the consequences of sin, a more practical and self-denying rule of
conduct, before such a blessed usage will be safely extended among our congregations. I really do trust, as
I have already said, that the effects of this observance
among ourselves have been such as we could desire; but
if ever it is introduced into our great towns, much evil
will come of it [1]. It is a very merciful provision, if we
may thus speak of error overruled for good, that there
should be so much opposition to it as there is at present.
People say that the Holy Communion obscures the
doctrine of Gospel grace; that in obeying Christ's
command we are forgetting His atonement; that in
coming for His benefits, we tend to deny His all-
sufficient merits. Can any imputation be more preposterous and wild, however estimable the persons may
be who cast it? Certainly none. But still I say
this strange apprehension is doing us service. I am
not at all sorry for it, and the clamour that follows
upon it; for it hinders a great evil, it represses a
luxuriant, rank, unhealthy vegetation in our religious
habits.

Many a man, and especially many a woman, may
abandon themselves to the real delight, as it will prove,
of passing hours in repeating the Psalms, or in saying
Litanies and Hymns, and in frequenting those Cathedrals and Churches where the old Catholic ideas are
especially impressed upon their minds; and they will

---

[1] Of course it must not be forgotten, that for the revival of the
practice altogether we are indebted to clergymen in great towns, as in
London and Leeds, whose instances cannot be supposed to come under
the remark in the text.

find, in the words of Scripture, that our Lord's "Name is like ointment poured forth [1]," and His "fruit is sweet to their taste [2]." Yet like the Prophet's roll, though "in the mouth sweet as honey"—nay, almost literally so in a strange way—yet as soon as they have eaten it, it will be bitter, if they have forgotten that "before honour is humility," sowing in tears before reaping in joy, pain before pleasure, duty before privilege. Nothing lasts, nothing keeps incorrupt and pure, which comes of mere feeling; feelings die like spring-flowers, and are fit only to be cast into the oven. Persons thus circumstanced will find their religion fail them in time; a revulsion of mind will ensue. They will feel a violent distaste for what pleased them before, a sickness and weariness of mind; or even an enmity towards it; or a great disappointment; or a confusion and perplexity and despondence. They have learned to think religion easier than it is, themselves better than they are; they have drunk their good wine instead of keeping it; and this is the consequence. I need not enter, however, into the full consequences of this incaution; they are very various and sometimes very awful. I am but calling attention to the fact. And then the persons in question will be ashamed or afraid to confide to others what their state is, or will not have the opportunity; and all this the more, because affectionate, sensitive, delicate, retired persons are perhaps more open than others to the danger I have been describing.

The most awful consequences of this untrue kind of devotion, which would have all the glories of the

[1] Cant. i. 3. [2] Cant. ii. 3.

Gospel without its austerities, of course are those into
which the dreadful heretics fell who are alluded to in
the text; and of which it is well not to speak. Yet it
must not be forgotten that even in these latter times,
though not in our own Church, and not certainly among
persons of high or refined minds, even immoralities have
been the ultimate consequents of religious enthusiasm.
But one need not dwell upon extreme results, in order
to be impressed with the danger to which our Church is
at present exposed. What indeed but evil can come
of living like the world, eating and drinking, marrying
and giving in marriage, faring sumptuously, dressing in
purple and fine linen, and increasing in goods, and yet
affecting to be the children of Apostles, and using the
devotion of Saints?

Christianity, considered as a moral system, is made
up of two elements, beauty and severity; whenever
either is indulged to the loss or disparagement of the
other, evil ensues. In heathen times, Greek and Barbarian in some sense divided these two between them;
the latter were the slaves of dreary and cruel superstitions, and the former abandoned themselves to a joyous
polytheism. And so, again, in these latter times, the
two chief forms of heresy into which opposition to
primitive truth has developed, were remarkable, at least
in their origin three hundred years ago, and at times
since, the one for an unrefined and self-indulgent religiousness, the other for a stern, dark, cruel spirit, very
unamiable, yet still inspiring more respect than the
other.

Even the Jews, to whom this earth was especially

given, and who might be supposed to be at liberty
without offence to satiate themselves in its gifts, were
not allowed to enjoy it without restraint. Even the
paschal lamb, their great typical feast, was eaten "with
bitter herbs [1]." And, as time went on, the Prophets
were given, who were more or less moulded after the
pattern of Elijah, in "suffering affliction and in
patience," and were typical of the one great Prophet of
the Church who was to come. Much more are Christians
bound to recollect, and to rejoice, that "the brother of
low degree" is to be "exalted," and "the rich" to be
"made low," and that the Apostles whose steps we are
to follow. (as we this day are especially reminded [2])
hungered and thirsted, and were naked, and were
buffeted, and had no certain dwelling-place, and were
accounted the filth of the world and the offscouring of
all things.

Let us thus enter upon the rich and happy months
which lie before us, when the earth puts forth all her
excellence, and robes herself in her bright garments, and
scatters her most precious gifts. Thus let us hallow
Rogation Sunday, which is to-day,—suitably to the
Church's intention which has made three days of
abstinence attend upon it, by way of warning us that
we must not enjoy our Father's temporal blessings
without reserve. "He visiteth the earth and blesseth
it; He maketh it very plenteous . . . He provideth for
the earth; He watereth her furrows. He crowneth the
year with His goodness, and His clouds drop fatness [3]."

---

[1] Exod. xii. 8.   [2] Feast of St. Philip and St. James.
[3] Ps. lxv. 9—12.

And we acknowledge His bountifulness, we commemorate His providence, we enter upon His gifts, by abstaining from them. As the Israelites brought the first fruits of their land in a basket[1] and left it in the priest's hand before the altar of the Lord their God, so do we in another way, but in the same spirit, begin our thankful use of God's blessings by a prudent delay and a lowly prayer. We deprecate wrath, we entreat mercy; as Job sacrificed for his sons, so we for ourselves. We remind ourselves that though " every creature of God is good," we ourselves, God's creatures, are the one exception to that rule; that though His gifts are holy and innocent, our hearts are frail and wayward; that they are good in the sending, yet dangerous in the taking—good in the use, but harmful in the enjoyment. As before meat, day by day, we say a grace and then begin, so now do we ask a blessing on the whole year by pausing ere we enter upon it.

This is to feed ourselves *with* fear. Thus let us proceed in the use of all our privileges, and all will be benefits. Let us not keep festivals without keeping vigils; let us not keep Eastertide without observing Lent; let us not approach the Sunday feast without keeping the Friday abstinence; let us not adorn churches without studying personal simplicity and austereness; let us not cultivate the accomplishments of taste and literature without the corrective of personal discomfort; let us not attempt to advance the power of the Church, to enthrone her rulers, to rear her palaces, and to ennoble her name, without recollecting that she

[1] Deut. xxvi. 1—11.

must be mortified within while she is in honour in the world, and must wear the Baptist's hair-shirt and leathern girdle under the purple ephod and the jewelled breastplate.

And lastly, let us beware, on the other hand, of dishonouring and rudely rejecting God's gifts, out of gloominess or sternness; let us beware of fearing without feasting. "Every creature of God is good, and nothing to be refused." Let us beware, though it must be a sad perversion of mind which admits of it,— let us beware of afflicting ourselves for sin, without first coming to the Gospel for strength to do so. And let us not so plunge ourselves in the sense of our offences, as not withal to take delight in the contemplation of our privileges. Let us rejoice while we mourn. Let us look up to our Lord and Saviour the more we shrink from the sight of ourselves; let us have the more faith and love the more we exercise repentance. Let us, in our penitence, not substitute the Law *for* the Gospel, but add the Law *to* the Gospel. Those who do despite to baptismal grace fall under the Law; but they do not fall *from* the Gospel, if they are repentant; they fall under the Law without the Gospel, if they continue in sin; they receive the Law with the Gospel, if they return. The Law which once introduced the Gospel, in such cases becomes its instrument. They fall indeed under bondage, but they have the power of Christ's grace to enable them to bear it.

And in like manner, as they must not defraud themselves of Christian privileges, neither need they give up God's temporal blessings. All the beauty of nature, the kind influences of the seasons, the gifts of sun and moon, and the fruits of the earth, the advantages of civilized life, and the presence of friends and intimates; all these good things are but one extended and wonderful type of God's benefits in the Gospel. Those who aim at perfection will not reject the gift, but add a corrective; they will add the bitter herbs to the fatted calf and the music and dancing; they will not refuse the flowers of earth, but they will toil in plucking up the weeds. Or if they refrain from one temporal blessing, it will be to reserve another; for this is one great mercy of God, that while He allows us a discretionary use of His temporal gifts, He allows a discretionary abstinence also; and He almost enjoins upon us the use of some, lest we should forget that this earth is His creation, and not of the evil one. I am not denying that there are certain individuals raised up from time to time to a still more self-denying life, and who have a corresponding measure of divine consolations. As some men are Apostles, others Confessors and Martyrs, as Missionaries in heathen countries may be called to give up all for Christ; so there are doubtless those, living in peaceable times and among their brethren, who acknowledge a call to give up every thing whatever for the sake of the Gospel, and in order to be perfect; and to become as homeless and as shelterless, and as resourceless and as solitary, as the holy Baptist in the wilderness: but extraordinary cases are not for our imitation, and it is as great a fault to act without a call as to refuse to act upon one.

May God give us grace to walk thus humbly, thus

soberly, thus without censoriousness in this day of confusion; enjoying His blessings, yet taking them with
fear and trembling; and disciplining ourselves without
gloom, yet not judging or slandering those who are
more rigid or less secular than ourselves!

SERMON X.

Connexion between Personal and Public Improvement.

(WHITSUNTIDE.)

"The earth shall be full of the knowledge of the Lord, as the water. cover the sea."—ISA. xi. 9.

IT was promised that "the waters should no more become a flood to destroy all flesh [1];" that "the waters of Noah should no more go over the earth [2];" and yet a flood there was to be, a mighty flood of waters, all-compassing, all-absorbing, in God's good time, and in His merciful foreknowledge, when He spake the former word; but not to destroy all flesh, but to save it. And in its season, as on this day, this second, and more wonderful and more gracious deluge came to pass; the rain of grace descended; "the heavens dropped down from above, and the skies poured down righteousness [3];" "the rain descended, and the floods came, and the winds blew [4];" "the sea made a noise, and all that therein is;

---

[1] Preached during a very wet season.
[2] Gen. ix. 15. Isa. liv. 9. [3] Isa. xiv. 8.
[4] Matt. vii. 25.

the round world, and they that dwell therein¹;" the earth began to fill with the knowledge of the glory of the Lord; for "the Spirit of the Lord filled the world; and that which containeth all things had knowledge of the voice²."

How different a fulfilment was this from that for which the Apostles had been waiting! For ten days had they waited for the fulfilment of a promise, the coming of a Comforter. And surely they imagined, that such as Christ had been, would be the Paraclete which was to come. Christ was a present, visible, protector; a man, with man's voice and man's figure. Who was to be their Comforter, how could they conjecture, seeing He was to be such, that it was expedient for them that Christ should depart? Some one greater than Elias, who was expected to come before the last day; greater than the Baptist, of whom Herod thought that he had risen again in Christ, with miracles; greater than "Jeremias, or one of the prophets;" greater than Moses, who saw God face to face; more than a prophet, more than any born of woman, more than man; perhaps an angel, such as had appeared in bodily form to the Patriarchs (for of a spiritual nature He was to be), but still surely a present, a visible Being, one whose individuality and intelligence they could not doubt, and need not take on faith.

For such an one they waited during ten days to guide them into all truth, little deeming that knowledge about Himself was one main portion of the truth He had to teach them; and then, when they were waiting for this

¹ Ps. xcviii. 8.   ² Wisd. i. 7.

Angelic Messenger, Prophet, and Lawgiver, One higher
than all created strength and wisdom, suddenly came
down upon them; yet not as a Lord and Governor, but
as an agency or power. " Suddenly there came a sound
from heaven, as of a rushing mighty wind, and it filled
all the house where they were sitting. And there
appeared unto them cloven tongues, like as of fire, and
it sat upon each of them; and they were all filled with
the Holy Ghost [1]."

Such was the coming of the Comforter; He who is
infinitely personal, who is one and individual above all
created beings, who is the One God, absolutely, fully,
perfectly, simply, He it was who vouchsafed to descend
upon the Apostles, and that, as if not a Person, but as
an influence or quality, by His attribute of ubiquity;
diffusing Himself over their hearts, filling all the house,
poured over the world, as wholly here, as if He were not
there; and hence vouchsafing to be compared to the
inanimate and natural creation, to water and to wind,
which are of so subtle a nature, of so penetrating a
virtue, and of so extended a range.

And most exactly have these figures, which He
condescended to apply to Himself, been fulfilled in the
course of the Dispensation; nay, even to this day. His
operation has been calm, equable, gradual, far-spreading,
overtaking, intimate, irresistible. What is so awfully
silent, so mighty, so inevitable, so encompassing as a
flood of water? Fire alarms from the first: we see it,
and we scent it; there is crashing and downfall, smoke
and flame; it makes an inroad here and there; it is

[1] Acts ii. 2 - 4.

uncertain and wayward;—but a flood is the reverse of
all this. It gives no tokens of its coming; it lets men
sleep through the night, and they wake and find themselves hopelessly besieged; prompt, secret, successful:—
and equable; it preserves one level; it is every where;
there is no refuge. And it makes its way to the
foundations; towers and palaces rear themselves as
usual; they have lost nothing of their perfection, and
give no sign of danger, till at length suddenly they
totter and fall. And here and there it is the same, as
if by some secret understanding; for by one and the
same agency the mighty movement goes on here and
there and every where, and all things seem to act in con-
cert with it, and to conspire together for their own ruin.
And in the end they are utterly removed, and perish
from off the face of the earth. Fire, which threatens
more fiercely, leaves behind it relics and monuments of
its agency; but water buries as well as destroys; it
wipes off the memorial of its victims from the earth;
it covers the chariot and the horsemen, and all the host
of Pharaoh, and sweeps them away; "the waters overwhelm them, there is not one of them left."

Such was the power of the Spirit in the beginning,
when He vouchsafed to descend as an invisible wind, as
an outpoured flood. Thus He changed the whole face
of the world. For a while men went on as usual, and
dreamed not what was coming; and when they were
roused from their fast sleep, the work was done; it was
too late for aught else but impotent anger and an
hopeless struggle. The kingdom was taken away from
them and given to another people. The ark of God

[s. d.] K

moved upon the face of the waters. It was borne aloft
by the power, greater than human, which had overspread the earth, and it triumphed, "not by might, nor
by power, but by My Spirit, saith the Lord of Hosts [1]."

And what the power of the Spirit has been in the
world at large, that it is also in every human heart to
which it comes; and by attending to the figure under
which it is represented in the text, we shall understand
(what concerns us most intimately) whether we are
personally under its influence, or are deceiving ourselves.
For if, as has been said, the characteristics of the
Spirit's influence are, that it is the same every where,
that it is silent, that it is gradual, that it is thorough;
not violent, or abrupt, or fitful, or partial, or detached;
and if, on the other hand, the stirrings of heart which
we experience, the impulses and the changes, are of this
imperfect character, we have cause to suspect that in no
sense do they come from the One True Sanctifier, the
Holy Ghost, the Comforter.

For instance: any spirit which professes to come to
us alone, and not to others, which makes no claim of
having moved the body of the Church at all times and
places, is not of God, but a private spirit of error;
because "the river of God is full of water; Thou
visitest the earth and blessest it; Thou makest it very
plenteous. Thou crownest the year with Thy goodness,
and Thy clouds drop fatness [2]." God's Spirit dwells in
the Catholic Church, and has visited the whole world.
New creeds, private opinions, self-devised practices, are
but delusions.

[1] Zech. iv. 6.   [2] Ps. lxv. 10—12.

Again; vehemence, tumult, confusion, **are no attri-**butes of that benignant flood with which God has replenished the earth. That flood of grace is sedate, majestic, gentle in its operation. **If at any time it** seems to be violent, that **violence is** occasioned by some accident **or** imperfection **of the** earthen vessels into which it vouchsafes **to pour** itself; and is no token of the coming of Divine Power. Sudden changes of feeling, restlessness, terror, vehement emotions, im-petuous resolves, ecstasies **and** transports, **are no signs of it; and often** they proceed from false spirits, who **are** but imitating heavenly influences **as best they may, and** seducing souls to their ruin.

And again: the Divine Baptism, **wherewith God** visits **us**, penetrates through our **whole soul and** body. It leaves no part of **us** uncleansed, unsanctified. It claims **the whole man for** God. **Any spirit** which **is** content with what is short **of this,** which does not lead us to utter self-surrender and devotion; which reserves something **for** ourselves; which indulges our **self-will;** which flatters this or that natural inclination or affec-tion; which does not tend to consistency of religious character;—is **not** from God. The heavenly influence which **He has given** us is as intimately present, **and as** penetrating—as catholic—in an individual heart **as it** is in the world **at large.** It is every where, in every faculty, **every** affection, every design, every work. And the surest test that **we are members** of the Catholic Church is the evidence of this Catholic influence, or **religious** consistency, "casting down imaginations, and **every high thing** that exalteth itself against the knowledge of God, and bringing into captivity every thought to the obedience of Christ[1]."

Thus the heart of every Christian ought to represent in miniature the Catholic Church, since one Spirit makes both the whole Church and every member of it to be His Temple. As He makes the Church one, which, left to itself, would separate into many parts; so He makes the soul one, in spite of its various affections and faculties, and its contradictory aims. As He gives peace to the multitude of nations, who are naturally in discord one with another, so does He give an orderly government to the soul, and set reason and conscience as sovereigns over the inferior parts of our nature. As He leavens each rank and pursuit of the community with the principles of the doctrine of Christ, so does that same Divine Leaven spread through every thought of the mind, every member of the body, till the whole is sanctified. And let us be quite sure that these two operations of our Divine Comforter depend upon each other, and that while Christians do not seek after inward unity and peace in their own breasts, the Church itself will never be at unity and peace in the world around them;—and in somewhat the same manner, while the Church throughout the world is in that lamentable state of disorder which we see, no particular country, which is but a part of it, but must be in great religious confusion too, within its own limits.

This is a point much to be kept in view in this day, as it will moderate our expectations, and sober us: we cannot hope for peace at home, while we are at war

[1] 2 Cor. x. 5.

abroad. We cannot hope for the recovery of dissenting bodies, while we are ourselves alienated from the great body of Christendom. We cannot hope for unity of faith, if we at our own private will make a faith for ourselves in this our small corner of the earth. We cannot hope for the success among the heathen of St. Augustine or St. Boniface, unless like them we go forth with the apostolical benediction. That we are thus at disadvantage may not be our fault; it may be our misfortune; but at any rate it is not, what we too often consider it, our boast. Break unity in one point, and the fault runs through the whole body. There is a jar and a dissonance throughout; from the sole of the foot even unto the head there is no soundness. The flood of God's grace keeps its level, and if it is low in one place it is low in another. Surely we have abundant evidence on all sides of us, that the division of Churches is the corruption of hearts.

As then we would forward that blessed time, when the knowledge of the Lord, as the text speaks, will in its fulness cover the earth, as the waters cover their bed, let us look at home, and wait on God for the cleansing and purifying of ourselves. Till we look at home, no good shall we be able to perform for the Church at large; we shall but do mischief, when we intend good, and to us will apply that proverb—"Physician, heal thyself." Let us learn first to "come" diligently "to the waters," and ask for that gift of God, which will be "a well of water in us springing up unto everlasting life [1]." And let us not doubt that if we do thus proceed, we

[1] Isa. lv. 1. John iv. 14.

shall advance the cause of Christ in the world, whether we see it or not, whether we will it or not, whether the world wills it or not.   Let us but raise the level of religion in our hearts, and it will rise in the world.   He who attempts to set up God's kingdom in his heart, furthers it in the world.   He whose prayers come up for a memorial before God, opens the "windows of heaven, and the foundations of the great deep," and the waters rise.   He who with Christ goes up into the mountain to pray, or with St. Peter seeks the house-top, or with Mary, the mother of Mark, is in company with many, praying, or with Paul and Silas, singing praises at midnight, he is overcoming the world, let the world do what it will.   Elijah went up to Carmel, and cast himself down upon the earth, and put his face between his knees, and bid his servant look towards the sea seven times, till at his prayers a little cloud rose out of the sea like a man's hand, which at length covered the whole heaven, and there was abundance of rain [1].

Let these instances be our encouragement now.   Let us try to serve God more strictly than heretofore; let us pray Him to send down that influence which converted the world in the beginning, and He surely will answer our prayers far beyond what we think or hope.   He will raise up for us saints and guides in this dreary time, when sanctity and wisdom seem well nigh to have failed; He will bring together the different parts of the Church, and restore peace and unity as at the first.   He will give us that true and perfect faith which was once delivered to the saints, and which our sins have forfeited.

[1]   1 Kings xviii. 42—46.

" He will finish the work, and **cut it short** in righteousness, because a short **work** will **the Lord make upon the** earth [1]."

And mean **time** we shall **have our** true reward, **which** is personal, consisting in **no** mere external privileges, however great, but in the " water of life [2]," of which we are allowed to take freely. " How excellent is Thy mercy, **O God !** and the children of men shall put their trust under the shadow of Thy wings. They shall be satisfied with the plenteousness of Thy house, and Thou **shalt** give them **drink of** Thy pleasures, **as out of the** river. For with Thee is the well of life, **and in Thy light** shall **we** see light [3]." We shall be **as** "**trees** planted by the water-side, that will **bring forth** their fruit **in** due season [4];" " trees **of righteousness**, the planting of the Lord, that **He** may be glorified [5]." Let the high mountain, and the awful solitude, and the sun-bright clime, and the **rich** and varied scene, be the boast of the foreigner and the heritage of the south. Enough for us, if we are allowed, what Scripture singles out as the choicest of God's blessings, the green meadow and the calm full stream, and the bounteous rain, and the thick foliage, and fruit in its season. Enough for us, in **this age and country,** if so be, to " dwell **in a peaceable habitation,** and **in sure** dwellings, **and in** quiet resting-**places [6];**" " **to be fed in a** green pasture, and led forth beside **the** waters **of comfort [7]."** " **The** mountain of myrrh, **and the hill of** frankincense, the orchard of pomegranates, **the** camphire **with spikenard** and saffron,

[1] Rom. ix. 28. [2] Rev. xxii. 1. [3] Ps. xxxvi. 7—9. [4] Ps. i. 3.
[5] Isa. lxi. 3. [6] Isa. xxxii. 18. [7] Ps. xxiii. 2.

calamus and cinnamon, myrrh and aloes, with all the chief spices [1]," let others taste, for it is their portion. But who shall find, except at home, "the rivers of water in a dry place, the shadow of a great rock in a weary land [2]"? Who shall find us elsewhere, "butter of kine, and milk of sheep, with fat of lambs, and rams of the breed of Bashan, and goats, with the fat of kidneys of wheat [3]"? Let us be content with what supports life, while that is given us, though we dwell in a humble place, and have not the riches of the world. Let us "take no thought for our life what we shall eat, or what we shall drink, or wherewithal we shall be clothed; but let us seek the kingdom of God and His righteousness, and all these things shall be added unto us [4]." "Let our conversation be without covetousness, and let us be content with such things as we have, for He hath said, I will never leave thee nor forsake thee." Let us nourish ourselves "in the words of faith and good doctrine, whereunto we have attained." Let us be "filled with the fruits of righteousness, which are by Jesus Christ unto the glory and praise of God." And let us not doubt, that "if in any thing we be otherwise minded, God shall reveal even this unto us [5]."

---

[1] Cant. iv. 6. 13, 14.   [2] Isa. xxxii. 2.
[3] Deut. xxxii. 14.   [4] Matt. vi. 25—33
[5] Heb. xiii. 5.   1 Tim. iv. 6.   Phil. i. 11; iii. 15.

SERMON XI.

Christian Nobleness.

(WHITSUNTIDE.)

" I will not leave you comfortless: I will come to you. Yet a little while, and the world seeth Me no more; but ye see Me."—JOHN xiv. 18, 19.

WHEN our Saviour was leaving His disciples, He told them that He would soon return to them, that their sorrow might be turned into joy. He was going away, yet they were to see Him, though the world saw Him not; for they were to be blessed with the presence of Him who was equal to Him and one with Him, and would unite them to Him, the Third Person in the Eternal Trinity, God the Holy Ghost.

He said that He was going away, and yet was coming again; for the Holy Ghost came, and His coming was really the coming of Christ. Christ said that it was to be but a short interval between His departure and His return; and such it was, ten days. He went on Holy Thursday; He returns on the day of Pentecost.

But, though our Lord and Saviour sent His Holy Spirit to be with us on His going away, still there was a difference between the Spirit's office, and that which He Himself graciously fulfilled towards His disciples in the days of His flesh; for their wants were not the same as before. Christ, while He was with them, had no occasion to console them under affliction, to stand by them in trial as their Paraclete; for trial and affliction did not visit them while He was with them; but, on the other hand, the Holy Spirit especially came to give them joy in tribulation. Again, He came to teach them fully, what our Lord had but in part revealed; and hence too it followed, that the consolation which the Spirit vouchsafed differed from that which they had received from Christ, just as the encouragements and rewards bestowed upon children, are far other than those which soothe and stimulate grown men in arduous duties. And there were, moreover, other circumstances, much to be dwelt upon, which altered the state of the Apostles' feelings and ideas, after their Lord had died and risen again, and which made them need a consolation different from that which His bodily presence gave them. There is no reason for supposing that, while He was with them, they apprehended the awful truth, that He is very God in our nature. "I am among you," He said, "as He that serveth." But on His resurrection He re-vealed the mystery. St. Thomas adored Him in the words, "My Lord and my God;" and He forthwith withdrew Himself from them, not living in their sight as heretofore, and soon ascending into heaven. It is plain, that, after such a revelation, the Apostles could not have returned to their easy converse with Him, even had He offered it. What had been, could not be again; their state of childhood, ere "their eyes were opened and they knew Him." Of necessity then, since they could not endure to see God and live, did He "vanish out of their sight." And if, according to His promise, He was to come to them again, it must be after a new manner, and with a higher consolation.

Accordingly, when the Spirit of Christ descended at the promised season, "He bowed the heavens and came down, and it was dark under His feet." He came invisibly, and invisibly hath He dwelt in the Church ever since. He does not manifest His glory to mortal sense. We do not hear the whisperings of His still small voice, nor do our hearts burn within us in token of His Presence. The truth is, we Christians know too much concerning Him to endure the open manifestation of His greatness. It is in mercy that He hides Himself from those who would be overcome by the sensible touch of the Almighty Hand. Still it is plain that, after all, in spite of this considerate regard for our frailness, His visitation cannot but be awful anyhow, to creatures who know what we know, and are what we are. This cannot be avoided; the very secrecy of His coming has its solemnity: is it not fearful to wait for Him, appalling to receive Him, a burden to have held communion with Him? and though we joy, as well we may, yet we cannot joy with the light hearts of children, who live by sight, but with the thoughtful gladness of grown men, who are anxious, who feel difficulties, who look out for dangers, who, in St. John's words, know both that "the whole world lieth in wickedness," and "that the Son of God is come, and hath given us an understanding that we may know Him that is true [1]," and discover His real majesty and power.

And hence, as we might expect, the Apostles' fellowship with Christ through the Spirit, after His ascension, was very different from their fellowship with Him on earth. Though they waited continually on Him for His peace, "not as the world giveth," and continually received it; yet, the history shows us, they feared the gift while they rejoiced in it. Consider, too, our Saviour's own most overpowering words, to be fulfilled in the coming of the Comforter,—"Whosoever speaketh a word against the Son of man, it shall be forgiven Him: but whosoever speaketh against the Holy Ghost, it shall not be forgiven him." Does not this Scripture imply thus much, whatever else it implies,—that our ascended Saviour, who is on God's right hand, and sends down from thence God's Spirit, is to be feared greatly, even amid His gracious consolations? Hence St. Paul says, "Work out your own salvation with fear and trembling;" and again, "Grieve not the Holy Spirit of God;" and again, "Know ye not that ye are the temple of God, and that the Spirit of God dwelleth in you? If any man defile the temple of God, him shall God destroy [2]."

This great truth is impressed upon the whole course

[1] John v. 19, 20.
[2] Matt. xii. 32.   Phil. ii. 12.   Eph. iv. 30.   1 Cor. iii. 16, 17.

of that sacred fellowship with Christ, which the Church
provides for her children; in proportion as it is more
high and gracious than that first intercourse, which the
Apostles enjoyed, so is it also more awful. When He
had once ascended, henceforth for unstudied speech
there were solemn rites; for familiar attendance there
were mysterious ministerings; for questioning at will
there was silent obedience; for sitting at table there
was bowing in adoration; for eating and drinking there
was fasting and watching. He who had taken his
Lord and rebuked Him, dared not speak to Him after
His resurrection, when He saw and knew Him. He
who had lain in His bosom at supper, fell at His feet as
dead. Such was the vision of the glorified Saviour of
man, returning to His redeemed in the power of the
Spirit, with a Presence more pervading because more
intimate, and more real because more hidden. And as
the manner of His coming was new, so was His gift.
It was peace, but a new peace, "not as the world
giveth;" not the exultation of the young, light-hearted,
and simple, easily created, easily lost: but a serious,
sober, lasting comfort, full of reverence, deep in contemplation.

And hence the keener, the more rapturous are the
feelings of the Christian, the more ardent his aspirations,
the more glorious his visions; so much the graver, the
more subdued, the more serene must be his worship and
his confession. Who was so intoxicated with divine
love as St. John? who so overcharged with the Spirit?
yet what language can be calmer than when He says,
" Behold what manner of love the Father hath bestowed

upon us, that we should be called the sons of God! . . . When He shall appear, we shall be like Him, for we shall see Him as He is [1]"? And who was possessed with a more burning zeal than St. Paul? yet observe his injunction to the spiritually-gifted Corinthians— "Let all things be done unto edifying; the spirits of the prophets are subject to the prophets; for God is not the author of confusion, but of peace. . . . Let all things be done decently and in order [2]." And in like manner, in anticipation of Gospel perfection, we read of the impressive gravity and saintly bearing of Samuel and his prophetic company, when Saul came to Ramah; while Saul's extravagance when he came within the Divine Influence, prefigures to us the wayward and unpeaceful behaviour of heretical sects in every age, who, in spite of whatever tokens they may bear of the presence of a good spirit among them, yet, whether they preach or pray, are full of tumult and violence, and cause wild alarm or fierce ecstasy, and even strange affections of body, convulsions and cries, in their converts or hearers.

But if gravity and sobriety were seen even in that time, when the heirs of promise were under age, as children submitted to a schoolmaster, and when holy David "danced before the Lord with all his might, leaping and dancing before the Lord [3];" much more is the temper of the Christian Church high and heavenly, noble, majestic, calm, and untroubled. For it is the state of heart imparted by the Divine Paraclete, who

---

[1] 1 John iii. 1, 2.   [2] 1 Cor. xiv. 26. 32, 33. 40.
[3] 2 Sam. vi. 14. 16.

stands by us to strengthen us and raise our stature, and, as it were, to straighten our limbs, and to provide us with the wings of Angels, wherewith to mount heavenward;—by Him who takes possession of us, and dwells in us, and makes us His agents and instruments, nay, in a measure, His confidants and counsellors, till we "comprehend the breadth and length and depth and height, and know the love of Christ, which passeth knowledge, that we may be filled with all the fulness of God[1]." Religious men, knowing what great things have been done for them, cannot but grow greater in mind in consequence. We know how power and responsibility change men in matters of this world. They become more serious, more vigilant, more circumspect, more practical, more decisive; they fear to commit mistakes, yet they dare more, because they have a consciousness of liberty and of power, and an opportunity for great successes. And thus the Christian, even in the way of nature, without speaking of the influence of heavenly grace upon him, cannot but change from the state of children to that of men, when he understands his own privileges. The more he knows and fears the gift committed to him, so much the more reverent is he towards himself, as being put in charge with it.

Consider the language in which our Lord and His Apostles describe the gift—"If a man love Me," says Christ, shortly after the text, "he will keep My words, and My Father will love him, and We will come unto him, and make Our abode with him." Again, in St.

[1] Eph. iii. 18, 19.

Paul's words, " Ye are the temple of the Living God;
as God hath said, I will dwell in them and walk in
them." Again, " Know ye not that your body is the
temple of the Holy Ghost, which is in you, which ye
have of God, and ye are not your own?" And St.
John, "Whosoever shall confess that Jesus is the Son of
God, God dwelleth in him, and he in God [1]." Is it not
plain, that such a doctrine as is here declared will
exceedingly raise the Christian above himself, and,
without impairing—nay, even while increasing his
humility, will make him feel all things of earth as little,
and of small interest or account, and will preserve him
from the agitations of mind which they naturally
occasion?

Alas! I am not speaking of ourselves in this
degenerate time, when we seem well nigh to have
forfeited the Gospel gifts through our sins; but,
without thinking of ourselves, surely it is not without its use to consider the high Gospel tone of
thought in itself. He then, who believes that, in
St. Paul's words, he is "joined to the Lord" as
"one spirit," must necessarily prize his own blessed
condition, and look down upon all things, even the
greatest things here below. "Ye are of God, little
children," says the beloved disciple, "and have overcome them; because greater is He that is in you
than he that is in the world. They are of the
world; . . . we are of God. He that knoweth God,
heareth us; he that is not of God, heareth not
us [2]." Here is the language of saints; and hence

[1] 2 Cor. vi. 16. 1 Cor. vi. 19. 1 John iv. 15.   [2] 1 John iv. 6.

it is that St. Paul, as feeling the majesty of that
new nature which is imparted to us, addresses himself in a form of indignation to those who forget
it. "What!" he says, "what! know ye not that
your body is the temple of the Holy Ghost?" As if
he said, "Can you be so mean-spirited and base-
minded as to dishonour yourselves in the devil's
service? Should we not pity the man of birth, or
station, or character, who degraded himself in the
eyes of the world, who forfeited his honour, broke
his word, or played the coward? And shall not
we, from mere sense of propriety, be ashamed to
defile our spiritual purity, the royal blood of the
second Adam, with deeds of darkness? Let us leave
it to the hosts of evil spirits, to the haters of
Christ, to eat the dust of the earth all the days of
their life. Cursed are they above all cattle, and
above every beast of the field; grovelling shall they
go, till they come to their end and perish. But
for Christians, it is theirs to walk in the light, as
children of the light, and to lift up their hearts, as
looking out for Him who went away, that He might
return to them again."

For the same reason Christians are called upon
to think little of the ordinary objects which men
pursue—wealth, luxury, distinction, popularity, and
power. It was this negligence about the world
which brought upon them in primitive times the
reproach of being indolent. Their heathen enemies
spoke truly; indolent and indifferent they were about
temporal matters. If the goods of this world came

in their way, they were not bound to decline them ; nor would they forbid others in the religious use of them; but they thought them vanities, the toys of children, which serious men let drop. Nay, St. Paul betrays the same feeling as regards our temporal callings and states generally. After discoursing about them, suddenly he breaks off as if impatient of the multitude of words; " But this I say, brethren," he exclaims, " the time is short."

Hence, too, the troubles of life gradually affect the Christian less and less, as his view of his own real blessedness, under the Dispensation of the Spirit, grows upon him ; and even though persecuted, to take an extreme case, he knows well that, through God's inward presence, he is greater than those who for the time have power over him, as Martyrs and Confessors have often shown.

And, in like manner, he will be calm and collected under all circumstances; he will make light of injuries, and forget them from mere contempt of them. He will be undaunted, as fearing God more than man ; he will be firm in faith and consistent, as "seeing Him that is invisible;" not impatient, as one who has no self-will; not soon disappointed, who has no hopes; not anxious, who has no fears ; nor dazzled, who has no ambition ; nor open to bribes, who has no desires.

And now, further, let it be observed, on the other hand, that all this greatness of mind which I have been describing, which in other religious systems degenerates into pride, is in the Gospel compatible— nay, rather intimately connected—with the deepest humility. It is true, that, so great are the Christian privileges, there is serious danger lest common men should be puffed up by them; but this will be when persons take them to themselves who have no right to them. Did I not begin with saying, that the Dispensation of the Spirit is one of awe, of "reverence and godly fear"? Surely, then, they who pride themselves on the gift have forgotten the very elements of the Gospel of Christ. They have forgotten that the gift is not only "a savour of life unto life," but "of death unto death;" that it is possible to "do despite unto the Spirit of grace;" and that "it is impossible for those who were once enlightened, if they shall fall away, to renew them again unto repentance [1]." Again; if they do aught well, "what have they which they have not received?" and how know they but He, by whom their souls live, will withdraw that life—nay, will to a certainty withdraw it—if they take that glory to themselves which is His? Why was it that Herod was smitten by the Angel? O awful instance of the jealousy of God! "The people gave a shout, saying, It is the voice of a god, and not of a man; and immediately the Angel of the Lord smote him, because he gave not God the glory [2]." He was smitten immediately: suddenly and utterly does our strength, and our holiness, and our blessedness, and our influence, depart from us, like a lamp that expires, or a weight that falls, as soon as we rest in them, and pride ourselves in them, instead of referring them to the Giver. God keep us in His mercy from this sin! St. Paul

---

[1] 2 Cor. ii. 16. Heb. x. 29; vi. 4—6.　　　[2] Acts xii. 22, 23

shows us how we should feel about God's gifts, and how to boast without pride, when He first says, " I laboured more abundantly than they all :" and then adds, " yet not I, but the grace of God which was with me [1]."

Accordingly, the self-respect of the Christian is no personal and selfish feeling, but rather a principle of loyal devotion and reverence towards that Divine Master who condescends to visit him. He acts, not hastily, but under restraint and fearfully, as understanding that God's eye is over him, and God's hand upon him, and God's voice within him. He acts with the recollection that his Omniscient Guide is also his future Judge; and that while He moves him, He is also noting down in His book how he answers to His godly motions. He acts with a memory laden with past infirmity and sin, and a consciousness that he has much more to mourn over and repent of, in the years gone by, than to rejoice in. Yes, surely, he has many a secret wound to be healed; many a bruise to be tended; many a sore, like Lazarus; many a chronic infirmity; many a bad omen of perils to come. It is one thing, not to trust in the world; it is another thing to trust in one's self.

But, alas ! I repeat it, how unreal in this age are such contemplations, when neither in ourselves nor in the Church around us have they a fulfilment ! How is it fit to speak of thoughts and tempers which men of the day not only fail to cherish, but are eager to reprobate ! Yet perchance what is lost upon the many, may gain a hearing with the few; what is lost to-day, may be recalled to-morrow; what is lost in fulness, may be

[1] 1 Cor. xv. 10.

retained in portions; what fails to convince, may excite misgivings; what fails with the heart, may create the wish. We must not grudge to speak, whether men will hear, or whether they will forbear; knowing that "he that observeth the wind shall not sow, and he that regardeth the clouds shall not reap[1]."

May we, one and all, set forward with this season, when the Spirit descended, that so we may grow in grace, and in the knowledge of our Lord and Saviour! Let those who have had seasons of seriousness, lengthen them into a life; and let those who have made good resolves in Lent, remember them in Eastertide; and let those who have hitherto lived religiously, learn devotion; and let those who have lived in good conscience, learn to live by faith; and let those who have made a good profession, aim at consistency; and let those who take pleasure in religious worship, aim at inward sanctity; and let those who have knowledge, learn to love; and let those who meditate, forget not mortification. Let not this sacred season leave us as it found us; let it leave us, not as children, but as heirs and as citizens of the kingdom of heaven. For forty days have we been hearing "the things pertaining to the kingdom of God[2]." The time may come, when we shall desire to see one of the days of the Son of man, and see it not. Let us redeem the time while it is called to-day; "till we all come in the unity of the faith and of the knowledge of the Son of God, unto a perfect man, unto the measure of the stature of the fulness of Christ[3]."

[1] Eccles. xi. 4.   [2] Acts i. 3.   [3] Eph. iv. 13.

SERMON XII.

Joshua a Type of Christ and His Followers.

(FIRST SUNDAY AFTER TRINITY.)

*" And it came to pass a long time after that the Lord had given rest
unto Israel from all their enemies round about, that Joshua waxed
old and stricken in age."*—JOSH. xxiii. 1.

THE Law came by Moses, and grace and truth came
by Jesus Christ; but as if to presage what was in
prospect, as if to give an omen and token of the good
things to come, immediately upon Moses' death, a sort
of momentary fulfilment, or at least a momentary vision
of fulfilment, of the promise took place. For who
succeeded Moses but Joshua? and as Moses led the
people to and from Mount Sinai, and disciplined them
in the barren wilderness of the Law, so Joshua, who
succeeded him, led them into the rich and happy land,
and prefigured the future Saviour, who was to be
gracious and true. I say, on Moses' death, a sudden
gleam of heaven, as it were, came over the elder Church;
the Law seemed for a while suspended, as regards its
threats and punishments; all was privilege on the one

side, all was obedience on the other. Joshua led the
people forward, conquering and to conquer; he led them
into rest and prosperity. His history is made up of
these two parts, triumph and peace. First, he fought,
when in his own words in the chapter which has formed
part of the Service, "one man of them chased a thousand;" and no man was able to stand before them.
And then he rested, and Israel with him,—"the Lord
gave them rest from all their enemies round about."
This morning we read of his victories, this evening of
the fruit of them. This was what God did for them;—
and on their side there was obedience. "Israel served
the Lord," we read in the twenty-fourth chapter, "all
the days of Joshua, and all the days of the elders that
overlived Joshua." It was indeed a wonderful time;
dutifulness and security; it had an end when Joshua
and his generation went the way of all flesh; but while
they lived, the gleam of sunshine still rested on the
Israelites, and was the promise of the New Covenant,
and of the times of the Gospel. Such a blessed season
never returned to the Church of Israel, till that Church
was made glorious by the coming of the Sun of Righteousness, and was brought forth out of the shadows and
dreariness of the Law into the fulness of grace and truth.

It will be appropriate then to this day, when the
history of Joshua is brought before us in our Services,
to consider it in its relation to the life and office of our
Lord Jesus Christ; nay, I will add, to that of His
servants and followers also; for in them in their degree,
as well as in Him in its fulness, is accomplished the type
which is contained in Joshua the successor of Moses.

1. Now, first, as is very obvious, Josnua is a type of our Lord Jesus Christ, as regards his name; for Joshua is in Hebrew what Jesus is in Greek. When we think what high things are told us in the New Testament concerning the Name of Jesus, what reverence towards it is enjoined us, and what virtue is ascribed to it, who can doubt that it is a very significant circumstance indeed, that the successor of Moses should bear it? This circumstance leads us from the first to expect that the history of Joshua will contain much in it bearing upon the blessed times of the Gospel. If that name is put upon him, which in due season the Angel was to announce as the earthly name of the Son of God—that Name which was to be above every name, at which every knee was to bow, of things in heaven, and things in earth, and things under the earth; that Name which was to cast out devils, to restore the crippled, and to do many wonderful works; that Name, which is like oint-ment poured out, and which shall endure for ever among the posterities—how should not some large bountifulness in act accompany such grace in word? Let it be observed, that his name was originally Oshea, and was changed into Joshua by Moses. Surely the change was not made for nothing. We see the meaning of it; it is as if a silent sign, made to us by the All-merciful God, that even then He had before Him the thought of redemption, and of us, and of the reign of grace and truth.

2. And again, this too should be observed: that whereas the successor of Moses was called Joshua, or Jesus, so did he singularly typify the Saviour of men by

an act of grace which he exercised, and that in the case
of an enemy. Up to his time, many instances as there
were of the faith of saints, there is no instance recorded
of the faith of a sinner. St. Paul says, that by "faith
the elders obtained a good report." He mentions the
faith of righteous Abel; of Enoch, who walked with
God; of Noah, that preacher of righteousness, whose
name was worthy to be associated with the names of
Daniel and Job, in exemplifying the holiness which
might save guilty cities; of Abraham, the friend of
God, whose sanctity so availed with God, that He hid
not from him what He was about to do; of blameless
Isaac; of Jacob, righteous and holy himself, even if his
history form a typical anticipation of Gospel grace; of
Joseph, tried and tempted, yet without transgressing,
from his youth up; of Moses, the meekest man upon
earth. Of him the Apostle speaks, the immediate predecessor of Joshua; nay, he speaks perchance of Joshua
himself, when he says, "By faith, the walls of Jericho
fell down, after they were compassed about seven days."
Down to Joshua's day, no instance appears but of the
faith of saints; but in the next verse, and in Joshua's
history, we have a different specimen. "By faith, the
harlot Rahab perished not with them that believed not,
when she had received the spies with peace." Now,
why this change? why have we at once a sinful
woman spared and admitted into covenant on her faith—
nay, privileged in the event to be the ancestress of our
Lord; except that in Joshua the reign of that Saviour
is typified, and that the pardon of a sinner is its most
appropriate attendant? The word "Jesus" means the

Saviour; it has reference then to sinners. He came, "not to call the righteous, but sinners to repentance." "Scarcely for a righteous man will one die;" but "while we were yet sinners, Christ died for us[1]." As then Joshua had the Name, so did he exercise the Office also of our Lord; and his first act is one of mercy. Before he enters the land, while he and she are yet a great way apart, she does an act of faith, and he, by his representatives, an act of grace. And so, when he comes to the city of evil, and encompasses it with trumpets, and takes and destroys it utterly; in that day of doom she has bound the scarlet line across her window, and her house becomes a Church, and she and all who take refuge in it are saved. Such is the history of Rahab, recalling to our minds that favoured and blessed penitent, "the woman which was a sinner," who came and stood at our Lord's feet behind Him, in silence and in tears; and to whom He uttered the gracious words, "Thy faith hath saved thee; go in peace[2]."

3. And as Joshua answers to our Lord in his name and in his clemency, so too does he in his mode of appointment. When Christ came, He inherited the earth by the right of His heavenly Father, and by no earthly pretension. He came not as the emperor of the world, or as a claimant of any earthly throne; nor was He of the priestly line; but "without father, without mother, without descent," as far as any temporal prerogative flowed from it; born miraculously; prospered miraculously; "not of blood, nor of the will of the flesh, nor

---

[1] Rom. v. 7, 8.   [2] Luke vii. 37—50.

of the will of man, but of God[1]." And here, too, Joshua was the type of Jesus. Moses was not told to appoint one of his own sons as his successor; nor did he betake himself to the family of Aaron; nor to the tribe of Judah, from which the Shiloh Himself was to be born. But he chose Joshua, who had no claim or title to be chosen; and when he had to set him apart for his work, what was his ceremonial? Did he use oil, or offer sacrifice, or in any other way comply with the rites of the Law? No; he consecrated him, not in a legal, but in a Gospel way; he prefigured in him the ministers of Christ and soldiers of His Church. "The Lord said unto Moses, Take thee Joshua the son of Nun, a man in whom is the Spirit, and *lay thine hand upon him;* . . . . and thou shalt put some of thine honour upon him, that all the congregation of the children of Israel may be obedient;" and this he was to do, that " the congregation of the Lord be not as sheep which have no shepherd." " And Moses did as the Lord commanded him;" "he took Joshua, . . . and laid his hands upon him, and gave him a charge, as the Lord commanded by the hand of Moses[2]."

4. And in the next place, let it be observed, that whereas Joshua was chosen not by man, but at God's will; so, too, in a special way did God's choice end in Him. He did not receive it by inheritance, nor are heirs mentioned to whom he left it. Others indeed, as Moses, and as Samuel, were vouchsafed God's favour, yet not allowed to transmit it to their children; but there is this peculiarity in Joshua's history, as recorded

---

[1] John i. 13.   [2] Numb. xxvii. 17—23.

in the book bearing his name, that at least there is no record of children, who might have been his heirs; nor mention of any special inheritance in Canaan. He who divided the land by lot, who gave to each his portion to enjoy, is allotted in the sacred history neither wife, nor children, nor choice possession. As to the other servants of God in the Old Testament, we read of their wives and their children, and their children's children. We read of their sitting under their vine and their fig-tree; of a blessing on "the fruit of their body, and the fruit of their ground," and the fruit of their "kine and sheep[1]." "Blessed of the Lord shall be his land," says Moses, of Joshua's own tribe, and of Manasseh; "for the precious things of heaven, for the dew, and for the deep that coucheth beneath, . . . and for the chief things of the ancient mountains, and for the precious things of the lasting hills, and for the precious things of the earth and fulness thereof[2]." And Solomon exhorts, "Go thy way, eat thy bread with joy, and drink thy wine with a merry heart; for God now accepteth thy works. Let thy garments be always white; and let thy head lack no ointment. Live joyfully with the wife whom thou lovest all the days of the life of thy vanity, . . . for that is thy portion[3]." And yet in spite of this, Joshua seems to lack these peculiar blessings of the covenant under which he lived.

Take, by way of contrast, the history of Caleb. He and Joshua were the two spies who alone had been faithful out of the twelve who went to view the land forty years before they entered it. Here are two

---

[1] Deut. xxviii. 4.   [2] Deut. xxxiii. 13, 14.   [3] Eccles. ix. 7—9.

servants of God, alike in their faithfulness, and in the
reward given them. They alone stood forward boldly
on God's side, and rent their clothes when the people
broke out into disobedience, and were on the point
of being stoned by them in consequence. They alone
had this privilege of all who came out of Egypt, that
they at length did enter the good land, while the rest
died in the wilderness. But observe the promise made
at the time to Caleb. " My servant Caleb, because he
had another spirit with him, and hath followed Me fully,
him will I bring into the land, whereinto he went; and
his seed shall possess it [1]." He was not only to enter,
but to obtain possession, and to be the head of a family.
But to Joshua, who was the greater, no such promise
was made. And accordingly, when they entered to take
possession of the land, we read of Caleb coming to
Joshua, and claiming the promise, and receiving from
him his own portion of land at Hebron. " Forty years
old was I," says he, " when Moses, the servant of the
Lord, sent me from Kadesh-barnea to espy out the land.
. . . . And Moses sware on that day, saying, Surely
the land whereon thy feet have trodden shall be thine
inheritance, and *thy children's* for ever, because thou
hast wholly followed the Lord my God. And now,
behold, the Lord hath kept me alive, as He said,
these forty and five years, . . . while the children of
Israel wandered in the wilderness: and now, lo! I am
this day fourscore and five years old. As yet I am
as strong this day as I was in the day that Moses
sent me. . . . Now therefore give me this mountain,

[1] Numb. xiv. 24.

whereof the Lord spake in that day. . . . . And Joshua
blessed him, and gave unto Caleb . . . Hebron for
an inheritance[1]." Joshua blessed him: the less is
blessed of the greater; Joshua was greater than
Caleb. Caleb had a promise, and its performance.
Joshua had none.

And again, we read of Caleb's daughter, and of Caleb
saying, " He that smiteth Kirjath-sepher, and taketh it,
to him will I give Achsah my daughter to wife;" and
then we read of her begging of her father some
land for a dowry, and obtaining it. " She lighted
off her ass; and Caleb said unto her, What wouldest thou? Who answered, Give me a blessing; for
thou hast given me a south land; give me also
springs of water. And he gave her the upper
springs, and the nether springs[2]." See what a pro-
minence in the history of Caleb has the history of
his family; but of Joshua we read of no honour or
reward in river or mountain; no daughters, no sons-in-
law, no children's children. No descendants follow him
to the grave; his name rests upon no earthly household.
He has an inheritance indeed as his brethren, but that
in no place of honour and excellence. He did not choose
before the rest; on the contrary, he took the last portion. For we read, " When they had made an end of
dividing the land for inheritance in their coasts, the
children of Israel gave an inheritance to Joshua the son
of Nun among them[3]." Do you not see what this
means? Is not the New Covenant anticipated in him,
even as it is at this day? Is he not the type of all

---

[1] Josh. xiv. 7—13.   [2] Josh. xv. 16—19.   [3] Josh. xix. 49

acceptable servants, "in the present distress," all faithful and wise stewards whom their Lord sets over His household to give them their meat in due season; "who are poor, yet making many rich; who have nothing, yet possess all things"? Is he not the type of their Lord Himself, the Giver of all good, "who, though He was rich, yet for our sakes became poor, that we through His poverty might be rich"? Who was it who had not a place to lay His head? Who was He who had no near relative but His Mother? Who is Joshua, but Christ in figure, the Priest of the New Covenant? Joshua gave away; "he dispersed abroad;" he made men wealthy; he blessed them; he provided for their family needs,—not for his own. And Christ has gone to prepare a place for us; and in His Father's house are "many mansions;" and He is the disposer of them all; and to His good and faithful servants who enter into His joy, He gives to one ten cities, and to another five, according to their works.

And all this brings to mind what Scripture says about Melchizedek also, to whom I have already alluded, who was the Priest of the Most High God, and a figure of the Christ who was to come; and, being "without father, without mother, without descent, having neither beginning of days nor end of life, but made like unto the Son of God, abideth a priest continually[1]."

5. And here perhaps it is in point to mention another circumstance closely connected with the foregoing, which meets us in the history of Joshua. We read of

---

[1] Heb. vii. 3.

no lamentation of friends, **no** special honours paid **him**
on **his** death.   Abraham was buried **by his sons Isaac
and Ishmael**; Isaac, by his sons **Esau and Jacob**[1]; for
Jacob they mourned threescore and ten days, **and** then
they carried him from Egypt to the field of Machpelah
in the land of Canaan[2].   Joseph took an oath of his
brethren, that **they would** carry his relics from Egypt
when they **left it;** and they did so.   Moses the Lord
buried, **and no** one **knew** of his sepulchre[3], that his
people (as is thought) might **not** honour him **in excess.**
On Samuel's death, again, **all the** Israelites **were**
gathered together, **and** lamented **him.   But** Joshua
was buried neither **by** sons **nor by the** assembled
people, as **if to** teach **us to raise up our** hearts to
Him, **for whom no mourning was to be** made, for
He was the Living among **the** dead; **and** though
for awhile He **laid** Himself down **in the** grave, He
did it that, **there lying,** He might quicken the dead
by His touch; that so, first He and then they, all might
rise again and live for ever.

6. Once more.   **We are told in the** chapter **we** have
read **in** this Service, that Joshua did not accomplish
all the work that was **to be done;** but left a remnant
of it **to those** who came **after** him.   And yet in one
sense he did **it all, for** "all these kings and their land
did Joshua **take *at one*** *time*[4]."   And, accordingly, he
divided out even the country which **he** had not conquered; for what he **had** done involved and secured,
as far as God's aid **was** necessary, the doing of the rest.

---

[1] Gen. xxv. 9; xxxv. 29.   [2] Gen. l. 3—13.
[3] Deut. xxxiv. 6.   [4] Josh. x. 42.

" Behold," he says, " I have divided unto you by lot these nations which remain, to be an inheritance for your tribes. . . . And the Lord your God, He *shall* expel them from before you. . . . Be ye therefore very courageous[1]." And so in like manner Christ has done the whole work of redemption for us; and yet it is no contradiction to say, that something remains for us to do : we have to take the redemption offered us, and that taking involves a work. We have to apply His grace to our own souls, and that application implies pain, trial, and toil, in the midst of its blessedness. He has suffered and conquered, and those who become partakers in Him, undergo in their own persons the shadow and likeness of that passion and victory. In them, one by one, is acted over again and again the history of the Son of God, so that as He died they die to sin,—as He rose again, so they rise again to righteousness; and in this imitation of His history consists their participation of His glory. He truly has planted us in the land of promise, and has given our enemies into our hands; but they are still in it, and they have to be expelled from it; and as the Israelites after Joshua's death entered into a truce with them instead of obeying his command, so we too, after our Lord's departure, instead of making that right-eousness our own, which He has of His free grace imputed to us at the first, too often are content with that nominal imputation, and think it enough that He has " divided out the nations which remain," careless about fulfilling His directions in destroying them.

[1] Josh. xxiii. 4—6.

To conclude: though Joshua is a figure of Christ and His followers in that he is a combatant and a conqueror, in one point of view he plainly differs from them. He was bidden use carnal weapons in his warfare; but of ours St. Paul says, "the weapons of our warfare are not carnal, but mighty through God to the pulling down of strong-holds[1]." And, again, as the Prophet says, "Not by might, nor by power, but by My Spirit, saith the Lord of hosts[2]." "Ride on," says the Psalmist, "because of the word of truth, of meekness and righteousness[3];" and the armies which follow Christ are "upon white horses, clothed in fine linen, white and clean;" and "fine linen is the righteousness of saints[4]." Such is the rule of our warfare. We advance by yielding; we rise by falling; we conquer by suffering; we persuade by silence; we become rich by bountifulness; we inherit the earth through meekness; we gain comfort through mourning; we earn glory by penitence and prayer. Heaven and earth shall sooner fall than this rule be reversed; it is the law of Christ's kingdom, and nothing can reverse it but sin. As Achan could cause the defeat of the armies of Israel, so sin, indeed, of whatever kind, habitual, or hidden, or scandalous, may disturb this divine provision, but nothing else. Let us pray that we may all of us be kept pure from sin; let us pray that at last, when we are well stricken with years, we may be as Joshua, not gifted with riches of this world, or with the blessings of life, or with "the precious things brought forth by

---

[1] 2 Cor. x. 4.
[2] Zech. iv. 6.
[3] Ps. xlv. 4.
[4] Rev. xix. 8. 14.

the sun," or "the precious things put forth by the moon ;" but with "a name better than of sons and of daughters," "the Eternal God for our refuge, and underneath the everlasting arms."

𝔈𝔩𝔦𝔰𝔥𝔞 𝔞 𝔗𝔶𝔭𝔢 𝔬𝔣 ℭ𝔥𝔯𝔦𝔰𝔱 𝔞𝔫𝔡 𝔥𝔦𝔰 𝔣𝔬𝔩𝔩𝔬𝔴𝔢𝔯𝔰.

(ELEVENTH SUNDAY AFTER TRINITY.)

" And Elisha said, I pray thee, let a double portion of thy spirit be upon me."—2 KINGS ii. 9.

THERE is so much alike at first sight in the history of Elijah and Elisha, that it is not surprising if many of us (as I suppose is the case) confuse them one with the other. Yet if we examine the sacred narrative carefully, we shall find that they differ from each other as widely as those children in the market-place, described by our Lord, the figures of Himself and St. John Baptist, who first piped and then mourned. Certainly there are many things which correspond in their respective histories. Both wrought miracles; both withstood kings; both, at God's bidding, visited in mercy the heathen in their neighbourhood; both lived in one age and one country, and apparently with one principal design in God's Providence, viz. that of witnessing against idolatry. Even the same miracles were wrought by the one and the other; both multiplied oil; both raised a dead child: so far they resemble each other.

Yet they differ in many important respects. Elijah led an ascetic and solitary life, and was the great Reformer of Israel; he was a preacher of repentance, and the avenger of God's honour upon false gods and their worshippers. What the kings Hezekiah and Josiah did in Judah, that work Elijah the Prophet did in Israel, and by the same weapon, the sword. On the other hand, Elisha lived in the world, mixed with all classes of people, had greater political influence (as we now call it), and the higher invisible gifts.

Of Elijah it is said, "He was an hairy man, and girt with a girdle of leather about his loins[1]." We read of him first as miraculously fed by ravens in concealment, then living on the oil and meal miraculously increased; and this for three years: next, as showing forth the great miracle on Mount Carmel before all the people, of calling down fire from heaven on the sacrifice, and as slaughtering the four hundred and fifty prophets of Baal; then, as fleeing to the wilderness, sustained miraculously by an Angel, going forty days and nights without food; then as returning and denouncing judgment upon Ahab; then as calling fire from heaven upon the messengers of Ahaziah; and, lastly, as taken up without dying in a whirlwind. Such is the course of his history, very mysterious throughout, as if he did not live on earth, but only appeared from time to time for special purposes. Like Melchizedek, he has neither beginning of days nor end of life; he is introduced

---

[1] 2 Kings i. 8.

abruptly, as "Elijah the Tishbite, who was of the inhabitants of Gilead[1]," and he is taken away as suddenly.
His special characteristics, however, are, on the one
hand, his austere mode of life; on the other, his destruction of idolatry.

Elisha, on the other hand, cannot be called a preacher
of repentance or a reformer: as if Elijah had done the
work for him, as far as it was attainable. Moreover,
he lived in public, in known dwellings; he presided in
the schools of the Prophets; and he had dealings with
the kings of Israel, Judah, Edom, and Syria.

The difference between the two Prophets is marked
in the circumstance that Elijah, and not Elisha, is taken
as the type of St. John the Baptist, our Lord's forerunner; and from our knowledge of what St. John was,
we may form some idea of Elijah's office. The Baptist
prepared the way for Christ; such seems to have been
Elijah's office, with reference to the age which succeeded
him.   Before his ministry, Baal's prophets had the
supremacy, and the true prophets were hid in caves, and
fed with bread and water; Elijah reversed the state
of things, reinstated the Lord's Prophets, and then he
was withdrawn. Thus he prepared the way for Elisha.
Elijah then, as being a forerunner, a reformer, a
preacher of repentance and righteousness, was the type
of St. John the Baptist; but of whom is Elisha the
type?   On this subject I proceed to say a few words.

We need not of course be surprised, even if the
Prophet Elisha was not the type of any servant of God
then to come. Yet God's providences are so marvel-

---

[1] 1 Kings xvii. 1.

lously conducted in the way of figure and token, that certainly it does seem likely that Elisha is meant to represent some person or persons in the times of the Gospel, as Elijah is the type of St. John. Nor is it to the purpose to object that Scripture is silent on the subject, for Scripture omits to tell us that Isaac is a type of Christ, or Joseph, or Job, or Jeremiah; yet we can scarcely doubt that all these were such; and as the Apostle had much to say (which he did not say) about Melchizedek, there is no reason why he might not also have had somewhat to say about Elisha too, had it so happened. Since specimens of a typical correspondence between the histories of the Old and of the New Testament are given us in Scripture, it is arbitrary to say that the correspondence ends with these specimens; probable, on the other hand, that we are intended dutifully to avail ourselves in our expositions of Scripture of the clue which Scripture itself has put into our hands.

Still, though Elisha be the representative of some Christian office or ministry, it does not follow that there should be any very accurate and conclusive correspondence between type and antitype. Thus Elijah, we know, represents the Baptist; yet there are points in his history which are unlike St. John, and more like Christ Himself. The Baptist did no miracles; Elijah even raised the dead, and so far was a type of Christ rather than of the Baptist. Again, when he ascended on high, he was rather a type of Christ than of Christ's forerunner.

We cannot, then, have such certainty in typical

expositions which we make for ourselves, as we feel when Scripture has supplied them; but it is a great mistake to suppose that religion is only occupied with such facts and doctrines as are certain. Faith has its duties towards what is probable or doubtful, as well as towards the express teaching of Scripture. Whom then does Elisha represent? does he prefigure Christ? All the Prophets are types of Christ, as being Prophets; and it is true besides that Elisha is the type of Christ, in some remarkable points of his history peculiar to himself. For instance, when he came from Jordan, gifted by the hand of Elijah with the power of the Spirit, surely he resembled our Lord, as baptized by St. John in Jordan, and receiving the Spirit in consequence. And when his bones after his death revived a dead man, he typified (one cannot doubt) the Everlasting Saviour, whose body, dying on the cross, is our life and resurrection. Yet, in spite of these parallels, one may hardly call Elisha a special type of Christ any more than Elijah.

Whom then does Elisha represent? in other words, What is the lesson for Christian times deducible from Elisha's history? What light does that history throw upon the present condition of the Church, and the present duties of us members of it? I think we may say that, as Elijah represents the Baptist, Christ's forerunner, so Elisha prefigures Christ's successors, His servants which come after Him and inherit His gifts; Christ Himself being exactly represented by neither, coming between them, or (if at all) represented by both at once, when the one was departing, and the other taking his place; at once the Antitype of Elijah ascending into heaven, and of Elisha standing by Jordan, and receiving the gift of the Spirit.

Let Elisha then be taken to be the figure of Christ's favoured servants and followers, and thus be made to throw light upon their duties and privileges. By Christ's favoured and special servants, I do not merely mean His ministers, such as bishops and others, but all who in any measure have upon them eminent marks of the Lord Jesus; such as evangelists, confessors, solitaries, founders of monastic orders, doctors, and the like. Of all these, the glorious company of the Apostles, the goodly fellowship of the Prophets, the noble army of martyrs, Elisha is the type. Let us go through some points of the resemblance.

1. Though Elijah was so great a prophet, yet Elisha had a double portion of his spirit. This seems to have its parallel in the Christian history. Our Saviour says, that though " among those that were born of women, there was not a greater than John the Baptist, yet he that was least in the kingdom of heaven," that is, the Christian Church, " was greater than he." This is explained by our being told by the Evangelist, that the Spirit was not given till Christ was glorified. St. John " was filled with the Holy Ghost, even from his mother's womb [1];" yet even this extraordinary gift was as nothing compared with that Presence of the Spirit which Christ's followers received, and by which they are regenerated. It is indeed a double, or rather a sevenfold portion of the Spirit, and gives us powers, in

[1] Luke i. 15.

proportion to our faith, above all that we can anticipate
or comprehend. This then is a first point of resemblance. Christ's followers, like Elisha, begin their
divine career from the waters of Jordan, with the power
of the Holy Ghost upon them.

2. Next I observe on the especial communion, or (as I
may call it) citizenship, which Elisha enjoyed with the
unseen world. Elijah thought himself solitary, though
he was not so; the world invisible was hid from him.
Though ministered to by Angels, though sustained
miraculously by Almighty God, yet, like St. John
Baptist, when he sent to ask Christ, "Art Thou He
that should come?" he seemed to himself one against
many. But Elisha had the privilege of knowing that
he was one of a great host who were fighting the Lord's
battles, though he might be solitary on earth. To him
was revealed in its measure the comfortable Christian
doctrine of the Communion of Saints. His eyes were
purged to see sights which the world could not see;
and that so clearly, that he could even comfort his
attendant, who felt that fear which had overtaken
Elijah when he fled from Jezebel. Hear Elijah's words
—"I, even I only, am left, and they seek my life to
take it away [1]." On the other hand, when Elisha's
servant, on finding the host of the Syrians round about
them, said to the Prophet, "Alas! my master, how
shall we do?" Elisha answered, "Fear not, for they
that be with us are more than they that be with
them [2]." And then he besought Almighty God to give
to his servant for an instant a glimpse of that glorious

[1] 1 Kings xix. 10.   [2] 2 Kings vi. 15—17.

vision which he in faith, or by inspiration, enjoyed
continually. He "prayed, and said, Lord, I pray Thee,
open his eyes, that he may see. And the Lord opened
the eyes of the young man; and he saw: and behold
the mountain was full of horses and chariots of fire
round about Elisha." How well does this vision correspond to that blessed privilege which, as the Apostle
assures us, is conferred upon us Christians! "Ye are
come unto Mount Zion, and unto the city of the Living
God, the heavenly Jerusalem, and to an innumerable
company of Angels, to the general assembly and Church
of the first-born, which are written in heaven, and to
God the Judge of all, and to the spirits of just men
made perfect, and to Jesus the Mediator of the New
Covenant, and to the blood of sprinkling, that speaketh
better things than that of Abel!" An innumerable
company of Angels, and the Spirits of the just;—we
dwell under their shadow; we are baptized into their
fellowship; we are allotted their guardianship; we are
remembered, as we trust, in their prayers. We dwell in
the very presence and court of God Himself, and of His
Eternal Son our Saviour, who died for us, and rose
again, and now intercedes for us before the Throne.
We have privileges surely far greater than Elisha's; but
of the same kind.

3. Another gift bestowed upon Elisha, and on the
Christian Church which he prefigured, that is on her
saints, and at times on her rulers, is the gift of discern-
ing of spirits. Of our Saviour it is said, "He knew
what was in man;" He knew the thoughts of His
disciples; He knew what was happening in other

places. Of His fulness His disciples received. St.
Peter detected Ananias; St. Paul speaks as if he could
have been in spirit at Corinth, while in the flesh he was
absent. And in all ages the Catholic Church is
promised an instinctive perception of Christian truth,
detecting the grosser or the more insidious forms of
heresy, though at a distance, as if by some subtle sense;
and thus transmitting the faith of the Gospel pure and
inviolate to the latest times. "The anointing," says
St. John, "which ye have received of Him abideth in
you, and ye need not that any man teach you; but as
the same anointing teacheth you of all things, and is
truth, and is no lie, and even as it hath taught you, ye
shall abide in Him[1]." Now observe how this spiritual
perception was granted in figure unto Elisha. When
Gehazi, after taking the silver and raiment from
Naaman, stood before Elisha, the prophet said to him,
"Went not mine heart with thee, when the man turned
again from his chariot to meet thee[2]?" At another
time he was enabled to reveal to the king of Israel all
the plans of the king of Syria: "The heart of the king
of Syria was sore troubled for this thing; and he called
his servants, and said unto them, Will ye not show me
which of us is for the king of Israel? And one of his
servants said, None, my lord, O king; but Elisha, the
Prophet that is in Israel, telleth the king of Israel the
words that thou speakest in thy bedchamber[3]." When
the king of Israel determined to put him to death, and
sent a messenger for that purpose, "Elisha sat in his
house, and the elders sat with him; and the king sent a

[1] 1 John ii. 27.   [2] 2 Kings v. 26.   [3] 2 Kings vi. 11, 12.

man from before him; but ere the messenger came to
him, he said to the elders, See ye how this son of a
murderer hath sent to take away mine head? look,
when the messenger cometh, shut the door, and hold
him fast at the door; is not the sound of his master's
feet behind him [1] ?" Further, when he saw Hazael, the
captain of the king of Syria, "he settled his countenance steadfastly, until he was ashamed; and the man of
God wept. And Hazael said, Why weepeth my lord?
And he answered, Because I know the evil that thou
wilt do unto the children of Israel [2];" he saw in his face
his future fortunes. Still more remarkable are his
words when he could not discover the trouble which
weighed upon the Shunammite, as implying that such
ignorance was unusual with him. "Her soul is vexed
within her: and the Lord hath hid it from me, and hath
not told me [3]."

4. A further power vouchsafed to Elisha, in which he
seems to have surpassed Elijah his predecessor, was the
power of inflicting spiritual censures and judgments. I
mean, that the punishments he awarded were accomplished, not by earthly, but by supernatural means.
Elijah indeed called down fire from heaven on the
messengers of Ahaziah; but his great judgment upon
the worshippers of Baal was effected by the sword. But
Elisha's recorded judgments and censures were of a
supernatural kind, bringing out into clearer view that
characteristic of the spiritual priesthood which was to
come, which Elijah only obscurely betokened. For
instance, when he passed through Bethel, little children

[1] 2 Kings vi. 32. [2] 2 Kings viii. 11, 12. [3] 2 Kings iv. 27.

came out of the city and mocked him, saying, "Go up, thou bald head!"—"and he turned back, and looked on them, and cursed them in the Name of the Lord; and there came forth two she-bears out of the wood, and tare forty and two children of them[1]." When Gehazi was convicted, he smote him with leprosy[2]; when the Syrians encompassed him, he "prayed unto the Lord, and said, Smite this people, I pray Thee, with blindness. And He smote them with blindness, according to the word of Elisha[3]." And when the unbelieving lord scoffed at his prophecy of plenty during the siege of Samaria by the Syrians, he said, "Behold, thou shalt see it with thine eyes, but shalt not eat thereof[4];" and accordingly, he was trampled to death in the gate by the people, as they went out to profit by the plenty, when this came to pass by the Syrians fleeing and leaving their camp behind them. This seems to be the meaning of the words, "Him that escapeth from the sword of Jehu shall Elisha slay." In like manner, under the Gospel, St. Paul smote Elymas with blindness; and St. Peter pronounced God's judgment upon Ananias and Sapphira, who, like Gehazi, were guilty of covetousness and lying; and St. Paul bade deliver the incestuous Corinthian to Satan. Nay, to all the ministers of Christ is committed the awful power of retaining and remitting sins, according to the words, "Whosoever sins ye remit, they are remitted unto them; and whosoever sins ye retain, they are retained[5]."

5. Further: Elisha's person seems to have been gifted

---

[1] 2 Kings ii. 23, 24.   [2] 2 Kings v. 27.   [3] 2 Kings vi. 18.
[4] 2 Kings vii. 2.   [5] John xx. 23.

with an extraordinary sanctity and virtue. Even the touch of his relics after his death raised a dead man. Our Saviour had this power, as all others, in its fulness; virtue went out of Him. And His Apostles inherited it in their measure. We are told that "the people brought forth the sick into the streets, and laid them on beds and couches, that at the least the shadow of Peter passing by might overshadow some of them[1]." And of St. Paul,—that "God wrought special miracles by the hands of Paul, so that from his body were brought unto the sick handkerchiefs or aprons, and the diseases departed from them, and the evil spirits went out of them[2]." Here, moreover, we see the superiority of the Apostles to Elisha; for on one occasion, when the Shunammite's son was dead, Elisha apparently tried the like means, but was not answered. He sent Gehazi forward with his staff, to lay it on the child's face; "and Gehazi passed on before them, and laid the staff upon the face of the child; but there was neither voice nor hearing[3];" though it may be that the employment of the hypocritical Gehazi was the cause of the disappointment, if it was one.

6. Further; there is much in Elisha's miracles—nay, and in Elijah's in a degree—typical of the Christian sacraments. Naaman's cleansing in Jordan is a manifest figure of Holy Baptism, in which the leprosy of the soul is washed away by water. Again, the multiplying of the oil is, like the miracle of the loaves, a type of Holy Communion, in which Christ is given to us again and again without failing, all over the world,—to all who

[1] Acts v. 15.   [2] Acts xix. 11, 12.   [3] 2 Kings iv. 31.

believe,—to each of them wholly and entirely, though
He is on the right hand of God in heaven.   At another
time, Elisha multiplied twenty loaves of barley and some
corn, so as more than to suffice for one hundred men.

7. Again, I might say much on what I alluded to in
the beginning of these remarks—I mean, Elisha's close
connexion and intercourse with matters of this world,
in which he resembles Christ and His Church.   Elijah,
like the Baptist, lived out of the world; but Elisha was
intimately connected with the great political movements
(as we now call them) of the day.   It was through him
that Jehoshaphat and Joram gained the victory over the
Moabites.   It was through him that Jehu was raised to
the throne, and Jezebel and Joram slain.   He interfered
in the counsels of Benhadad, king of Syria; and his last
act in his "sickness, whereof he died," was to promise
Joash king of Israel three victories over the Syrians [1].
Yet he pretended to no earthly power in all this; he
acted from God, and on supernatural claims; thus
answering to our Lord's account of His kingdom, as
being not of this world, else would His servants fight [2].

8. Lastly, it is well to notice the dignity and state
which he assumed in his dealings with men, high and
low; in which he was a fit type of that Holy Church
Catholic to whom it is promised, "The nation and kingdom that will not serve Thee shall perish; yea, those
nations shall be utterly wasted."

For instance, consider his conduct to the Shunammite.
She was "a great woman," as Scripture tells us, wealthy
and honourable; he was a poor man and a wanderer.

[1] 2 Kings xiii. 14—19.   [2] John xviii. 36.

She, in her piety, finding him pass by often, constrained him to eat bread at her house, and gave him a room in it. If this were now to take place, she would be called the patron of Elisha, and he would be thought highly indebted to her, and bound to look up to her. But what was the actual bearing of Elisha and this pious woman towards one another? they both felt that his presence conveyed far more to her than any thing she could do for him. Accordingly, in spite of her riches and his poverty, he in her house acted as the lord, and she as the servant. We read that, "it fell on a day that he came thither, and he turned into the chamber, and lay there. And he said to Gehazi his servant, Call this Shunammite. And when he had called her, she stood before him. And he said unto him, Say now unto her, Behold, thou hast been careful for us, with all this care; what is to be done for thee? wouldest thou be spoken for to the king, or to the captain of the host? And she answered, I dwell among mine own people. And he said, What then is to be done for her? And Gehazi answered, Verily, she hath no child, and her husband is old. And he said, Call her. And when he had called her, she stood in the door. And he said, About this season, according to the time of life, thou shalt embrace a son[1]." Such a deportment would in this day be called pride in such as Elisha,—so different are God's ways and our ways. It would indeed have been gross pride and arrogance, had he so acted as from himself; but he was in his day a steward of the mysteries of God, and only behaved himself as became his rank and his office as

---

[1] 2 Kings iv. 11—16.

[S. D.]   N

God's representative. Again; consider his conduct towards Naaman, which so grievously offended the proud Syrian. Instead of waiting upon him, he sent him a mere message to wash in Jordan. Thus he magnified his heavenly office, to remind Naaman that there was a God in Israel; whereas Naaman and his master had considered him a mere servant of the king of Israel, bound to do whatever he was bidden to do. Consider, too, his conduct to the messenger of Jehoram, already referred to, when he "sat in his house and the elders with him;" and to Joash, on his death-bed, with whom "the man of God was wroth," because "he smote thrice and stayed[1]." What have we here but a figure of that Church to whom kings were to "bow down with their face toward the earth, and lick up the dust of her feet[2]"?

To conclude. These remarks lead us to this reflection. If Elisha be in spirit still among us, I mean, if the Church of Christ, viewed in her rulers, her confessors, her ascetics, and her doctors, be represented in the prophetic writings, such as Elisha is described in the history of Israel, how much have we to learn before we gain a clear and simple view of its real character! What a veil is on the eyes of men who treat it as a mere institution of this world! Surely, we are under a supernatural dispensation, though we do not realize it; and did we realize it, we should be given to see it, I mean we should doubtless have more sensible proofs given us of it. God asks of us, first, faith, and then He vouchsafes to give us sight. Did we

---

[1] 2 Kings v. 10; vi. 32, 33; xiii. 14—19.　　[2] Isa. xlix. 23.

believe that we were under His immediate governance, He would reward us by tokens of such a privilege which we know not of at present. Did we cry out, " Where is the Lord God of Elijah ?" the waters would divide. Never then, my brethren, come to Church, or to Holy Communion, never be present at a baptism, marriage, or burial, or at any other rite, without feeling that there is a great deal more there than you see. Where two or three are gathered together in Christ's Name, He is in the midst of them. Believe that, were your eyes opened, as the young man's were, you would see horses and chariots of fire round about. God's arm is not shortened, though man does not believe. He does His wonders in spite of us. Elijah went to heaven by miracle, and one man only saw it; but a miracle was done nevertheless. Angels are among us, and are powerful to do any thing. And they do wonders for the believing, which the world knows nothing about. According to our faith, so it is done unto us. Only believe, and all things are ours. We shall have clear and deeply-seated convictions on our minds of the reality of the invisible world, though we cannot communicate them to others, or explain how we come to have them.

SERMON XIV.

𝔗𝔥𝔢 𝔆𝔥𝔯𝔦𝔰𝔱𝔦𝔞𝔫 𝔆𝔥𝔲𝔯𝔠𝔥 𝔞 𝔆𝔬𝔫𝔱𝔦𝔫𝔲𝔞𝔱𝔦𝔬𝔫 𝔬𝔣 𝔱𝔥𝔢 𝔍𝔢𝔴𝔦𝔰𝔥.

" The remnant that is escaped of the house of Judah shall again take root downward, and bear fruit upward."—Isa. xxxvii. 31.

WHEN the power and splendour of the family of David were failing, and darkness was falling on the Church, and religious men were fighting against dismay and distrust, then the Prophets foretold that the kingdom of the saints should one time be restored; and that, though its glories were then setting, a morrow would come in due course, and that a morrow without an evening. Has this promise yet been fulfilled or no? and if fulfilled, in what sense fulfilled? Many persons think it has not yet been fulfilled at all, and is to be fulfilled in some future dispensation or millennium; and many think that it has indeed been fulfilled, yet not literally, but spiritually and figuratively; or, in other words, that the promised reign of Christ upon earth has been nothing more than the influence of the Gospel over the souls of men, the triumphs of Divine

Grace, the privileges enjoyed by faith, and the conversion of the elect.

On the contrary, I would say that the prophecies in question have in their substance been fulfilled literally, and in the present Dispensation; and, if so, we need no figurative and no future fulfilment. Not that there may not be both a figurative and a future accomplishment besides; but these will be over and above, if they take place, and do not interfere with the direct meaning of the sacred text and its literal fulfilment.

In the text, the prophet Isaiah, upon Sennacherib's invasion, makes to Hezekiah the encouraging promise, that, in spite of present misfortunes, " the house of Judah should again take root downward and bear fruit upward." Other prophecies, parallel to the text, are such as the following :—" Behold, the days come, saith the Lord, that I will make a new covenant with the house of Israel, and with the house of Judah. . . . I will put My law in their inward parts, and write it in their hearts, and will be their God, and they shall be My people[1]." Again : " Behold, the days come, saith the Lord, that I will perform that good thing which I have promised unto the house of Israel and to the house of Judah. . . . For thus saith the Lord, David shall never want a man to sit upon the throne of the house of Israel, neither shall the priests, the Levites, want a man before Me to offer burnt offerings, and to kindle meat offerings, and to do sacrifice continually[2]." Ezekiel speaks the same lan-

---

[1] Jer. xxxi. 31—33.   [2] Jer. xxxiii. 14—18.

guage as Jeremiah : " I will set up one shepherd over
them, and He shall feed them, even My servant
David; He shall feed them, and He shall be their
shepherd. And I, the Lord, will be their God: and
My servant David a prince among them : I, the Lord,
have spoken it [1]." And Zechariah: "Thus saith the
Lord, I am returned unto Zion, and will dwell in the
midst of Jerusalem; and Jerusalem shall be called
a city of truth ; and the mountain of the Lord of Hosts,
the holy mountain [2]." And the prophet Isaiah again :
" Fear not, thou worm Jacob, and ye men of Israel : I will
help thee, saith the Lord, and thy Redeemer, the Holy
One of Israel. Behold, I will make thee a new sharp
threshing instrument, having teeth ; thou shalt thresh
the mountains, and beat them small, and shalt make
the hills as chaff [3]." And again : " For Zion's sake
will I not hold my peace, and for Jerusalem's sake I
will not rest, until the righteousness thereof go forth
as brightness, and the salvation thereof as a lamp that
burneth. And the Gentiles shall see thy righteousness
and all kings thy glory; and thou shalt be called by
a new name, which the mouth of the Lord shall
name [4]."

Now, first, that these and a number of other prophecies which speak still more distinctly of a conquest,
a kingdom, a body politic, a ritual, and a law, are
fulfilled in the Dispensation under which we live, which
immediately succeeded upon the Jewish, not in one
future and disconnected, is plain from the express asser-

[1] Ezek. xxxiv. 23.   [2] Zech. viii. 3.
[3] Isa. xli. 14, 15.   [4] Isa. lxii. 1, 2.

tions of inspired persons. Such as the Apostle St.
James in the Acts, who, after declaring with St. Peter,
"how God at the first did visit the Gentiles, to take out
of them a people for His Name," adds, "to this agree
the words of the Prophets, as it is written, After this
I will return, and will build again the tabernacle of
David which is fallen down, and I will build again the
ruins thereof, and I will set it up; that the residue of
men might seek after the Lord, and all the Gentiles
upon whom My Name is called, saith the Lord, who
doeth all these things." You see that, according to the
Apostle, at that very time the fulfilment of the prophecy
was commencing; the reconstruction of the kingdom
of David was no future and detached event, it was then
in progress; it was coming to pass in the conversion of
the heathen. What confirms this view of the subject
is, that it serves as an explanation of the strong
language of Moses, in which the perpetual obligation of
the Law is asserted, in spite of inducements of whatever
kind to abandon it. "Ye shall not add unto the word
which I command you, neither shall ye diminish aught
from it;" for the Gospel was but a development of the
Law. "Thou shalt teach them diligently unto thy
children, and shalt talk of them when thou sittest in
thine house, and when thou walkest by the way, and
when thou liest down, and when thou risest up." "If
ye shall diligently keep all these commandments, . . .
then shall no man be able to stand before you." And
after punishment, return of prosperity was promised
them, on condition of their returning to the Law.
"When thou art in tribulation, and all these things are

come upon thee, even in the latter days, if thou turn to the Lord thy God, and shalt be obedient unto His voice, . . . He will not forsake thee, neither destroy thee, nor forget the covenant of thy fathers, which He sware unto them [1]." The latter days are mentioned, yet without a hint that obedience to the Law was to be relaxed, which holds only on the principle that the Gospel is its continuation.

And, on the other hand, it is no mere figurative sense in which such words as " power," " kingdom," " rule," " conquest," " princes," " judges," " officers," and the like are used (as if the promised dominion were to be but moral, the promised Church invisible, the promised reign of Christ but spiritual), for this simple reason, that there *has* been, in matter of fact, in Christian times a visible Church, a temporal kingdom, a succession of rulers, such as the prophecies do describe; which have been most variously and minutely fulfilled in their literal sense; and we know, in such cases, what has been laid down by a great authority in our Church, —"I hold it," he says, "for a most infallible rule in expositions of sacred Scripture, that where a literal construction will stand, the farthest from the letter is commonly the worst [2]." Indeed, these figurative interpretations have given special occasion to the infidel to scoff against the Bible, as if the prophecies had failed even by the confession of their friends, who, to hide their failure, are forced to pretend that they never were intended to have a literal fulfilment, only a spiritual one.

[1] Deut. iv. 2. 30; vi. 7; xi. 22—25.

[2] Hooker, Eccles. Pol. v. 59. § 2.

History indeed shows their fulfilment, but *we* enable him to deny it.

Temporal, then, as well as spiritual greatness, a visible dominion as well as a secret influence, was both, under the Law, promised to the Church in the future, and according to the promise has already come to pass in Gospel times. And now I will observe upon one or two difficulties, which at first may be felt in receiving a view of God's dealings with His Church, which in itself is most simple and satisfactory.

1. First, it may be said that the prophecies have not been, and never will be, fulfilled in the letter, because they contain expressions and statements which do not admit, or certainly have not, a literal meaning. Thus, in one of the passages just now quoted, it is said that David shall feed the chosen people. Now, by David, cannot be meant any one but Christ; that is, the prophecy is figurative; for if one part is not literal, why should another be? Again, it is said that "the Sun of Righteousness shall arise with healing in His wings[1];" and "behold I will bring forth My Servant the Branch[2];" and again, "The wolf shall dwell with the lamb, and the leopard shall lie down with the kid[3]." Again, "I will write My law in their hearts." The fulfilment of the prophecy then is either spiritual, or, where it admits of being taken literally, it is future.

Now this objection is surely not well grounded, and presents no real difficulty at all, as a very slight consideration will show us; for it stands to reason that the use of figures in a composition is not enough to make it

---

[1] Mal. iv. 2.　　　[2] Zech. iii. 8.　　　[3] Isa. xi. 6.

figurative as a whole. We constantly use figures of speech whenever we speak; yet who will say on that account that the main course of our conversation is not to be taken literally? We talk of a cutting wind and a threatening sky, without meaning that literally the sky is able to threaten, or the wind to cut; yet, in spite of these figures, we mean what we say, as to the general run and drift of our sentences.

One of the two disciples said that their heart "burnt" within them, as our Lord talked to them; are we not literally to understand that He conversed with them, because their heart did not literally burn? St. Paul calls the Church "the pillar and ground of the truth;" is Church not literal, and truth not literal, because pillar is not literal? And in like manner we speak of the Christian minister as a pastor, and his charge as his flock; yet without any intention to be allegorical or poetical.

Again, to take another class of instances, St. Peter calls Rome Babylon; does that make his epistle an allegory? our Lord calls Herod "that fox;" does this show that His whole speech is a figure, and that He did not mean in a literal sense, what He said, that He was casting out devils and doing cures, and that "no prophet could perish out of Jerusalem"? And again, when He calls Simon by the name of Peter or Rock, what is this more than giving him a *name?* Peter, which is in its origin a figure, becomes a mere proper name. And so when He Himself is called a Lamb, this is but His sacred Name, taken from His gracious office; and when St. John Baptist said, " Behold the Lamb of

God, which taketh away the sin of the world," he must
be taken to mean, that our Lord does really and literally
take away the world's sin, though He is called the
Lamb by a figure.

Now this will apply to the language of the Prophets:
the words "David," "Israel," "Jerusalem," and the
like, are not so much figures, as proper names which
have a figurative origin, or words which, having first
had a confined sense, come, as language proceeds, to
have a wide one. Of course, there are in the Prophets
figurative words and sentences too, because they write
poetically; but even this does not make the tenour of
their language figurative, any more than occasional
similes show an heroic poem to be an extended allegory.
It does not follow, because they speak figuratively of
the lion lying down with the kid, with an allusion to
the state of brute animals before the fall, or of the desert
blossoming, that therefore all they say about the temporal greatness of the Church, its power over high and
low, rich and poor, one with another, is figurative too.
Again, in the text, hardly any one word admits of a
literal interpretation; yet to give it a mere spiritual
sense, as if no house or family were spoken of, and no
extension or triumph of a family, would be to explain it
away. However, such passages as these are not of
common occurrence; the more common figures, if they
must be so called, are the use of David for Christ, Israel
for the chosen people, Jerusalem for the Church, and so
on. Now is it a difficulty with any one, that Christ
should be called David, or the second David, as Simon
may be called Peter? is it not quite consistent with a

literal announcement that He was to come upon earth, being the very God, and to redeem us? And if so, why should we find it a difficulty that Israel does not mean simply the Israelites, but the chosen people, wherever they are, in all ages; and that Jerusalem should be used as a name for the body politic, or state, or government of the chosen people, in which the power lies, and from which action proceeds? according to the Psalm, "there are set thrones of judgment, the thrones of the house of David[1]." Thus, when it is said, that Jerusalem shall be called a city of truth, the sacred text will mean, that that divinely appointed seat of revelation and power, which then happened to be at Jerusalem, and had then fallen into error, should in time to come be illuminated with heavenly knowledge. And when it is said, "Neither shall the priests, the Levites, want a man before Me to offer burnt-offerings," this indeed implies, of course, that there would ever in the Church be priests, and ever offerings; yet these need not be a Levitical priesthood, or offerings of burnt victims. And when it is said, "Fear not, thou worm Jacob, and ye men of Israel," this will mean, "Fear not, little flock, My elect people, who at present are children of Israel, and are called by the name of Jacob." All these words, I say, convey a literal truth in their substance; the meaning need not be explained away, though it is conveyed in a figure; the persons and things spoken of existed then and exist now.

2. But then it may be asked, whether it is possible to consider the Christian Church, which is so different

---

[1] Ps. cxxii. 5.

from the Jewish, a continuation of it; or to maintain that what was promised to the Jewish, has been
fulfilled in substance in the Christian. It may be
argued that our Lord founded His Church as a new
thing in the earth; and that it is manifestly distinct
from the elder Church; that the one was local, Jewish,
carnal; the other Catholic, Gentile, spiritual. Perhaps
the following considerations will lessen this difficulty.

(1.) Let it be observed, then, that the chosen people
had in former ages gone through many vicissitudes,
many transformations, before the revolution which followed on the coming of the promised Saviour, and
which was the greatest of all. There are nations on the
face of the earth which have remained for thousands of
years the same, in site, in institutions, in relations to
the rest of mankind. Such were not the people of
God's choice. They had led a wandering life as shepherds in the land of Canaan, in the time of the Patriarchs; they had been slaves in Egypt; and then again,
after a time of miracles in the wilderness, they had
gained renown as conquerors and kings in the land
where their forefathers sojourned. And again had they
been slaves, and in a farther country; and again, quite
as strangely, though not so marvellously, had they been
restored. The place of God's presence had moved about,
being first in the wandering tabernacle, then at Shiloh,
then at Jerusalem. They had been governed first by a
. lawgiver, then by occasional judges, then by kings, then
by priests. This then is what must be carefully considered, should it at first sight be thought that the Gos-

pel made changes in the state of religion, too great to
allow of the Jewish Church being reckoned one with the
Christian.   If it be asked, What likeness is there
between a Church spread over the whole earth, and a
Church pent up in one corner of it, between a national
Church and a Catholic?   I answer, Surely the mere
extent of a Church, and its fortunes generally, are but
an accident of its being: externals cannot destroy
identity, if it exists, which is something inward.   In
spite of the vast, nay, even organic changes in its constitution, which had taken place before, its identity had
remained.   When the Church was made up of Abraham's household, to external appearance a mere Arab
horde or family, roaming through the desert or sojourn-
ing in the vale, it was as unlike itself in its regal form,
as that local sovereignty in Canaan was unlike its
Catholic state under the Gospel.   Again, that Joseph, a
foreign slave, should become governor of all Egypt, or
that Pharaoh's carnal and cowardly bondsmen should
become Joabs and Abners, was as startling a change as
that by which twelve fishermen and peasants were set
over the world to bind and to loose.   Consider again
the state of Israel in Babylon; or its state when Christ
came, partly settled in a part of Canaan, partly in
Alexandria, with a rival temple, and partly scattered all
over the face of the earth, like a mist, or like the drops
of rain.   And let it be observed, as this last instance
suggests, its change when Christ came, from a local into
a Catholic form, was not abrupt but gradual.   What
was first a dispersion, became a diffusion; during the
last centuries of Judaism, the Church was in great

measure Catholic already. Besides Jerusalem and Alexandria, it had a number of centres or metropolitan posts scattered over the Roman empire, as we read in the book of Acts; and about these were collected a number of proselytes from the heathen, waiting for the promised Paraclete to make the dead bones live. And, in matter of fact, these centres did become the first channels of the Gospel, and starting-points of its propagation, as we learn from the same inspired history. Such changes, however, whether gradual or not, do not interfere with the Church's being considered one and the same under them. How different is a human being in different stages of his existence! how different all his states here below from that body which shall be! yet the same body shall rise which dies, though it be made a spiritual body. It is no objection, then, rather it gives countenance, to the notion of the identity of the Jewish Church with the Christian, that it is so different from it; for the Jewish Church was at various eras very different from itself; and worms of the earth at length gain wings, yet are the same, and man dies in corruption, and rises incorrupt, yet without losing his original body.

And, let it be observed, a change in externals, for instance, of name and site, was anticipated as regards the city of God in the Old Testament. "Thou shalt be called by a new name," says the Prophet, implying that the old name of Jerusalem would no longer apply. And much stress is laid in the Law upon God's free choice of the place where He was to fix His presence, as if to show that it might change. "There shall be a place which the Lord thy God shall choose, to cause His Name to dwell there[1]."

(2.) But, further, it may be objected, that the change was internal, not external only: not only did the Church change from local to Catholic, but it became a Church of Gentiles instead of a Church of Jews. Its members were changed as well as its locality, though Christ and His Apostles happen to have been Jews. This certainly is a weightier objection, yet this too will perhaps be removed on an attentive consideration of the subject.

Consider, then, that changes also of this kind had already occurred in the history of Israel, yet the Church remained one and the same. How unexpected, for instance, was the change which destroyed the substantive existence of the ten tribes, which amalgamated Judah and Benjamin almost into one, and absorbed into them the fragments of the ten whose sceptres were broken! At first, the principle of continuity seemed to lie in the twelve sons of Jacob; then one is set apart for a peculiar office in the body politic,—the priesthood, and is deprived of its share of the territory; and another of the twelve is divided into two to make up the full number without that one; and then, at length, the favoured line is narrowed to Judah. Again, in an earlier age, only two of those who left Egypt with Moses entered the promised land. The line of continuity, surely, was not less definite when the Church became Christian. Christ and His Apostles were all Jews; the first converts were Jews; the centres of conversion throughout the Roman empire were com-

[1] Deut. xii. 11.

posed of Jews. In one place, we are even told, that "a great company of the priests were obedient to the faith[1]."

And let it be observed, that the sacred writers show themselves quite aware of this peculiarity in the mode in which God's purposes are carried on from age to age. They are frequent in speaking of a "remnant" as alone inheriting the promises; the phenomenon of a remnant has been a sort of law of the Divine Dispensations towards man hitherto, and is declared, especially by St. Paul, to be such. "God hath not cast away His people which He foreknew. Wot ye not what the Scripture saith of Elias? . . . but what saith the answer of God unto him? I have reserved to Myself seven thousand men;" and then the Apostle adds, "Even so then at this present time also there is a *remnant*, according to the election of grace[2]." No word is more frequent in the Prophets than this word *remnant*, as we must be very well aware. Thus, in the first chapter of the prophet Isaiah, "Unless the Lord had left us a very small *remnant*, we should have been as Sodom." And it was promised that "the Lord should set His hand to recover the *remnant* of His people." And the very threat denounced against the people was, not that the *nation* should be lost, for that was too certain, but that even the *remnant* should perish. "I will take the *remnant* of Judah," says Almighty God by Jeremiah, "that have set their faces to go into the land of Egypt to sojourn there, and they shall all be consumed[3]." And Ezekiel asks, "Wilt Thou make a full end of the *remnant*[4]?"

---

[1] Acts vi. 7.
[2] Rom. xi. 2—5.
[3] Jer. xliv. 12.
[4] Ezek. xi. 13.

And Johanan wishes to take a certain course, lest "the *remnant* of Judah perish." And Ezra confesses the sin of his people, who had sinned again, when, "now for a little space grace had been showed from the Lord their God, to leave them a *remnant* to escape[1]." And Haggai says, that "the Lord stirred up the spirit of all the *remnant;*" as if it were an acknowledged and almost technical term. And, in like manner, to the remnant is the great recovery and the victory promised, as in the text, "The *remnant* that is escaped of the house of Judah shall again take root downward, and bear fruit upward." And in Joel, "Whosoever shall call on the name of the Lord shall be delivered; for in Mount Zion and in Jerusalem shall be deliverance, as the Lord hath said, and in the *remnant* whom the Lord shall call[2]." And Micah, "The *remnant* of Jacob shall be in the midst of many people, as a dew from the Lord, . . . and the *remnant* of Jacob shall be among the Gentiles, in the midst of many people, as a lion among the beasts of the forest, as a young lion among the flocks of sheep, who, if he go through, both treadeth down and teareth in pieces, and none can deliver." And Zephaniah, "The coast shall be for the *remnant* of the house of Judah; . . . the residue of My people shall spoil them, and the *remnant* of My people shall possess them[3]." And Zechariah, after promising that "the seed shall be prosperous, and the vine shall give her fruit, and the ground shall give her increase, and the heavens shall give their dew," adds, in the Name of the

---

[1] Jer. xl. 15. Ezra ix. 7, 8.   [2] Hagg. i. 14. Joel ii. 32.
[3] Micah v. 8. Zeph. ii. 7—9. Zech. viii. 12.

Lord, " I will cause the *remnant* of this people to possess all these things." It was not promised then that all Israel should be a light of the earth, and should possess the nations, but that the remnant should thus be favoured: to the remnant it was promised; and how small the remnant might be, is plain from St. Paul's reference to the time of Elijah, when it was but seven thousand men. As then no one would say that the chosen people did not continue one and the same after the captivity in Babylon, though instead of Israelites they had become Jews; as the Church remained the same as before, though the nation was gradually changing; so when it changed altogether and became Gentile for Jewish, still there was no substitution of a new Church for an old: it was but a manifestation of the old law of "the remnant," by which the many were called and the few were chosen. And so it has been ever since; the Church has lasted, but as a pilgrim upon earth, having a secure dwelling-place in no country; first identified with one nation, then with another; losing children and gaining them; sure of a sojourn nowhere, yet sure of it somewhere; Israel being but the first of many nations in which she had been lodged, and from which she takes her name in prophecy.

I consider, then, that the word "remnant," so constantly used in Scripture, is the token of the identity of the Church, in the mind of her Divine Creator, before and after the coming of Christ. Express and precise as are the sacred writers in declaring that the Gentiles shall be called, and again, that the Jews as a body shall be rejected, still, instead of stating the solemn appointment of God in a simple contrast like this, and thus drawing a line of demarcation between His two Dispensations, they are accustomed to speak of the *remnant* of Israel *inheriting* the Gentiles; as if to make the Law run into the Gospel, and to teach us, as St. Paul expressly inculcates, that the promises made to Israel are really accomplished, without any evasion, in the Divine protection accorded to Christians.

To conclude : the object of the foregoing remarks has been to remove some difficulties in the way of looking upon the prophecies made in the Old Testament to the Church, as having been already fulfilled, and literally fulfilled, in Gospel times.   At first sight, any one, looking first at the prophecies, then at the history of the Christian Church, would say that they *have* been strikingly fulfilled; but still, in spite of this broad fulfilment, there are certain points to clear up, and with these I have been engaged.

1. I will but observe, first, that whether we can clear them up satisfactorily or no, they are not greater than the difficulties which attend on other confessedly fulfilled and very chief and notable prophecies, as that of the dispersion of the Jews.   No one surely can read the twenty-eighth chapter of Deuteronomy, and then survey the actual state of the Jews at this time and since our Lord came without being sure that their present state is indeed a fulfilment of the prophecy; yet, observe, they were threatened with the evils which have befallen them, supposing they did *not* keep their Law; whereas in the event the punishment has come upon them, apparently *for keeping* it; because they would not

change the Law for the Gospel, *therefore* have they been scattered through the nations. If then the prophecy of Moses is really fulfilled in their case, as we believe it to be, it is implied of necessity, that in rejecting the Gospel they in some way or other rejected their Law; or that the Gospel is the continuation or development of the Law. But if the Gospel may be considered as a new state or condition of the Law, surely it is not stranger or harsher to consider the Church of the Gospel as a continuation of the Church of the Law; and as the prophecies concerning the reprobate *body* of the nation are fulfilled in the past and present history of the Jews, in spite of this difficulty, whatever it is, so, in spite of a less difficulty, are the prophecies concerning the elect *remnant* fulfilled in the history of the Christian Church.

2. Secondly, and lastly, let it be observed, that if the prophecies in their substance certainly have had a literal fulfilment, as I think any one might see who considered the matter, so that the Jewish Church and Christian are really one, then this will follow, viz. that that very appearance of separation and contrast between them which I grant does exist, does but make it more necessary that there should be some great real agreement and inward unity between one and the other, whether we can discover what it is or not, on account of which they are called one. What has taken place in the Christian Church is of course no fulfilment at all of promises made to the Jewish, *unless* in some very true sense they may be called one Church. The greater the difficulty on the surface, so much the firmer and stronger must be the principle of continuity and identity within, to

counterbalance it.   And what are these points of intimate union between the Church in her Jewish and in
her Christian form, it is of course important to inquire.

All Scripture has its difficulties; but let us not, on
account of what is difficult, neglect what is clear.   Let
us be sure there are many things said in Scripture most
clearly, many things which any one, under God's grace,
might gain for himself from Scripture, which we do not
gain from it; many truths, which all men, if they
carefully thought over the sacred text, would one and
all agree in finding there.   Perchance, if we had learnt
from it what we *can* learn by our own private study, we
should be more patient of learning from others those
further truths which, though in Scripture, we cannot
learn from it by ourselves

SERMON XV.

The Principle of Continuity between the Jewish and Christian Churches.

" If ye be dead with Christ from the rudiments of the world, why, as though living in the world, are ye subject to ordinances, (Touch not, taste not, handle not, which all are to perish with the using;) after the commandments and doctrines of men?"—COL. ii. 20—22.

THE whole passage of which these words form part is often brought to show that any regard to outward religion is unchristian, and a mere remnant of Judaism. St. Paul just before seems to condemn, or at least to set aside, observance of meats and drinks, of holy days, of sabbaths, as being but a shadow of the good things which are given us in the Gospel, and perishable, or rather perished and dead ordinances, and of one family with those more dangerous and destructive superstitions which substituted Angels as the objects of our worship instead of the one Lord and Saviour. This, I say, is what is argued from this passage,—that the Gospel is quite contrary to the Law in this respect, that it has no ritual, no regimen, no ordinances; and that to submit to any such, is to do injury to the simplicity of the Christian religion.

Now, so far from this being true, I think even the contrary may be laid down; that the existence of a polity, a ceremonial, and a code of laws, under the Gospel, is the very point in which Christianity *agrees* with Judaism, and in consequence of which the Christian Church may be considered the continuation of the Jewish. And I think this very passage of St. Paul, which many consider to warrant them in the rejection of external religion, if it does not prove its obligation, as I consider it does, at least is quite consistent with it.

1. First, then, I observe, that certainly not all ordinances are done away under the Gospel, considering our Lord Himself instituted two Sacraments, and set up the Church as a city on a hill, and bade us hear her, and is frequent in laying down rules and directions as to what is to be done in indifferent matters. And further, St. Paul expressly says to the Corinthians, " I praise you, brethren, that ye remember me in all things, and keep the ordinances, as I delivered them to you [1];" and again, to the Thessalonians, " Brethren, stand fast, and hold the traditions which ye have been taught, whether by word or our epistle [2]." And we read in the Acts of the Apostles, that St. Paul and his brethren, " as they went through the cities, delivered them the decrees," or (as the same word is translated in the text) the ordinances, " for to keep, that were ordained of the Apostles and elders which were at Jerusalem [3]."

It is quite certain, then, that St. Paul did not mean

---

[1] 1 Cor. xi. 2.   [2] 2 Thess. ii. 15.   [3] Acts xvi. 4.

to speak against all ritual ordinances and rules of discipline whatever, in the passage in which the text is found, because he himself enjoined and enforced certain such, at least on other occasions.

2. And in truth, a very little consideration will show, that the text does not at all speak against ordinances generally, but against those particular ordinances which did not come from Christ. Let it be observed, that the Apostle-expressly adds, " after the commandments and doctrines *of men.*" He does not forbid all ordinances, but mere human, unsanctioned, and therefore unchristian, ordinances. He does not say simply, " Why are ye subject to ordinances?" but " Why keep ye ordinances after the commandments of *men ?*" Nor can this be treated as an accidental addition, because he uses the same language elsewhere. For instance, in the beginning of the chapter, " Beware, lest any man spoil you through philosophy and vain deceit, after the tradition *of men,* after the rudiments *of the world,* and not after Christ." The fault of the tradition was, that it came, not from Christ, but from man. And so, writing to the Galatians, " I certify you, brethren, that the Gospel which was preached of me is not *after man;* for I neither received it of man, neither was I taught it, but by the revelation of Jesus Christ[1]." And accordingly, when he enjoins Christian ordinances, he is very particular, as indeed in the passage just quoted, to say that they, on the other hand, come from Christ; " Be ye followers of me, *even as* I also am of Christ: now I praise you, brethren, that ye remember me in all

[1] Gal. i. 11, 12.

things, and keep the ordinances, as I delivered them
to you." Again, "For I have received of the Lord that
which also I delivered unto you[1]." And those ordinances which he published in the course of his apostolic
journey, from whom did they come? Hear the Apostles'
own account of them: "It seemed good to the Holy
Ghost and to us[2]." Not to man merely, but to God;
and therefore the ordinances put forth were not traditions of men, but traditions of God.   -

Our Saviour had made the same distinction in His
own ministry. He had found fault with the Pharisees
for their traditions; but why? because they were traditions of men, and such as obscured and resisted the
tradition of God. "Why do ye," He says, "transgress
the commandment *of God* by *your* tradition[3]?" and
again, "In vain they do worship Me, teaching for doctrines the commandments *of men.*" Again; "laying
aside the commandment *of God*, ye hold the tradition *of
men*[4];" and again, "Full well ye reject the commandment *of God*, that ye may keep *your own* tradition;"
and again, "making the word *of God* of none effect,
through *your* tradition which *ye have delivered.*" And
then He adds, "Every plant which My Heavenly Father
hath not planted, shall be rooted up[5]."

3. Now let us turn back to the text, and the passage
connected with it. Here, as elsewhere, the Apostle lays
down the great principle, that every thing, to be done
acceptably, must be done in Christ. "Other foundation

---

[1] 1 Cor. xi. 1, 2. 23.   [2] Acts xv. 28. Vide also 1 Thess. iv. 8.
[3] Matt. xv. 3. 9.   [4] Mark vii. 8, 9. 13.
[5] Matt. xv. 13.

can no man lay [1]." Every plant, but the Cross, shall
be rooted up; no fruit is good but what its branches
bear. No person, no work of any kind will endure the
judgment, but what comes of Christ, and is quickened
by His Spirit. Every thing out of Him is dead. And
as no virtue is real virtue, nor service true service, nor
work good work, if He is not the life of it; so in like
manner, no rite or ordinance is good, unless as grafted
into Him and sanctified by Him. St. Paul does not
speak against ordinances in themselves, but ordinances
which are done beside or against Christ's grace and will.
Such were those of the Pharisees which our Lord Himself denounced; such were those of the Galatians which
St. Paul protested against; such were the ordinances of
those Jews or Gnostics, or whoever they were, whom,
in the passage connected with the text, he has in view.
These teachers of error refused to take Christ as their
Head,—"not holding the Head," he says; they would
not believe that Christ was all-gracious, all-powerful;
so the Apostle reminded them, " In Him dwelleth all
the fulness of the Godhead bodily." Again, " Ye are
complete in Him which is the Head of all principality
and power." Instead of remembering this, these false
teachers made Angels their hope and their worship;
" in a voluntary humility and worshipping of Angels."

And, in consequence, nothing they did, or said, or
taught, or practised, was right. Their services, their
rites, their ordinances were all reprobate. How does
this show that there are no ordinances *in* Christ? why
must ordinances in Christ be unacceptable, because they

[1] 1 Cor. iii. 11.

are unacceptable out of Christ? St. Paul says, " Let no man judge you in meat or in drink, or in respect of a holy day, or of the new moon, or of the Sabbath days." Why? Because these were not of the body. You see, then, there *is* a body; yes, but it is not the body of any angelic lord or teacher; it is not the body of Abraham, Isaac, and Jacob, though they are members of it; it is not the body of Moses, for Moses " was faithful in all his house," but "as a *servant.*" It is Christ, who is Lord over His own house; it is Christ's, whose, and whose only, is the body. In Him only are we sanctified; in Him only are our works, our services, our ordinances sanctified; but in Him we *are* sanctified; in Him our works, our rites, our forms, our observances, are sanctified. We are wrong, not when we have works, rites, and observances, but when they are not in Him. All these make up the body of Christ:—first of all in the body are our persons; next our order and polity; then our rites and ceremonies; lastly, our professions and works. All are parts, each in its own way, of Christ's Body, in which is life; or in the words of the Apostle, from Him, as the Head, " all the body by joints and bands having nourishment ministered, and knit together, increaseth with the increase of God."

4. Nay, something more is yet to be said on this point. Not only do forms and ordinances remain under the Gospel equally as before; but, as is plain from the very chapter on which I am commenting, what was in use before is not so much superseded by the Gospel ordinances, as changed into them. What took place under the Law is a pattern, what was commanded is a

rule, under the Gospel. The substance remains, the use, the meaning, the circumstances, the benefit is changed; grace is added, life is infused; "the body is of Christ;" but it is in great measure that same body which was in being before He came. The Gospel has not put aside, it has incorporated into itself, the revelations which went before it. It avails itself of the Old Testament, as a great gift to Christian as well as to Jew. It does not dispense with it, but it dispenses it. Persons sometimes urge that there is no code of duty in the New Testament, no ceremonial, no rules for Church polity. Certainly not; they are unnecessary; they are already given in the Old. Why should the Old Testament be retained in the Christian Church, but to be used? *There* are we to look for our forms, our rites, our polity; only illustrated, tempered, spiritualized, by the Gospel. The precepts remain; the observance of them is changed.

This, I say, is what many persons are slow to understand. They think the Old Testament must be supposed to be our rule directly and literally, or not at all; and since we cannot put ourselves under it absolutely and without explanation, they conclude that in no sense it is binding on us; but surely there is such a thing as the *application* of Scripture; this is no very difficult or strange idea. Surely we cannot make any practical use even of St. Paul's Epistles, without application. They are written to Ephesians or Colossians; we apply them to the case of Englishmen. They speak of customs, and circumstances, and fortunes, which do not belong to us; we cannot take them literally; we must adapt them to

our own case; we must apply them to us. *We* are not
in persecution, or in prison; we do not live in the south,
nor under the Romans; nor have we been converted
from heathenism; nor have we miraculous gifts; nor
live we in a country of slaves; yet still we do not find it
impossible to guide ourselves by inspired directions,
addressed to those who were thus circumstanced. And
in somewhat a like manner, the directions of the Old
Testament, whether as to conduct, or ritual, or Church
polity, may be our guides, though we are obliged to
apply them. Scripture itself does this for us in some
instances, and in some others we ourselves are accustomed to do so for ourselves; and we may do so in a
number of others also in which we are slow to do it.
For instance, the Law says, "Thou shalt love thy
neighbour as thyself[1]." Does the Gospel abrogate this
command? of course not. What does it do with it? it
explains and enlarges it. It answers the question,
"*Who* is my neighbour[2]?" The substance of the
command is the same under Law and under Gospel;
but the Gospel opens and elevates it. And so again the
Ten Commandments belong to the Law, yet we read
them still in the Communion Service, as binding upon
ourselves; yet not in the mere letter; the Gospel has
turned the letter into spirit. It has unfolded and
diversified those sacred precepts which were given from
the beginning.

To this, however, it may be answered, that what is
true of the Moral Law is not true of the Ritual. That
the Moral Law remains, that the rites and ceremonies

---

[1] Lev. xix. 18.   [2] Luke x. 29.

are abrogated. They *are* abrogated, yet only in the letter; and not in such sense abrogated, but they are in their substance continued still. Let us recollect *why* they are abrogated, and we shall understand *in what sense.* They are abolished, because they were types, and because Christ, their Antitype, is come. True, *so far then* as they are types they are abolished; but not as they are religious services, and principles and elements of religious worship. That is, we must distinguish between the precept itself, and the particular fulfilment of it under the Jewish Law, that is, the Jewish rite. As the duty to love our neighbour continues still; but by our neighbours are no longer meant merely inhabitants of Palestine, nor our own countrymen, but all men; so also the duty remains of coming to God's house for His favours, of obeying His priests, of offering Him our sacrifices, though the particular forms in which these duties were fulfilled under the Law, being types of Christ, were abolished when Christ came. The Jewish temple, the Jewish priesthood, and the Jewish sacrifices, then, were abolished because they were but shadows, and "the body was of Christ;" but the precepts remain though the types disappear.

5. This, as I have already observed, is taught us in the chapter from which the text is taken, as is very plain. For instance, it tells us that the Sabbath is a shadow, and its observance not binding, since Christ is come, of whom is "the body." The Sabbath, according to St. Paul, is of the rudiments of this world, a carnal ordinance, and brings us into bondage. It had been a witness of the creation of heaven and earth, which was

no longer needed. It was a memorial of past mercies to
the Jews, which are surpassed in the Gospel. It was a
type of the Gospel rest, which is now come. The type
is fulfilled; the *whole* period of the Christian Church,
from the day of Pentecost to the end of all things, is
one holy and spiritual Sabbath. Again, the whole life
of each individual Christian, from his baptism to his
death, is also an antitype of the Jewish Sabbath. The
heaven on earth, which abides in the Christian Church
and in the regenerate soul, this is that true spiritual
rest which God promised of old time; in the words of
Zacharias, "that we, being delivered out of the hands
of our enemies, might serve Him without fear, in holiness and righteousness before Him all the days of our
life." Yet, though this be so, shall we therefore say,
that the Fourth Commandment is abrogated? surely
not. The Sabbath indeed is abolished, but the commandment which enjoins it remains; it is fulfilled in
another manner. The Sabbath, with other shadows of
the Law, has flitted away; but "the word of God
endureth for ever," and has a real and imperishable
substance, issuing forth in ever fresh manifestations,
fresh duties, fresh promises, as its older forms successively
do their work and dissolve. The old fulfilment of this
commandment, with its observance of the seventh day,
its memorial of the creation, and of the deliverance from
Egypt, its ceremonial inactivity, its preciseness and
formality, is at an end; but the duty of keeping it, with
new objects, and new acts of service, remains. It is
observed still in substance, though not in the letter.
And what is true of the institution of the Sabbath, is

true also of other ritual precepts in the Old Testament; that they are typical, and, as such, fulfilled, is quite consistent with their ecclesiastical obligation, and their perpetual abidance.

The Sabbath then is one instance in point; though the Apostle implies that it has come to nought, yet it endures, though in a new manifestation. Another instance, suggested by the passage before us, is the rite of circumcision. This is altogether done away with in the Gospel; yet not so done away with, but it leaves behind it a representative. It is abolished as a type fulfilled, a type of Christian renewal; yet still there is such a rite as Christian circumcision, and it is called Baptism. This is what St. Paul expressly says in the chapter before us. "Ye are complete in Christ," he says, "which is the Head of all principality and power. In whom all ye are circumcised with the circumcision made without hands, in putting off the body of the sins of the flesh by the circumcision of Christ: buried with Him in baptism." Here he says, first, that the Colossians *had* received a circumcision, though not the Jewish; and then names what it is, "buried with Him in Baptism." Thus, though circumcision is abolished, Scripture has not left us without its substitute, lest the great and fundamental rule which circumcision implied, of entering God's service by a formal act of dedication, should be slighted. And on account of this correspondence between the two rites, we infer the duty of baptizing infants, because infants were circumcised, though there is no command to that effect in Scripture. Nor need there be, if, as I am here showing, the Law

[S. D.]   P contains in it the ecclesiastical and ritual rules of the Gospel, only under a veil.

6. These two instances, of the Sabbath and of circumcision, are suggested by the very chapter of which I am speaking; but what is true of these, is true of many other parts of the Law, as in some particulars all will allow; and if in them, why not in others? No one will deny that the principle or spirit of the commandment concerning the Paschal feast is still fulfilled in our feast of Holy Communion. It is true, that the Paschal feast was a type of our Lord's atoning death, and therefore has come to an end, as being a type fulfilled; but it has not come to an end without leaving behind it a rite in its place, without reviving, as it were, in a new form; why? because the Jewish Church and the Christian Church are one; and the rules given to the Jewish are in some sort the ritual and the canons of the Christian, though not *as* Jewish rules; the form, the manner, the virtue being different, the substance the same.

I say, without looking for directions in the New Testament, we shall be able to see at once the reason of other institutions and usages, which have ever existed in the Christian Church, by merely referring to the Old. For instance, the three orders of the Jewish ministry, high-priest, priests, and Levites, are done away in Christ in their Jewish form; yet, let us suppose that the commandment on which they rested remains in force now, and needs not to be repeated in the New Testament, and we see it fulfilled in our three orders of bishops, priests, and deacons.

Again: we learn from the histories of Nadab and

Abihu, of Korah, Dathan, and Abiram, and of Uzziah, that no one could intrude upon the priestly office, or rebel against the priest, without the most fearful responsibility.   What was the rule of the Law is the rule of the Gospel, as St. Jude expressly teaches us; for he speaks of the opposers of Church authority in his day as "perishing in the gainsaying of Core;" nay, and St. Paul, who lays down the general principle, "No man taketh this honour unto himself, but he that is called of God, as was Aaron."

Again: under the Jewish law, the ministerial office was continued by a succession; it was not committed to men here and there, as it might be, but passed from father to son.   The carnal form of this ordinance is now at an end, but the succession remains; spiritual sons succeed spiritual fathers.   As under the Law, each preceding generation of priests begat the following, so each generation ordains the next, under the Gospel.

Again: the Jewish temple is abolished, because the True and Spiritual Temple, the Communion of Saints, has been established by Christ.   Yet, though the type is at an end, the precept remains.   Temples are to be built to God's honour under the Gospel, and to be consecrated, and to be treated as His dwelling-places; and in other respects, as far as suitable, to be conformed to the model of that ancient building once commanded.

Once more: under the Law there were altars and sacrifices; these very altars, these very sacrifices, have come to nought, for they were a shadow of good things to come: but still Altars and Sacrifices endure, though with a different virtue, and a different purpose; they are part of that body which is of Christ.   He has taken possession of them, and made them spiritual.

I will add, in corroboration, that as other Prophets, so especially Malachi, the last of them, in whom, as being the last, we might expect some clearer intimations of the destruction of ordinances on Christ's coming, if they were to be destroyed, when prophesying of Gospel times and speaking of the preparation necessary thereunto, builds up, instead of pulling down, the ritual system. For instance, " Even from the days of your fathers," he says, " ye are *gone away from Mine ordinances*, and have not kept them.   Return unto Me, and I will return unto you, saith the Lord of Hosts."   Again, as to the ordinance of tithes : " Bring ye all the tithes into the storehouse, that there may be meat in Mine House, and prove Me now herewith, saith the Lord of Hosts, if I will not open you the windows of heaven, and pour you out a blessing, that there shall not be room enough to receive it."   And as to the priesthood, far from its abolition, Christ was but to purify and refine it.   " He shall sit as a refiner and purifier of silver, and He shall *purify the sons of Levi*, and purge them as gold and silver."   Nor was He to abolish sacrifice, for the Prophet proceeds, " He shall purge them as gold and silver, that they may offer unto the Lord an offering in righteousness."   And what this offering was to be, the Prophet tells us, speaking of it as a rite of the Church in its universal or Catholic form.   " From the rising of the sun even unto the going down of the same, My Name shall be great among the Gentiles; and in

every place incense shall be offered unto My Name, and
a pure offering[1];" that is, the offering of fine flour or
bread. What is thus instanced from Malachi might be
drawn out from other Prophets also.

7. It seems, then, that making what allowance we
will for the changes which were introduced by the
Gospel, which in point of knowledge, grace, and influence upon the world, were incalculably great, and
cannot be overrated, yet as regards the substantial form
of religion, ecclesiastical order, ritual, polity, observance,
the change was not considerable. Indeed, religion
viewed as an institution, and that of a social nature,
does not admit of any great variety. As all civil
governments are one in their great characteristics, as
all sciences proceed on common principles, else they
would not be called by that one name, so in one sense
religion, wherever found, is one thing, and one thing
only. A true religion is a religion based on truth,
and a false religion is a religion based on falsehood;
but they would not be called by the same name, unless
there were a substantial agreement between them. And
if true and false religions are like each other, as to their
bodily substance, much more are Judaism and Christianity alike, which are both from God; and, consequently, Catholic Christians must not be surprised, if
on their submitting to Christianity *as* a religion, and
not as a mere philosophy, or an opinion, or a sentiment, they are charged by those who do so treat it,
with being Jews or even Pagans.

8. And what has just been said leads to another

[1] Mal. iii. 7. 10. 3; i. 11.

reflection. The Jews might quite as justly be charged with Paganism for their rites, as we with Judaism for ours; for ours are not so like the Jewish, as the Jewish were like those of the Pagans. This ought to be insisted on. It has been shown by learned men, that considerable portions of the Mosaic system were either taken from the heathen religions which surrounded it, or at least, from their likeness, must have had a common origin with them. In truth, Judaism was, in God's mercy, the correction, the restoration, of those degenerate and corrupt religions, just as Christianity is the development and spiritual perfection of the Jewish. Now, if it is a good argument against our Christian priesthood, Christian sacrifices, Christian Sabbaths, and Christian sacraments, that they are like ordinances of the Jewish Law, which came from God, much more would it be an argument against that Law in Samuel's time or David's, as infidels have made it since, that in some chief portions of it, it is like the paganism of Egypt or Syria. And if it is a good argument against our Church system, that St. Paul denounces Judaism, surely it is not a worse argument against the Jewish system, that Moses denounces Paganism. If St. Paul says of Judaism, "Let no man judge you in meat or in drink;" or, "Ye observe days, and months, and times, and years," I suppose Moses says still more sternly of Paganism, "Ye shall overthrow their altars, and break their pillars, and burn their groves with fire [1]." And if Moses adds the reason, as regards Paganism, viz. because they were dedicated to *false*

[1] Deut. xii. 3.

gods; so does St. Paul give the reason, as regards Judaism, "which are a *shadow* of things to come." And as the ordinances of the Jewish Church were not paid to false gods, though they were ordinances like the Pagan; so those of the Christian are not a shadow, though they are ordinances like the Jewish. And since, supposing in the time of Samuel or of David, a reformer had arisen to set things to rights out of his own mind, he might have forcibly urged against all that he found established—rite, and ordinance, and government—that it was like heathenism, and that Moses, speaking from Almighty God, had denounced heathenism, and that, therefore, the existing system could not come from heaven,—and yet this in truth would have been a very bad argument, therefore, let us not be moved from our steadfastness by the arguments of innovators and heretics, who pretend that the Church system is a corruption, because it is like the Jewish, which St. Paul repudiates. For it is *not* Jewish *in spirit*, though it *is* Jewish in certain externals; nor was the Jewish system Pagan in spirit, though it was Pagan in externals. At one time, God dwelt in the Jewish ritual, though it was like the Pagan; and now He dwells in the Christian ritual, though it be like the Jewish. Forms are nothing without God's presence; but with His presence they are all things.

Thus then I answer the question, What is that substantial unity and identity of the Jewish and Christian Churches, since they so differ in their members, circumstances, and objects? Thus, too, I would answer that other question, How can the Jews be said to have rejected their Law, in rejecting the Gospel? The Gospel is but a development of the Law; and creeds and systems may at first sight be very far removed from certain known originals, and yet, after all, be but developments of them.

I conclude with one observation, viz. that a view of the Old Testament, such as I have been taking, makes it a book much more level to the comprehensions of the unlearned than the theories concerning it which have of late years prevailed. It is difficult to make an unlearned person understand, who comes to Scripture with reverence, that the commands of the Law are not binding on us now. To tell him that the Sabbath is a mere type, and that it does not concern him, and that it now means merely a life of religion, is too subtle an idea for him; but to tell him that the Fourth Commandment does bind him (though it bind not in the sense in which it bound the Jews), approves itself to him as natural and true. It is a refinement, again, in his judgment, to tell him that the Jewish temple was a mere type of the communion of saints, and is not a model for our cathedrals and churches. In like manner, he will easily understand, if he is so taught, that the other precepts of the Old Testament apply to us Christians; that what is said about holy rites, and holy days, and holy persons, has a literal sense now, though not the particular sense it had before Christ came. Thus we see how inconsistent is the false philosophy of modern religion. It professes to give the Bible to the poor that they may judge

for themselves; yet it will not let them read it in a
plain way, lest they read it like the saints of former
ages—lest they become too catholic and primitive; but
it interposes with its own officious note and comment,
to fix upon it a strained figurative meaning.

SERMON XVI.

The Christian Church an Imperial Power.

*"And it shall come to pass in the last days, that the mountain of the
    Lord's house shall be established in the top of the mountains, and
    shall be exalted above the hills; and all nations shall flow unto it."*
—ISA. ii. 2.

WHEN Christ came and took possession of His own
House, it could not be but that some great changes
would take place in its economy, and its condition.
And such there were; it was exalted and established
above all earthly power, and became a refuge and home
for all nations. It remained what it had been before, a
Church, in its inward and characteristic structure the
same; but it became what it had never been before, or
only in a partial measure in the time of David and some
other princes, and that in type of what was to come, it
became an imperial Church. It was the head of an
empire.

And hence so much stress is laid upon its being a
kingdom, and Christ a King. It was a prophecy even
among the heathen at the time of His coming, that they
who were to rule the world were to issue from Judæa.
Much more had Micah, with the voice of inspiration,

said of Bethlehem, "Though thou be little among the thousands of Judah, yet out of thee shall He come forth unto Me, that is to be ruler in Israel[1]." And Daniel saw "one like the Son of man," "brought near before" the Ancient of days, "and there was given Him dominion and glory, and a kingdom, that all people, nations, and languages, should serve Him[2]." And the patriarch Jacob, long before them, had said, "The sceptre shall not depart from Judah, nor a lawgiver from between his feet, until Shiloh come, and unto Him shall the gathering of the people be[3]." Well, then, might His own brethren rejoice and shout for joy, and sing Hosanna, when their King came unto them, "just and having salvation, lowly, and riding upon an ass, and upon a colt the foal of an ass[4]." And for Him, His first and last words were about His kingdom, or empire, as we now speak. For He began His ministry with the words, "Repent, for the kingdom of heaven is at hand[5]." And before He ascended, He committed the work to His disciples, "being seen of them forty days," says St. Luke, "and speaking of the things pertaining to the kingdom of God[6]."

1. When He was ascending, He said, "All power is given unto Me in heaven, and *in earth*." We believe in His power in heaven, but, strange to say, it is usual with us to grudge Him His power upon earth. We believe that He exercises His powerful intercession with the Father in heaven; but we seem to think that the Mediator has no earthly kingdom. As God indeed, of

---

[1] Micah v. 2. [2] Dan. vii. 13, 14. [3] Gen. xlix. 10.
[4] Zech. ix. 9. [5] Matt. iv. 17. [6] Acts i. 3.

course, we accord Him a rule upon earth; but that rule
He had from the time He created land and sea, and all
things therein.   But on His resurrection as Mediator, a
kingdom was given unto Him; do we believe that He
has a kingdom?   We know what is meant by a kingdom.   It means a body politic, bound together by common laws, ruled by one head, holding intercourse part
with part, acting together.   We know what is meant by
the kingdom of Chaldea, or of Persia, or of Rome, which
the Prophet Daniel mentions; do we believe that Christ
now has a kingdom, as those earthly powers once had?
" Yes;" we reply, " He has a kingdom; it is an invisible kingdom."   An *invisible* kingdom on *earth?* what
is meant by an invisible kingdom?   A kingdom is an
organized body : do we mean then a secret society? no;
what we really mean by the words is, that He has no
earthly kingdom at all.   We admit a truth and explain
it away.   We explain away His words into a mere
metaphor, as when we speak of the animal kingdom, or
the vegetable kingdom.   When we say that Christ has
an invisible kingdom, we mean, I suppose, that He has
servants on earth, and gives them laws; that He interposes in the world's history, and punishes the guilty;
but all this surely He did before He came in the flesh;
and all this surely does not come up to the idea, does not
answer to the name, of kingdom.   It is as unmeaning
to speak of an invisible kingdom on earth, as of invisible
chariots and horsemen, invisible swords and spears,
invisible palaces : to be a kingdom at all it must be
visible, if the word has any true meaning.

But it may be said, that Christ Himself, the King, is

invisible, and therefore His kingdom may well be invisible also. It is true, He is the *invisible* King of a *visible* kingdom; for it does not at all follow, because a monarch is withdrawn from view, that therefore His kingdom must cease to be a fact in the face of day also. It is seldom that the monarch of any kingdom is seen, and then not by many, except on certain occasions. Kings are within their palaces, yet their power is in the public world. It is seldom they rule by themselves; they rule by instruments. Such is Christ's mode of governing; He is away; He has not resigned His rule; He does not simply abandon it to His servants: but still He rules *through* His appointed servants, and has committed His subjects to *them*. He resembles earthly sovereigns, not only in having a kingdom, but in His mode of governing it.

Now this description of Christ's kingdom is what He gives us of it Himself. "*The kingdom of heaven,*" He says, "is as a man travelling into a far country, who called his own servants, and *delivered unto them his goods*. And unto one he gave five talents, to another two, and to another one [1]." Another parable, spoken in warning, represents the officers of the kingdom under the image of a steward : "Who then is that faithful and wise steward, whom his lord shall make ruler over his household, to give them their portion of meat in due season? .... If that servant say in his heart, My Lord delayeth His coming, and shall begin to beat the men-servants and maidens, and to eat and drink, and to be drunken, the Lord of that servant will come in a day

[1] Matt. xxv. 14, 15.

when he looketh not for Him, and at an hour when he is not aware[1]."

2. So much is spoken in general; but next *who* are spoken of as the rulers in the kingdom, Christ's viceroys? the Twelve Apostles, and first of all Peter. To him our Lord addressed these wonderful words: "I say unto thee, That thou art Peter, and upon this rock I will build My Church; and the gates of hell shall not prevail against it. And I will give unto thee the keys of the kingdom of heaven: and whatsoever thou shalt bind on earth shall be bound in heaven; and whatsoever thou shalt loose on earth shall be loosed in heaven[2]." By the "Church" must be meant a community or polity of men, and you see that St. Peter had the keys of this Church or kingdom, or the power of admitting into it, and excluding from it: and besides that, an awful power of binding and loosing, about which it does not fall within our present subject to inquire.

What is here spoken of St. Peter, is elsewhere spoken of the other Apostles. They too are rulers in Christ's kingdom. Christ said to them all, "Whatsoever ye shall bind on earth shall be bound in heaven, and whatsoever ye shall loose on earth shall be loosed in heaven[3]."

And more distinctly on another occasion: "I appoint unto you a kingdom, as My Father hath appointed unto Me, that ye may eat and drink at My table, in My kingdom, and sit on thrones, judging the twelve tribes

[1] Luke xii. 42. 45, 46. [2] Matt. xvi. 18, 19.
[3] Matt. xviii. 18.

of Israel[1]." It had been prophesied of Christ that He should sit on the throne of David. Accordingly, they too, as His representatives, in His absence, were to sit on twelve thrones.

And their authority was equal to that of Him who appointed them. " He that receiveth you," He saith, "receiveth Me; and he that receiveth Me, receiveth Him that sent Me[2]." And as He had said to the seventy, " He that heareth you, heareth Me; and he that despiseth you, despiseth Me; and he that despiseth Me, despiseth Him that sent Me[3]." Nay, it would seem as if their authority were even greater than that which it pleased our Lord to possess in the days of His flesh; for, whereas He breathed on them and said, " Receive ye the Holy Ghost," He had formerly said, " Whosoever speaketh a word against the Son of man, it shall be forgiven him; but whosoever speaketh against the Holy Ghost, it shall not be forgiven him, neither in this world, neither in the world to come[4]." Thus the Apostles, the ministers of the kingdom, as being the organs of the Spirit, were arrayed in more awful sanctions even than the King Himself during His abode upon earth; and hence St. Paul says, " He that despiseth, despiseth not man, but God; who hath also given unto us His Holy Spirit[5]." And when St. Peter inflicted judgment upon Ananias, he said, " Thou hast not lied unto men, but unto God[6]."

Moreover, this kingdom was to extend all over the

---

[1] Luke xxii. 29, 30. [2] Matt. x. 40. [3] Luke x. 16.
[4] Matt. xii. 32. [5] 1 Thess. iv. 8. [6] Acts v. 4.

earth; "Go ye therefore and teach all nations[1]," or rather, "make disciples of all nations, baptizing them." And, especially, consider the parable of the mustard seed. "The kingdom of heaven," says our Lord, "is like to a grain of mustard seed, which a man took and sowed in his field; which indeed is the least of all seeds; but when it is grown, it is the greatest among herbs, and becometh a tree; so that the birds of the air come and lodge in the branches thereof." Now what is especially remarkable here, is the concluding clause, which seems to refer us, by way of parallel, to the Chaldean power, as described by the Prophet Daniel, of which Nebuchadnezzar was the head. "The tree grew and was strong, and the height thereof reached unto heaven . . . the beasts of the field had shadow under it, and the fowls of the heaven dwelt in the boughs thereof[2]." The parable then of the mustard seed, not only represents the kingdom of Christ as the greatest of kingdoms, but, like Nebuchadnezzar's, as a kingdom under which things external to it find shelter, or as an empire.

And further, let it be observed, that the visible appearance and display of this one kingdom in all lands, seems to have been intended as the means (which no doubt it really was in the event) by which all lands were to be converted. For our Lord prays for His followers, that they may be *one ;* " *that* the world may *believe* that Thou hast sent Me." Again, " that they may be made perfect in one, *that* the world may *know*

---

[1] Matt. xxviii. 19.
[2] Dan. iv. 11, 12.   Vide also Ezek. xvii. 23 ; xxxi. 6.

that Thou hast sent Me, and hast loved them as Thou hast loved Me [1]."

3. Now the only question that can here arise is this: whether this imperial power was vested only in the Twelve Apostles, or in others besides and after them.

I answer, we must conclude that the power was vested in others also, from the size of the empire; for a few persons, though inspired, cannot be supposed to have been equal to the care of all the Churches. As Moses found his charge too great for him, and was permitted to have associates in his office, so doubtless would it be with the Apostles.

But again, it is expressly said, that the Church is to last to the end of time, and the gates of hell are to fail in their warfare against it. But the Apostles were soon cut off; therefore the Church's power was vested in others besides the Apostles.

But further, let this be observed, that the promise was neither made nor fulfilled exactly to the Twelve Apostles; one of them fell, and another took his place. Again, St. Paul was "not a whit behind the very chiefest Apostles," yet he was added to their original company. Further, when, after His resurrection, He breathed on the Apostles, and gave them power to remit sins, St. Thomas was not present; was he then without the power which the rest had? Surely not; therefore others had it besides them on whom our Lord personally or primarily bestowed it. It appears from all this, that the Twelve

[1] John xvii. 21. 23.

to whom our Lord first spake, were but representatives
of the full number of His ministers, not commensurate
with them.

This conclusion is strengthened by considering our
Lord's language on another occasion, which certainly
seems to show that the Apostles were not regarded
by Christ in a personal light, but as representatives
of others, or rather, I should say, of Himself. He truly
is the only One, properly speaking, who sits on the
throne of the kingdom; He is the sole Ruler in His
empire, though invisible. They are but regents, or
viceroys, in His absence; and whatever be their power,
it is not their own, it comes from Him; and as it did
not begin in them, so with them it did not terminate.
They were but the accidental, though specially favoured,
organs of His wonder-working operation. The text
I allude to is as follows:—" Be not ye called Rabbi,
for One is your Master, even Christ, and all ye are
brethren. . . . Call no man your father upon the
earth; for One is your Father, which is in heaven.
Neither be ye called masters; for One is your Master, even Christ [1]." What words can be clearer to
show, that no honours which were accorded to the
Apostles, were accorded to them for their own sake,
or were, strictly speaking, vested in *them?* that
they were theirs only as being instruments of Him
who, being "immortal, invisible," governs His kingdom in every age in His own way, the one Master,
the one Lord, the one Teacher, the one Priest,
alone glorified in all His saints, while they live

[1] Matt. xxiii. 8—10.

and when they die? Whatever honours, then, and powers the Apostles possessed, needed not to die with them, for they never had really belonged to them.

It would seem then, that the ecclesiastical power held by the Apostles was intended for others also; but let us suppose the contrary, and see what will follow. This will follow: that we have no warrant in Scripture for any ministry under the Gospel at all; a ministry like the Apostles' being the only ministry for which we have *any* precedent in the New Testament. If we will be scriptural in our view of the Church, we must consider that it is a kingdom, that its officers have great powers and high gifts, that they are charged with the custody of Divine Truth, that they are all united together, and that the nations are subject to them. If we reject this kind of ministry, as inapplicable to the present day, we shall in vain go to Scripture to find another. If we will form to ourselves a ministry and a Church bereft of the august power which I have mentioned, it will be one of our own devising; and let us pretend no more to draw our religion from the Bible. Rather, we are like Jeroboam, who made his own religion. "Jesus I know, and Paul I know," said the evil spirit in the demoniac; "but who are ye?" Men now-a-days consider the Christian minister to be merely one who teaches the unlearned, rouses the sinful, consoles the afflicted, and relieves the poor. Great and Gospel offices these indeed, but who made them the privilege of a particular order of men? Great and Gospel offices, so great, so full of Gospel savour, that they are the prerogatives of all Christians, and may not be confined to a class.   If the ministerial office consist in these alone, then all Christians are ministers.   Men have a notion, that the mere function of reading prayers in public worship, and preaching sermons, constitutes a minister of Christ: where is this found in Scripture? Let us be honest; we are but deceiving ourselves, if we keep up the name of a Church, and deny its Scripture definition.

4. These then being the characteristics of the Christian Church, as we find them stated in the New Testament, let us next turn to the Prophets of the Old, and observe whether the same are not represented to us even more explicitly in their inspired pages.   If even from the texts which have been cited from the Gospels we might infer the imperial nature of Christ's kingdom, much more is this peculiarity of it drawn out in the prophetical writings.   By an imperial state, or an empire, is meant a power which has wide extent over the earth, and that beyond its own limits.   Thus, the kingdom of which we are subjects is small, consisting of two islands; but the empire vested in that kingdom extends all over the earth, consisting of our colonies, dependencies, fortified places, subject and tributary nations, and such allies as are materially under our influence and authority.   It is the peculiarity of an imperial state to bear rule over other states; and it is another peculiarity, not indeed essential, but almost necessary, that it should be always in movement, advancing or retiring, never stationary, aggression being the condition of its ex-

istence. Conquest is almost of the essence of an empire, and when it ceases to conquer it ceases to be.

Such is an empire of this world; and it is not difficult to show from Scripture, that such also in its substance is the kingdom of Christ. "In the days of these kings," says Daniel, speaking of the heathen empires, " shall the God of heaven set up a kingdom, which shall never be destroyed; and the kingdom shall not be left to other people, but it shall break in pieces and consume all these kingdoms, and it shall stand for ever[1]." Christ's religion was not a mere creed or philosophy. A creed or a philosophy need not have interfered with kingdoms of this world; but might have existed under the Roman empire or under the Persian. No; Christ's kingdom was a counter kingdom. It occupied ground; it claimed to rule over those whom hitherto this world's governments ruled over without rival; and if this world's governments would not themselves acknowledge and submit to its rule, and rule under and according to its laws, it "broke in pieces" those governments—not by carnal weapons, but by Divine Power—"without hands," to use the Prophet Daniel's language. Or, as another Prophet expresses it, "The nation and kingdom that will not serve thee shall perish; yea, those nations shall be utterly wasted[2]."

The royal Prophet and the other Psalmists give the same account of the promised kingdom, as an enterprising, active, advancing power, or empire, conquering and ruling. "Gird Thee with Thy sword upon Thy

[1] Dan. ii. 44.   [2] Isa. lx. 12.

thigh, O Thou Most Mighty, according to Thy worship
and renown. . . . . Thy arrows are very sharp, and the
people shall be subdued unto Thee; even in the midst,
among the King's enemies[1]." And while conquest is
spoken of, and sharp weapons, in order to conquest, it is
also signified that these weapons are of a heavenly
nature; "Ride on, because of the word of truth, of
meekness, and righteousness." Again, "A sceptre of
righteousness is the sceptre of Thy kingdom; Thou hast
loved righteousness and hated iniquity[2]." Parallel to
this are the passages in the book of Revelation, where
our Lord is represented as on a white horse, the emblem
of holiness: "I saw, and behold a white horse; and He
that sat on him had a bow, and a crown was given unto
Him; and He went forth conquering and to conquer[3]."
Again: "I saw heaven opened, and behold a white
horse; and He that sat upon him was called Faithful
and True, and in righteousness He doth judge and make
war. . . . And the armies which were in heaven followed Him upon white horses, clothed in fine linen,
white and clean. And out of His mouth goeth a sharp
sword, that with it He should smite the nations; and
He shall rule them with a rod of iron[4]."

These last words remind us of another celebrated
Psalm, in which the conflict is described between Christ
and the world, and the conquest of Christ predicted.
"The kings of the earth stand up, and the rulers take
counsel together, against the Lord and against His
Anointed. . . . Thou shalt bruise them with a rod of

---

[1] Ps. xlv. 4. 6.   [2] Heb. i. 8, 9.
[3] Rev. vi. 2.   [4] Rev. xix. 11. 14, 15.

iron, and break them in pieces like a potter's vessel. Be wise now, therefore, O ye kings; be learned, ye that are judges of the earth. Serve the Lord in fear, and rejoice unto Him with reverence[1]." You see that Christ breaks whom He does not bend; and that it is the wisdom of kings of the earth to bow down to Christ.

In another Psalm: "They that dwell in the wilderness shall kneel before Him. His enemies shall lick the dust. . . . All kings shall fall down before Him; all nations shall do Him service. For He shall deliver the poor when he crieth, the needy also, and him that hath no helper[2]." You see that Christ persuades or destroys; and that kings of the earth must fall down before Him, or lick the dust.

Again: "Let the saints be joyful with glory; let them rejoice in their beds. Let the praises of God be in their mouth, and a two-edged sword in their hands; to be avenged of the heathen, and to rebuke the people; to bind their kings in chains, and their nobles with links of iron[3]." Such is the battle of the Saints, such the victory of the Christian army, though their weapons be not carnal.

Once more: "Let God arise, and let His enemies be scattered: let them also that hate Him flee before Him. . . . The chariots of God are twenty thousand, even thousands of Angels; and the Lord is among them, as in the holy place of Sinai. . . . God shall wound the head of His enemies, and the hairy scalp of such a one as goeth on still in his wickedness. The Lord hath

[1] Ps. ii. 2. 9—11.   [2] Ps. lxxii. 9. 11, 12.   [3] Ps. cxlix. 5—9.

said, I will bring My people again, as I did from Basan; Mine own will I bring again, as I did sometime from the deep of the sea. . . . When He hath scattered the people that delight in war, then shall the princes come out of Egypt; the Morian's land shall soon stretch out her hands unto God [1]." You see God promised to fight for His people, and His people were to make progress, and to spread while He fought as of old time.

If we next take up the book of the Prophet Isaiah, we shall find promises made to the kingdom of Christ so many, and so high and awful, that there is neither time nor necessity to quote them at length. Thus in the text: "It shall come to pass in the last days, that the mountain of the Lord's house shall be established in the top of the mountains, and shall be exalted above the hills; and all nations shall flow unto it. . . . And He shall judge among the nations, and shall rebuke many people; and they shall beat their swords into plough-shares, and their spears into pruninghooks. . . . The lofty looks of man shall be humbled, and the haughtiness of men shall be bowed down, and the Lord alone shall be exalted in that day [2]." "In that day there shall be a root of Jesse, which shall stand for an ensign of the people: to it shall the Gentiles seek: and His rest shall be glorious [3]." Again, "The extortioner is at an end, the spoiler ceaseth, the oppressors are consumed out of the land. And in mercy shall the throne be established, and He shall sit upon it in truth, in the tabernacle of

---

[1] Ps. lxviii. 1. 17. 21, 22. 30, 31.   [2] Isa. ii. 2. 4. 11.
[3] Isa. xi. 10.

David, judging and seeking judgment, and hasting righteousness[1]."

But, you will say, such passages in the Prophet speak rather of the victory of the faith than of the Church; and that the faith might spread, even though there were no Church. Let us, then, consider the following passages in addition, and see whether, taken all together, they admit of being thus explained. "Arise, shine," says the Prophet to the Church, "for thy light is come, and the glory of the Lord is risen upon thee. . . . And the Gentiles shall come to thy light, and kings to the brightness of thy rising. . . . The sons of strangers shall build up thy walls, and their kings shall minister unto thee. . . . The nation and kingdom that will not serve thee shall perish; yea, those nations shall be utterly wasted. . . . The sons also of them that afflicted thee shall come bending unto thee; and all they that despised thee shall bow themselves down at the soles of thy feet[2]." Again, " Behold I will make thee a new sharp threshing instrument, having teeth; thou shalt thresh the mountains, and beat them small, and shalt make the hills as chaff." Again, " Enlarge the place of thy tent, and let them stretch forth the curtains of thine habitations: spare not, lengthen thy cords, and strengthen thy stakes. For thou shalt break forth on the right hand and on the left; and thy seed shall inherit the Gentiles, and make the desolate cities to be inhabited. . . . No weapon that is formed against thee shall prosper; and every tongue that shall rise against thee in judgment thou shalt condemn[3]." Again,

[1] Isa. xvi. 4, 5.　　[2] Isa. lx. 1. 3. 10. 12. 14.　　[3] Isa. liv. 2, 3. 17.

" Strangers shall stand and feed your flocks, and the sons of the alien shall be your plowmen and your vinedressers. But ye shall be named the priests of the Lord, men shall call you the ministers of our God ; for ye shall eat the riches of the Gentiles, and in their glory shall ye boast yourselves." And again, " Kings shall be thy nursing fathers, and their queens thy nursing mothers : they shall bow down to thee with their face toward the earth, and lick up the dust of thy feet [1]."

What is wanting in such passages to the picture of a great empire, comprising all that a great empire ordinarily exhibits ? Extended dominion, and that not only over its immediate subjects, but over the kings of other kingdoms ; aggression and advance; a warfare against enemies ; acts of judgment upon the proud ; acts of triumph over the defeated ; high imperial majesty towards the suppliant; clemency towards the repentant ; parental care of the dutiful. Again, these passages imply, in the subjects of the kingdom, a multitude of various conditions and dispositions ; some of them loyal, some restrained by fear, some by interest, some partly subjected, some indirectly influenced. They involve, in consequence, though they do not mention, a complex organization, and a combination of movements, and a variety and opposition of interests, and other similar results of extended sway. Of course, too, they involve vicissitudes of fortune, and all those other characteristics of the history of a temporal power which ever will attend it, while men are men, whether, as in the case of the Jews, they are under a supernatural Providence or no.

[1] Isa. xlix. 23.

5. After this view of the Gospel Church, as set before us in our Lord's announcements, and in the prophecies which preceded His coming, let us turn, in conclusion, to its history, and see whether they have not been most exactly and marvellously fulfilled.

Even in the Apostles' life-time the Gospel had spread east, west, and south, far and wide, and the Church with it. Multitudes had been converted in all nations, and the Apostles were the acknowledged rulers of those multitudes. So wide and well-connected a polity there was not on the earth, even before their martyrdom, except the Roman Empire itself, which was the seat of it.

And much more have the prophecies been fulfilled in later times. Many persons among us think that the history of the Church has been the fulfilment of those dark and fearful predictions, which speak of the city of confusion, and the man of sin. Now here I put the matter to a simple issue. Here are two sets of prophecies: one about the Gospel Dispensation, in the Prophet Isaiah and his brethren; the other in Daniel, St. Paul, and St. John, about the great enemy of the Gospel. I ask, then, *which* of the two sets of prophecy is the more *literally* fulfilled in the history of the Church? In which have we the less need to betake ourselves to allegories, and explanations, and forced statements? which of the two has the fewer difficulties? Has there not, in fact, been a great corporation, or continuous body politic, all over the world, from the Apostles' days to our own, bearing the name of Church —one, and one only? Has it not spread in spite of all opposition, and maintained itself marvellously against the power of the world? Has it not ever taken the cause of the poor and friendless against the great and proud? Has it not succeeded by the use of weapons, not earthly and carnal, but by righteousness and mercy, as was foretold? Has it not broken in pieces numberless kingdoms and conquerors which opposed it, and risen again, and flourished more than before, after the most hopeless reverses? Has it not ever been at war with the spirit of the world, with pride, and luxury, and cruelty, and tyranny, and profaneness? Let us, then, glorify our Lord and Saviour for what He has said, what He has done. Surely we may use, and with fuller reason, if it be possible, the words of Solomon, "Blessed be the Lord, that hath given rest unto His people Israel, according to all that He promised; *there hath not failed one word* of all His good promise, which He promised by the hand of Moses His servant. The Lord our God be with us, as He was with our fathers: let Him not leave us, nor forsake us: that He may incline our hearts unto Him, to walk in all His ways, and to keep His commandments, and His statutes, and His judgments which He commanded our fathers; . . . that He maintain the cause of His servant and the cause of His people Israel, at all times, as the matter shall require; that all the people of the earth may know that the Lord is God, and that there is none else[1]."

[1] 1 Kings viii. 56—60.

SERMON XVII.

Sanctity the Token of the Christian Empire.

" *With righteousness* shall *He judge the poor, and reprove* **with equity**
for the meek of the earth; and He shall **smite** the earth **with the**
rod of His mouth, and with the **breath of His lips** shall He slay the
wicked."—ISA. xi. 4.

WHEN Christ visited His Church in the flesh, He
left it what it was, yet made it what it was not;
He left it a Church, and He made it a kingdom. He
made it a kingdom or empire, like those four ungodly
kingdoms which Daniel saw in vision, to which His
Church was successively subjected, and to which His
own kingdom succeeded. But though it was as really a
kingdom as it was a Church; yet, as it differed from its
former state under the Law, though still a Church, so,
though a kingdom, it differed in some essential respects
from those heathen kingdoms to which the Prophet
compares it.

What this great difference is, the text expresses.
Kingdoms of this world are supported by weapons of
this world; but Christ's kingdom, though a visible
temporal kingdom, is *in* this world, but not *of* this

world, and is maintained by weapons, not carnal, but heavenly. "With righteousness," says the Prophet, speaking of His rule, "and with equity;" "with the rod of His mouth," by preaching and teaching, by exhortation and confession; and "with the breath of His lips," by judgment and sentence, by denunciation and anathema.

As then it may in many ways be shown that the Church of Christ, though one Church with the Jewish, differs from it as being a kingdom; so now let me dwell on this point, that though a kingdom like empires of the earth, it differs from them in being a Church, i. e. a kingdom of truth and righteousness.

Few words are necessary to show that it is thus described in Scripture; but some explanation may be necessary, in order to reconcile the description with its fulfilment.

First, then, as to Scripture. Our Lord, we know, calls it not only a kingdom, but a kingdom *of heaven;* or, as He says elsewhere, "My kingdom is not of this world." Now the Prophets comment largely by anticipation on this title, and show what it implies. For instance, the work is attributed to Almighty God, not to man. "Not by might, nor by power, but by My Spirit, saith the Lord of hosts[1]." Again, "Thou sawest," says Daniel to Nebuchadnezzar, "till that a stone was cut out without hands, which smote the image upon his feet[2]." Again, "The word that goeth forth out of My mouth . . . shall not return unto Me void, but it shall accomplish that which I please, and it

[1] Zech. iv. 6.   [2] Dan. ii. 34.

shall **prosper** in the thing whereto **I** sent it[1]." Again,
we **read** of "the Spirit being poured upon **us from on**
high, and the wilderness being **a fruitful field,** and the
fruitful field being **counted for a forest**[2]." Again, " So
shall they fear the **Name of the** Lord from the west, and
His glory from **the rising of the sun :** when the enemy
shall come in **like a** flood, the Spirit of the Lord shall
lift up a standard against him[3]." And again, "**I will**
pour My Spirit upon **thy** seed, and My blessing upon
thine offspring; **and** they shall spring up as among the
grass, as **willows by** the water-courses. One shall **say,**
I am **the Lord's, and** another **shall call** himself by the
name of Jacob[4]."

Thus the empire **was to be of a moral nature ; and
this is** further seen by **such** words **as** "law," "light,"
and "righteousness," **which** are **used in** describing its
progress. "Out **of** Zion shall go **forth the Law** and the
Word of the Lord **from Jerusalem**[5]." Again, "A Law
shall proceed from Me, **and I will make** My judgment
to rest for a light of the people[6]." And again, " For
Zion's sake **will I** not **hold My** peace, and for Jerusalem's sake I will not rest, until the righteousness
thereof go forth as brightness, and the salvation **thereof**
as a **lamp that** burneth[7]." And all such passages as
the text, **which** speak of righteousness, equity, truth,
and wisdom, being the attributes of the kingdom ; or as
the words in **the** Psalm, "Ride **on** because of the word
of truth, of meekness, and righteousness."

[1] Isa. lv. 11.   [2] Isa. xxxii. 15.   [3] Isa. lix. 19.
[4] Isa. xliv. 3—5.   [6] Isa. ii. 3.
[5] Isa. li. 4.   [7] Isa. lxii. 1.

The same thing is shown by such descriptions of the heavenly kingdom as speak of its rise as a creation; implying thereby that it was an inward change resulting from moral influence, or the like cause, not an outward conquest. "I will say to the north, Give up; and to the south, Keep not back: bring My sons from far, and My daughters from the ends of the earth; even every one that is called by My Name; for I have created him for My glory, I have formed him: yea, I have made him. Bring forth the blind people that have eyes, and the deaf that have ears." Again, "Behold, I will do a new thing. . . . . I will even make a way in the wilderness, and rivers in the desert. . . . . . This people have I formed for Myself; they shall show forth My praise[1]."

And to the same purport are such passages as speak of the subjugation of the nations to Christ's kingdom being voluntary on their part. It is a conquest by persuasion, a winning over, not a tyrannous compulsion. "Many people shall go and say, Come ye, and let us go up to the mountain of the Lord, to the house of the God of Jacob; and He will teach us of His ways, and we will walk in His paths[2]." And in the Prophet Zechariah, "There shall come people, and the inhabitants of many cities: and the inhabitants of one city shall go to another, saying, Let us go speedily to pray before the Lord, and to seek the Lord of hosts: I will go also. Yea, many people and strong nations shall come to seek the Lord of hosts in Jerusalem, and to pray before the Lord. Thus saith the Lord of hosts;

[1] Isa. xliii. 6—8. 19—21. [2] Isa. ii. 3.

In those days . . . ten men shall take hold out of all languages of the nations, even shall take hold of the skirt of him that is a Jew, saying, We will go with you: for we have heard that God is with you[1]."

That Scripture then speaks of the Kingdom of Christ as not an earthly kingdom, not supported by strength of arm, or force of mind, or any other faculty or gift of the natural man, is plain. But now let us consider some objections to which the circumstances of its actual history and condition give rise.

1. And first, it may be said that the event has not fulfilled the prophecies, in this very respect in which I have been speaking of them; that the kingdom has indeed been large and powerful, but it has not ruled according to justice and truth; that at times it has had very wicked men among its rulers, and that great corruptions, religious and moral, have been found in it; and that, as has sometimes been said, worse crimes have been perpetrated under colour of religion than in any other way. But this may be granted in the argument, and yet the Scripture account of the Church remain uncompromised. That there have been things that offend, and those that commit iniquity, in Christ's kingdom, in great abundance, is true indeed; but of this we are forewarned in Scripture itself. "The kingdom of heaven," says our Lord, "is like unto a net that was cast into the sea, and gathered of *every kind*[2]." Nor does the one truth interfere with the other. It is true there have been "many called and few chosen" in this kingdom; yet it is true also, that it is a kingdom

---

[1] Zech. viii. 20—23.   [2] Matt. xiii. 47.

of righteousness, for this reason, because it is a kingdom *founded, based* in righteousness. This is how the prophecies speak of it. "In righteousness shalt thou be *established*[1];" "in mercy shall the throne be *established*," "by liberal things shall He *stand*[2]." "A king shall reign in righteousness, and princes shall rule in judgment[3]." "Righteousness shall be the girdle of His loins, and faithfulness the girdle of His reins[4]." It is a kingdom which, from first to last, in every age, endures *because* of the righteousness which is in it. Earthly kingdoms are founded, not in justice, but in injustice. They are created by the sword, by robbery, cruelty, perjury, craft, and fraud. There never was a kingdom, except Christ's, which was not conceived and born, nurtured and educated, in sin. There never was a state but was committed to acts and maxims which it is its crime to maintain, and its ruin to abandon. What monarchy is there but began in invasion or usurpation? What revolution has been effected without self-will, violence, or hypocrisy? What popular government but is blown about by every wind, as if it had no conscience and no responsibilities? What dominion of the few but is selfish and unscrupulous? Where is military strength without the passion for war? Where is trade without the love of filthy lucre, which is the root of all evil? But Christ's kingdom was of another sort. It was destined to be powerful and wide-spreading above other kingdoms; it was to be the abode of proud, covetous, ambitious, sensual hearts; it was to look like

[1] Isa. liv. 14.   [2] Isa. xvi. 5; xxxii. 8.
[3] Isa. xxxii. 1.   [4] Isa. xi. 5.

the kingdoms of this world, first, because of its wealth and power; next, because there were many among its subjects who sought these things. But this is the indelible distinction between it and all other kingdoms, that they spring from evil, and depend on evil; they have their life and strength in bold deeds and bad principles: but that the life of the Church lies, not in inflicting evil, but in receiving it; not in doing, but in suffering; in all those things which the world despises, as being fitter in themselves to pull down an empire than to build it up; in patience, in simplicity, in inno-cence, in concession, in passiveness, in resignation.

True it is that numberless offences occur in the king-dom; but when its members sin, its original principle is abandoned, and its life is imperilled: on the other hand, by truth, by justice, by mercy, by sanctity, it arose, it gained power, and it keeps it. It awes men into obedience, not by strength of arm, by a soldiery, imple-ments of war, strongholds, silver and gold; for of these it has none: but by its visible tokens of a Divine ministry; by the weapons of God. When the Church displays her proper gifts, she prospers: when she disuses them, she declines. "Put up again thy sword into his place," said our Lord to St. Peter, "for all they that take the sword shall perish with the sword[1]." "Lord," said James and John, "wilt Thou that we command fire to come down from heaven and consume them, even as Elias did? And He turned and rebuked them, and said, Ye know not what manner of spirit ye are of; for the Son of man is not come to destroy men's lives, but

[1] Matt. xxvi. 52.

to save them [1]." We conquer by turning the cheek to
the smiter; by repaying good for evil; by praying for
the persecutor; by giving to him that asks; by suffering for the feeble; by sheltering the widow and the
fatherless; by being champions of the poor; by forti-
tude, firmness, constancy, disinterestedness, fairness,
moderation, nobleness, bountifulness, self-sacrifice, and
self-command; by patience in enduring ill, and perseverance in doing well. Thus the heavenly kingdom
rose at the first: thus, and thus only, in spite of its
untrue members, which cumber it, is it still maintained.
Thus it fulfils the paradox of being a holy Church, yet
containing "not only vessels of gold and of silver, but
also of wood and of earth; and some to honour, and
some to dishonour [2]."

2. What has been said brings to mind another
paradox, which is fulfilled in the kingdom of Christ,
and which may require some explanation. In the
Gospel, Christ's followers are represented as poor,
despised, weak, and helpless:—such pre-eminently were
the Apostles; but in the Prophets, especially in Isaiah,
the kingdom is represented as rich, and flourishing,
and honoured, and powerful, and happy. So much is
this the language of prophecy, that the Apostles, till
our Lord enlightened them, thought that, in being
rulers in His kingdom, they were to inherit the goods
of this world. They had been led to look out for a
throne like David's, and a king's house like Solomon's:
but far different is the nature of Christ's kingdom. At
length they learned, what is the truth, that under the

---

[1] Luke ix. 54—56.　　　　[2] 2 Tim. ii. 20.

Gospel, they who look out for such a throne and such a palace, do never obtain them, or, if so, obtain them to their harm, not to their benefit. In truth, so has it been ordered by Divine Providence, that in the Gospel kingdom is instanced a remarkable law of ethics, X. which is well known to all who have given their minds to the subject. All virtue and goodness tend to make men powerful in this world; but they who aim at the power have not the virtue. Again: virtue is its own reward, and brings with it the truest and highest pleasures; but they who cultivate it for the pleasure-sake are selfish, not religious, and will never gain the pleasure, because they never can have the virtue. So is it with the Church of Christ. If she were to *seek* power, wealth, and honour, this were to fall from grace; but it is not less true that she *will* have them, though she seeks them not, or, rather, *if* she seeks them not. For when men see disinterested goodness, and holiness which has no selfish aims, and conscientiousness which is strictly bound by a sense of duty, and faith which sacrifices this world for the next, they cannot help giving to those who display these excellences that which such persons are content to lose, and for which they ask not,—credit and influence. He who withdraws himself, is courted; he who solicits favour, is disdained. Satan offered our Lord the glory of all the kingdoms of the world, and He repelled the Evil One; but He gained from His Father what He refused from the Tempter.

So is it with all His followers. The Saints live in sackcloth, and they are buried in silk and jewels. The Church refuses the gifts of this world, but these gifts come to her unbidden. Power, and influence, and credit, and authority, and wealth flow into her, because she does not ask for them : she has, because she does not seek : but let her seek them, and she loses them. She cannot help the accumulation of worldly goods, except *by* seeking them, except by showing anxiety about them. Men aim at robbing her of them, when they see that she prizes them. They envy her them, when she makes much of them. They grudge her them, and stint her of them, when they see that her ministers squander them on themselves, on their own persons, on their families, their relations, and their dependents; when they convert them into private property, and desecrate them, and leave them away by will for purposes not religious. In this way indeed the Church *can* keep herself from power and dignity, by making them the direct object of her thoughts. And this the Holy Apostles at first supposed they ought to do. And so *is* it with the kingdoms of this world. Revenue and property, tribute and tax, are weighty matters necessarily with states and governments; and power, dignity, and honour, wealth and splendour, are considered great prizes by the children of men. But so must it not be with us. "Before honour is humility." "Ye know," says our Lord, "that the princes of the Gentiles exercise dominion over them, and they that are great exercise authority upon them. But it shall not be so among you; but whosoever will be great among you, let him be your minister. And whosoever will be chief among you, let him be your servant. Even as the Son of man came, not to be ministered unto, but to minister, and to give His life a ransom for many[1]." "He became obedient unto death, even the death of the Cross;" and therefore "God also hath highly exalted Him, and given Him a Name which is above every name[2]." So is it with us; we rise by self-abasement.

The case is the same in the matter of eating, drinking, and clothing. If we seek them not, we shall have them. "Take no thought, saying, What shall we eat? or what shall we drink? or wherewithal shall we be clothed? For after all these things do the Gentiles seek; for your heavenly Father knoweth that ye have need of all these things. But seek ye first the kingdom of God and His righteousness, and all these things shall be added unto you[3]." We are to seek, not temporal things, but God's righteousness; and temporal things will come, as it were, of their own accord.

Again; what is the command given us about the riches of this world? "Love not the world, neither the things that are in the world: if any man love the world, the love of the Father is not in him. For all that is in the world, the lust of the flesh, and the lust of the eyes, and the pride of life, is not of the Father, but is of the world[4]." Such is the Church's *rule*. But now, let us hear from the Prophet what the *result* of it is. "The multitude of camels shall cover thee, the dromedaries of Midian and Ephah. All they from Sheba shall come: they shall bring gold and incense; and they shall show forth the praises of the Lord[5]." What is this but to

---

[1] Matt. xx. 25—28. [2] Phil. ii. 8, 9. [3] Matt. vi. 31—33.
[4] 1 John ii. 15, 16. [5] Isa. lx. 6.

say, that *while* gold and silver are applied by the
Church to the purpose of showing forth the praises of
the Lord, they will be given, and may be accepted; but
that directly they are loved for their own sake, then
they return to their original dust, lose their sanctification, and become "not of the Father, but of the
world"?

Again, universal dominion, or Catholicity, is what all
empires of this world have sought after; and what the
Church alone has obtained, and obtained from the first:
and how? I said it just now, by the bond of gentleness
and charity. Other empires have attempted it by
ambition; but the kingdom of God by meekness. And
such was our Lord's declaration before He set it up.
"Blessed are the meek," He said, "for they shall
inherit the earth[1]." They shall gain without effort,
what the children of men have ever with great efforts
been seeking. They shrink and flee from the episcopate
of the world, and they are crowned with an ecumenical
dominion: they write themselves servants of servants,
and they become vicars of Christ. "Lift up thine eyes
round about, and see: all they gather themselves
together: they come to thee: thy sons shall come from
far, and thy daughters shall be nursed at thy side.
Then shalt thou see, and flow together, and thine heart
shall fear, and be enlarged; because the abundance of the
sea shall be converted unto thee, the forces of the Gentiles shall come unto thee[2]." "Then shalt thou say in
thine heart, Who hath begotten me these, seeing I have
lost my children, and am desolate, a captive, and

[1] Matt. v. 5.   [2] Isa. lx. 4. 5.

removing to and fro? and who hath brought up these? Behold, I was left alone; these, where had they been [1]?" The Church finds what she sought not for; and hence our Lord says to St. Peter, "There is no man that hath left house, or brethren, or sisters, or father, or mother, or wife, or children, or lands, for My sake and the Gospel's, but he shall receive an hundredfold, *now in this time*, houses, and brethren, and sisters, and mothers, and children, and lands, *with persecutions*[2]." And in this respect, the Christian Church is prefigured in the history of Solomon, to whom God appeared in a dream, and said, "Ask what I shall give thee;" and next, when he asked for an understanding heart, answered, "Because thou hast *not* asked for thyself long life, neither hast asked riches for thyself, nor hast asked the life of thine enemies, but hast asked for thyself understanding to discern judgment; behold, I have done according to thy words: Lo, I have given thee a wise and an understanding heart . . . and I have *also* given thee that which thou hast not asked, both riches and honour[3]."

Such, then, is the law of Christ's kingdom, such the paradox which is seen in its history. It belongs to the poor in spirit; it belongs to the persecuted; it is possessed by the meek; it is sustained by the patient. It conquers by suffering; it advances by retiring; it is made wise through foolishness. "If any man among you seemeth to be wise in this world, let him become a fool, that he may be wise[4]." Again: "Ye see your calling, brethren, how that not many wise

---

[1] Isa. xlix. 21.
[2] Mark x. 29.
[3] 1 Kings iii. 5. 11—13.
[4] 1 Cor. iii. 18.

men after the flesh, not many mighty, not many noble,
are called. But God hath chosen the foolish things of
the world to confound the wise: and God hath chosen
the weak things of the world to confound the things
which are mighty; and base things of the world, and
things which are despised, hath God chosen; yea, and
things which are not, to bring to nought things that
are: that no flesh should glory in His presence[1]." Or,
as He says elsewhere, contrasting their apparent weakness with their real power, " By honour and dishonour;
by evil report and good report; as deceivers, and yet
true; as unknown, and yet well known; as dying, and,
behold, we live; as chastened, and not killed; as sor-
rowful, yet alway rejoicing; as poor, yet making many
rich; as having nothing, and yet possessing all
things[2]."

But here we are brought to a third and very large
question, with some mention of which I shall conclude.

3. Temporal power and wealth, though not essential to the Church, are almost necessary attendants
on it, as I have already implied. They cannot long
be absent from it; it is but a matter of time, as
we speak, when they will be added. But if so, the
question rises, whether, for instance, Herod had not
cause to fear Him who was born King of the Jews
in Bethlehem. For if the spiritual power of the Gospel
Kingdom is followed, as a matter of necessity, by
temporal power, what matter to him whether such
temporal power was of the essence of the Church or
not? He did not care for theological distinctions; any

1 Cor. i. 26—29.   2 2 Cor. vi. 8—10.

how it belonged to the Church, or was henceforth to belong; that was the practical issue of the whole matter, and it was enough for him to know this. If so, he was right in being jealous of One who was going to resume in His own person, and delegate to His ministers, all power, temporal and spiritual, all over the earth. And again, the Romans too had cause to be jealous, and the cry of the Jews would seem to have reason in it: " Whosoever maketh himself a king speaketh against Cæsar;" and all this in spite of our Lord's most solemn and impressive statement, " My kingdom is not of this world." Such is the objection.

I answer, in the first place, by granting that Herod and other irreligious kings and states certainly had much reason to fear what was coming on them : especially since we have the plain prophecy in Scripture addressed to the Church, " The nation and kingdom that will not serve thee shall perish." And the event confirms this conclusion. The Roman power would not serve the Church. It was sagacious enough to discern her aggressive, imperial character from the first. It followed the steps of Herod and Pilate, and it inflicted a series of cruel persecutions upon her. We know well what resulted. The prophecy was accomplished. The nation and kingdom that did not serve the Church perished. The empire was broken; the Church triumphed; and then the empire humbled itself. It fell down and worshipped the King of the new kingdom, and it was allowed to live. It rose from its ruins. Rome, that guilty Pagan city, lives to this day (though Babylon is destroyed), because it has become Christian.

Still, granting that Christ's Church, as being a temporal power, does necessarily interfere in the concerns of this world, still is the Church not of this world, because she does not use the instruments of this world. For instance : Are there not many alterations going on in civil and political matters now, of which the Gospel is the author altogether; which nevertheless no one would feel an infringement of the spiritual nature of its kingdom? If then it may alter or modify the states of this world in one respect, it may do so in another. Who can deny that the treatment of prisoners has been much improved by Christianity? Who can deny that the laws for the poor are considerably influenced by its precepts? Take, again, the case of duelling : Does not the voice of Christian feeling among us support the law of the land in a special way, in denouncing it as a sin, in spite of most specious arguments in its favour? or rather, as far as it is discountenanced, is it not discountenanced, not by the power of the law, though the law is against it, but by an influence issuing now, as five hundred years ago, from the Church? Or, to come to a more apposite instance,—what greater revolution has there been in society, than the liberation of slaves? a revolution which is going on even now, as in times past. *This* has been owing to the Kingdom of the Saints. It has ever exalted those of low degree. It has changed the structure of the body politic all through Christendom. Is it a greater revolution that it should tend to humble the great, than that it should raise the low? or, rather, are not both achievements predicted as prerogatives of Him who is the glorious

Lord and King of the new kingdom? "He hath showed strength with His arm; He hath scattered the proud in the imagination of their hearts. He hath put down the mighty from their seats, and exalted them of low degree [1]." So it was of old time; so it is now: whenever the Kingdom of the Most High fulfils its mission, the mighty bow down, and the despised are exalted.

And, moreover, we see from this instance of the abolition of slavery, as in the other instances I mentioned, *how* the Church conquers—not by force, but by persuasion. It is written, "Thy people shall be *willing* in the day of Thy power [2];" and so it is fulfilled. And hence in the prophecies of the book of Isaiah the *willingness* of the kings of the earth to humble themselves to the Church, is noted as a special characteristic of the spread of the Church. They are overcome by the beauty of holiness, and they yield freely. "Lift up thine eyes round about, and behold: all these *gather themselves* together, and come to thee [3]." "The Gentiles shall come to thy light, *and kings to the brightness* of thy rising." "The isles shall wait for Me, and the ships of Tarshish first, to bring thy sons from far, their silver and their gold with them. . . . Thy gates shall be open continually, . . . that men may bring unto thee the forces of the Gentiles, and that their kings may be brought [4]." It is by influence only that the Church reigns, or by what is sometimes called *opinion.* Kings and states still have the power of the sword, and

---

[1] Luke i. 51, 52.
[2] Ps. cx. 3.
[3] Isa. xlix. 18.
[4] Isa. lx. 3—11.

they only. They must still be obeyed by the Church, *if* they prefer to command and rule over her, to honouring her. They must be obeyed, and they will come to nought. She must leave her cause to God, who has promised to avenge it on every proud kingdom and nation. For herself, she has no arms, but peace, quietness, cheerfulness, resignation, and love. "Being reviled, she blesses; being persecuted, she suffers it; being defamed, she intreats;" she does not defend herself: like her Master, she does not "cry in the streets, or strive;" but she prevails, because God fights for her.

Lastly. If the Kingdom of Christ be what this view, drawn from the prophecies, represents it, you will say a very heavy responsibility lies upon those parties at present, civil or religious, who withstand that heavenly Kingdom, and a miserable destiny lies before them. You will say that it follows that such men of power or influence as insult the Church, and such professors of religion as speak against her, are in very great peril. I do not wish to undervalue their perilous condition, in charity to them. But I will observe this one thing, that it is very different to resist the Kingdom of Christ when it was at unity with itself, and now, when it is broken up into sections. Christ said, that whoso spake against Himself should be forgiven; but whoso spake against the Spirit should not be forgiven. I hope it is not presumptuous to say, that to many of us the Kingdom of the Saints comes, or before now has come, not in demonstration of the Spirit, but as Christ was in His Passion, broken, defaced, with its glory hidden, and its power more or less suspended. And as then our Saviour, as if in fulfilment of His promise that His own persecutors should receive pardon, prayed for them on the Cross; so I trust now, without intruding into things unseen, we may hope that whatever hard things some among us speak or have spoken against that Heavenly Stranger which sojourns on the earth, yet, considering how she is disfigured and deformed by strife and calamity, Christ says for us continually, "Father, forgive them ; for they know not what they do."

SERMON XVIII.

Condition of the Members of the Christian Empire.

" Lord, Thou hast heard the desire of the poor ; Thou preparest their heart, and Thine ear hearkeneth thereto ; to help the fatherless and poor unto their right, that the man of the earth be no more exalted against them."—Ps. x. 19, 20.

THE book of Psalms has ever been one main portion of the devotions of the Christian Church, in public and in private, since that Church was. In the east and west, north and south, in quiet times, in troubled times, in the rise, and now in the decline, of the Kingdom of the Saints, the inspired words of the Prophets of Israel have been in the mouth of the children of grace. In consequence, it is natural to suppose that the Psalter has a Christian meaning: Since it has held its place at all times, it surely has a sense for all times. Since we especially use it, this surely must be because to us it is especially useful. Some free-thinkers have said, What is the book to us, relating, as it does, the history and expressing the feelings of a people who lived two or three thousand years ago ? I grant it: if the book of

Psalms be but a Jewish book, it is not a Christian book; but the question on which all turns is, whether the Psalms are the mere devotions of an extinct religion or no.

The very circumstance, then, that Christians use the Psalter, proves that they consider that it has a meaning over and above that Jewish meaning which lies on the surface of it. And when we consider how intimately it has been received into the Christian Church, how it is made the form of so great a portion of our devotions, how it enters into almost all our Services, equally with the Lord's Prayer—nay, it may be said, even more than the Lord's Prayer, because of its greater length and variety—it cannot be supposed that this Christian meaning contained in it is but occasional or faint; it must run through it; it must be strong, definite, and real; else why should Christians turn aside to use Jewish forms? They have ever acted as if no state of their minds but found its appropriate expression in the Psalms; no sentence in the Psalms but had its appropriate sense in their own mouths.

Now as to a great portion of this sacred Book, we all know full well, and shall be able to reply at once, that it relates to our Lord and Saviour. Whatever is said in the first instance of David and his labours, trials, and sufferings in the cause of God, whatever is said of Solomon and his glory, and much beside which is more or less of a directly prophetic, and not of a mere typical character, is fulfilled in Christ. Much as we revere the memory of holy David, such reverence would not account for our commemorating him in preference to all saints,

[s. D.]   s

and him alone, in our daily devotions; but we know
well, that in reading the 22nd, or the 69th, or the 109th
Psalm, we are reading, not of David's trials, which are
gone and over, but of the mediatory and expiatory work
of Him who ever liveth, a Priest for ever after the order
of Melchizedek; and in like manner, when we read the
2nd, or the 45th, or the 72nd, we read of the triumph
and exaltation, not of the monarchs of Israel, but of the
same Lord and Saviour.

And further, much that does not on the surface bear
tokens of a relation to the same great truths, and which we
cannot absolutely pronounce to relate to them, doubtless
may be interpreted of them by the pious mind for itself
as it reads;—from its own intimate apprehension and
continual contemplation of the details of the history of
Christ. And in this way the book of Psalms may
certainly be made to abound in edifying lessons, and
to breathe of Christ. But, allowing this fully, still it
is not a sufficient reason for using the devotions of the
Jewish Church, that they admit of being turned to good
account. Moreover, there are, after all, large portions
of the Psalms which cannot be said to support such a
sense at all, which do not carry it on and carry it
out continuously, which give it forth but at intervals;
and which, in consequence, if they are to be considered Christian devotions, would seem to require
some other interpretation, more natural, obvious and
uniform.

Great part of the Psalms, for instance, is employed in
lamenting, entreating, hoping, about certain subjects;
what is the Christian meaning of all this? I mean,

what is a Christian to be thinking of when he uses the words?

Again, a Christian's devotion does and must consist, in great measure, in lamenting, entreating, hoping. What is the meaning then of making the Psalms the channel of his devotion, unless they do faithfully express that lamenting, intreating, and hoping, which a Christian exercises?

What, for instance, do we mean when we say, in the words of the text, " Lord, Thou hast heard the desire of the poor; Thou preparest their heart, and Thine ear hearkeneth thereto; to help the fatherless and poor unto their right, that the man of the earth be no more exalted against them "?

Either the Psalms are ever applicable to the state of the Christian Church, or one does not see why they have always formed so necessary a part of her devotions. And, as I have hinted, many persons feel this, and not understanding what is the present meaning of the Psalms, advocate their disuse.

Now it is obvious what a remarkable evidence is afforded us of the substantial agreement and the unity existing between the Christian and Jewish Church, by the continuation in the Christian of the Jewish devotions. For what is religion but worship? and whatever changes we make in the sense of its letter, these cannot be of a nature to reverse that letter; they can but enlarge the letter; they can but introduce a sense parallel to it; the substance of the ideas expressed by it must remain the same. This should be seriously thought of by those who disparage certain ordinances and customs

as Jewish; such as reverence for sacred places, observance of holy days, adoption of a minute ceremonial, and
the like; for if there be one thing more than another
Jewish in our received form of religion, it is the use of
the Psalter. If we may safely use the very same prayers
and praises used by God's former people, it does not
appear why we may not adopt ceremonies, not the same,
but like those, which were divinely given to them; if
the Psalter admits of a Christian and spiritual sense, it
does not appear why rites and ceremonies may not be
practised spiritually also.

But our business at present is to inquire *what* that
sense is, in which we Christians are to use the Psalms
in our devotions.

Now, if we bear in mind what Scripture teaches us
concerning the Christian Church, as the Kingdom of
heaven upon earth, if we consider what the Church is
in office, and in circumstance, we shall, I think, see that
the Psalms are no foreign tongue, but do speak the
very language which is natural to her; that if Isaiah
has given her picture, David has supplied her voice;
that the two inspired writers harmonize with each other;
—and again, with the four Evangelists, and our Lord's
own account of the kingdom of the Saints, as recorded
by them.

For what is this kingdom as I have already described
it? a universal empire without earthly arms; temporal
pretensions without temporal sanctions; a claim to rule
without the power to enforce; a continual tendency to
acquire with a continual exposure to be dispossessed;
greatness of mind with weakness of body. What will

be the fortunes of such an empire in the world? persecution; persecution is the token of the Church; persecution is the note of the Church, perhaps the most
abiding note of all. The world is strong: men of the
world have arms of the world; they have swords, they
have armies, they have prisons, they have chains, they
have wild passions. The Church has none of these, and
yet it claims a right to rule, direct, rebuke, exhort,
denounce, condemn. It claims the obedience of the
powerful; it confronts the haughty; it places itself
across the path of the wilful; it undertakes the defence
of the poor; it accepts the gifts of the world, and
becomes involved in their stewardship; and yet it is at
the mercy of these said powerful, haughty, and wilful
men, to ill-treat and to spoil. Is not this too great a
temptation for sinful nature to resist? Can it be
otherwise, but that a kingdom which claims so much,
which professes so much, yet can resist so little, which
irritates the world's pride, which inflames its cupidity,
which interferes with its purposes, which terrifies its
conscience, yet does nothing in its defence but threaten;
which deals with unseen ill and unseen good, whose
only arms are what an unbelieving world calls priestcraft—is it not certain that such a kingdom will be the
prey and sport of the world?

Moreover, the mustard-seed, small and vile though it
be, was destined to spread and thrive; to thrive in spite
of all the world's power. Here is a distinct provocation.
What so irritating, so mortifying to the proud, who are
conscious that they are in high place in the world, and
have great worldly power or influence, the world's arms,

the world's homage, as to find a despised doctrine
"grow and multiply" in spite of them, and by means
which they cannot investigate, by powers which they
cannot analyze? Such was the nature of the Church's
triumph over heathenism; and what the counter triumph of heathenism would be over the Church, was
plain before the event. "It shall bruise thy head, and
thou shalt bruise His heel[1]." The Church made progress, and the world persecuted. The Kingdom was set
up, but it was set up in obloquy, ill-usage, suffering, in
much weakness, in fear and trembling. It triumphed
as a Church, it suffered in its members. Such, in its
measure, has been its lot ever since. The age of Martyrs, indeed, is well nigh over; but scarce a Saint, but
has been in his place and degree a Confessor. Hardly
has any one done right without provoking the world to
do him wrong. "All that will live godly in Christ Jesus
shall suffer persecution[2]," says St. Paul; and our Lord,
"Blessed are ye, when men shall revile you, and persecute you, and shall say all manner of evil against you
falsely, for My sake[3]."

But now to return to the Psalter. If the Church be
what has been described; if it be great, and wide-
spreading, yet ever open to attack; if it be ever strong,
yet ever weak, weak in itself, strong in the Lord; ever
persecuted, yet ever blessed and prospered; do you not
see that the tenour of the book of Psalms does most
exactly and minutely express what the feelings of the
Church will be under such circumstances? The Church
is holy, and the Church is defenceless. Now what is

---

[1] Gen. iii. 15.   [2] 2 Tim. iii. 12.   [3] Matt. v. 11.

the Psalter, from beginning to end, but a supplication to God to rescue the poor and needy, and to justify the righteous? the very petitions which the Church has such urgent cause to offer.

It contains two main ideas; the defeat of God's enemies, yet the suffering of God's people. I will now quote passages from it at some length, in illustration and proof of what I have said; that is, not merely isolated texts, such as we all know to be prophetic, or to admit of a reference to the great events of the New Testament, but such prayers and aspirations as occur in course, and in a context which cannot be applied merely to our Lord's history; which need a sense if they are to be used by Christians, and which find a sufficient one in the view of the Gospel Church which I have been taking.

1. Now, on the one hand, when we sing the Psalms we triumph in the Church's exultation over the might of this world. "In Jewry is God known, His Name is great in Israel[1]." What is meant by Israel, but the chosen people, even us Christians? The Psalm must say that God's Name is great in *us;* else, why read we the Psalms? Let us proceed. "At Salem is His tabernacle, and His dwelling in Sion. There brake He the arrows of the bow, the shield, the sword, and the battle. Thou art of more honour and might than the hills of the robbers." The earth is filled with robbery, plunder, violence, cruelty, except so far as it is Christian. All states of the world, all governments, except so far as they are Christian, except so far as they act upon Christian principles, are scarcely more than robbers and

[1] Ps. lxxvi.

men of blood; and against these God exalts Himself;
against these He is ever exalting Himself; against
these at this very time is He rising, as in all times;
against all states, all governments, all power of man
which does not acknowledge Him, and bow before Him.
And "the nation and kingdom that will not serve"
Him, or rather, as the Prophet says, His Church, "shall
perish." To proceed: "The proud are robbed, they
have slept their sleep, and all the men whose hands
were mighty have found nothing. At Thy rebuke,
O God of Jacob, both the chariot and horse are fallen."
Do we ask how this is fulfilled *now?* Have we not seen
in our own time, or did not our fathers see a great anti-
christian power in the world, exalting itself against
religion, and especially against Christ's Church? and
did it not seem sure of success? and yet has it not,
after all its threats and triumphs, ceased to be, leaving
nought behind it but the Egyptians upon the seashore,
and a small dust and ashes, for its worshippers fondly to
hang over? And this is but one instance of what takes
place in every age, the triumph of the Church over the
world. "Thou, even Thou art to be feared, and who
may stand in Thy sight when Thou art angry? Thou
didst cause Thy judgment to be heard from heaven; the
earth trembled, and was still, when God arose to judgment, and to help all the meek upon earth." The meek
of the earth; for it is pledged to them that they shall
"inherit" it. "The fierceness of men shall turn to Thy
praise, and the fierceness of them shalt Thou refrain.
. . . He shall refrain the spirit of princes, and is wonderful among the kings of the earth."

Again; the same triumph of God's Name in His chosen people over the mighty of the earth is spoken of in Psalm 93 : " The floods are risen, O Lord, the floods have lift up their voice, the floods lift up their waves. The waves of the sea are mighty, and rage horribly ; but yet the Lord who dwelleth on high is mightier."

Or again, in the 82nd, " God standeth in the congregation of princes; He is a Judge among gods," that is, among princes and rulers. " How long will ye give wrong judgment, and accept the persons of the ungodly? Defend the poor and fatherless ; see that such as are in need and necessity have right. Deliver the outcast and poor ; save them from the hand of the ungodly." **Here** the Church in her devotions speaks to the world, exhorting great men, and those who are rich in this world, to justice, impartiality, and mercy, and defending the poor, needy, and desolate—two of her special offices; but they will not listen : " they will not be learned, nor understand, but walk on still in darkness." Accordingly the Psalm ends, " Arise, O God, and judge *Thou* the earth ; for *Thou* shalt take all heathen to Thine inheritance :" which is, in other words, calling on God to extend His kingdom into all lands.

Other notes of triumph at the sovereignty of the chosen people over the powers of the earth are such as the following :—" He shall subdue the people under us, and the nations under our feet. . . . The princes of the people are joined unto the people of the God of Abraham[1]." Again, " Great is the Lord, and highly to be praised in the city of our God, even upon His holy hill.

[1] Ps. xlvii. 3. 9.

The hill of Sion is a fair place, and the joy of the whole earth. . . . God is well known in her palaces as a sure refuge. For lo, the kings of the earth are gathered, and gone by together. They marvelled to see such things; they were astonished and suddenly cast down. . . . Walk about Sion "—that is, the Church of Christ—" and go round about her, and tell the towers thereof. Mark well her bulwarks, set up her houses, that ye may tell them that come after [1]." And again, " Jerusalem is built as a city that is at unity in itself. . . . There are set thrones of judgment, the thrones of the house of David. . . . O pray for the peace of Jerusalem : they shall prosper that love thee. Peace be within thy walls, and plenteousness within thy palaces [2]." And again, " The Lord hath chosen Sion to be an habitation for Himself: He hath longed for her. This shall be My rest for ever; here will I dwell, for I have a delight therein [3]." Who or what is Sion? What do we mean when we read this Psalm, and say, " The Lord hath chosen Sion"? We mean the Church which He set up when He went away. The Psalm proceeds to speak of David—by whom, in like manner, is meant Christ: " As for His enemies, I shall clothe them with shame; but upon Himself shall His crown flourish."

2. So much on the one side. But now let us turn to the other aspect of the Christian Kingdom, which is much more frequently brought before us in the Psalms, and to which I wish principally to draw attention: the suffering, troublous state which, in this world, naturally befalls an empire so large, so aggressive, so engrossing,

---

[1] Ps. xlviii. 1—12.   [2] Ps. cxxii. 3. 5. 7.   [3] Ps. cxxxii. 14—18.

so stately and commanding, yet so destitute of weapons of earth. It provokes persecution at all times, both from its claims and from its weakness.

(1.) Thus then we cry out to God against our enemies. " When the wicked, even mine enemies and my foes, came upon me to eat up my flesh, they stumbled and fell. Though an host of men were laid against me, yet shall not my heart be afraid; and though there rose up war against me, yet will I put my trust in Him. . . . . Teach me Thy way, O Lord, and lead me in the right way, because of mine enemies [1]." Again, " O let not the foot of pride come against me, and let not the hand of the ungodly cast me down [2]." Again, " Strangers are risen up against me, and tyrants, which have not God before their eyes, seek after my soul [3]." And again, " Mine enemies are daily in hand to swallow me up, for they be many that fight against me, O Thou Most Highest [4]." And again, " Hide me from the gathering together of the froward, and from the insurrection of wicked doers [5]." Are the Psalms a dead letter, or are they spirit? Do we use them as a form, or as the voice of our hearts? If we have any meaning when we use them, surely we imply that the Church is always militant, always in warfare, never at ease, never well with the world, never shielded from its hatred, malice, and violence. And you will observe, that it is especially the proud and tyrannical who are her enemies. " Let not the foot of pride come against me." " Tyrants seek after my soul." " Princes also did sit and speak

---

[1] Ps. xxvii. 2, 3. 13.   [3] Ps. xxxvi. 11.   [3] Ps. liv. 3.
[4] Ps. lvi. 2.   [5] Ps. lxiv. 2.

against me [1] . . . I will speak of Thy testimonies also even before kings [2]. . . . The proud have had me exceedingly in derision; . . . the proud have imagined a lie against me; . . . the proud have digged pits for me. . . . Princes have persecuted me without a cause [3]."

(2.) Next, we lay before Almighty God our desolations. As, for instance, "Thou lettest us be eaten up like sheep, and hast scattered us among the heathen. Thou sellest Thy people for nought, and takest no money for them [4]." "O God, wherefore art Thou absent from us so long? why is Thy wrath so hot against the sheep of Thy pasture? O think upon Thy congregation, whom Thou hast purchased and redeemed of old [5]." For though the kingdom of the Saints extends and flourishes as a whole, yet it is open to reverses of any magnitude, schisms, defections, losses, in its separate parts.

(3.) And, further, we complain of our captivity. "Who shall give salvation unto Israel out of Sion? When the Lord turneth the captivity of His people, then shall Jacob rejoice, and Israel shall be glad [6]." "O that the salvation were given unto Israel out of Sion! O that the Lord would deliver His people out of captivity [7]!" "Turn our captivity, O Lord, as the rivers in the south [8]."

(4.) Again, the Psalms say much concerning the poor and needy, and God's protecting them against bad men.

---

[1] Ps. cxix. 23. 46. 51. 69. 85.

[2] Ps. cxix. 46.

[3] Ps. cxix. 51. 69. 85. 161.

[4] Ps. xliv. 12, 13.

[5] Ps. lxxiv. 1, 2.

[6] Ps. xiv. 11.

[7] Ps. liii. 7.

[8] Ps. cxxvi. 5.

"The Lord also will be a defence for the oppressed. . . . The poor shall not alway be forgotten; the patient abiding of the meek shall not perish for ever. Up, Lord, and let not man have the upper hand [1]." "The ungodly for his own lust doth persecute the poor. . . . The poor committeth himself unto Thee, for Thou art the helper of the friendless [2]." And in the text, "Lord, Thou hast heard the desire of the poor; . . . to help the fatherless and poor unto their right, that the man of the earth be no more exalted against them." "They smite down Thy people, O Lord, and trouble Thine heritage; . . . the Lord will not fail His people, neither will He forsake His inheritance [3]." "Our soul is filled with the scornful reproof of the wealthy, and with the despitefulness of the proud [4]." Now consider the state of Christendom during many centuries, when tribes of fierce barbarians poured over its face, or settled in its territory; or when tyrannical kings and nobles oppressed its people, or rose against its rulers and pastors; or when power, whether barbarian or constituted, broke in upon its sacred retirements, ill-treated their holy or studious inmates, destroyed the work or scattered the fruits of years of tranquil diligence; and say whether the Psalter is not just the book which all those variously tried, equally helpless multitudes would choose, as more fitting than any other to express their sorrows and their faith, their prayers and their hopes?

(5.) Once more, the Psalms speak especially of the righteous being in trouble, plead for them, and wait for

---

[1] Ps. ix. 9—19. [2] Ps. x. 2. 16.
[3] Ps. xciv. 5. 14. [4] Ps. cxxiii. 4.

their deliverance. " The righteous cry, and the Lord heareth them[1]." " Fret not thyself because of the ungodly, neither be thou envious against the evil doers. . . . The righteous shall inherit the land, and dwell therein for ever[2]." " I was grieved at the wicked; I do also see the ungodly in such prosperity. . . . O how suddenly do they consume, perish, and come to a fearful end[3]!" " The righteous shall flourish like a palm-tree, and shall spread abroad like a cedar in Libanus[4]." " Do well, O Lord, unto those that are good and true of heart[5]." Now, is it not just the peculiarity of the Christian Church, not only that it is slandered, scorned, ill-used by the world, but that all this happens to it *because* it is holy,—for its righteousness' sake?

Thus, on the whole, we see that in the Psalms a very wonderful provision is made by anticipation for the wants of the Christian Church. It is just the book of devotions needed by it, as it ever has been used; supposing it to be so great and so weak, so vast a kingdom, but not of this world, as the Prophets and the Evangelists describe it to be.

Now here, of course, it is obvious to make this objection—*we* are *not* in persecution; for us to use the language of the Psalms is unreal. Christians in our own happy country have every thing their own way. The profession of the Gospel is an honour, the rejection of it a disgrace. Either, then, we are not a part of the Kingdom of Heaven, or that Kingdom is not what Gospels,

---

[1] Ps. xxxiv. 17.   [2] Ps. xxxvii. 1. 30.
[3] Ps. lxxiii. 3. 18.   [4] Ps. xcii. 12.
[5] Ps. cxxv. 4.

Prophecies, and Psalms describe it to be. But many answers may be made to this objection.

1. First, it is not necessary that all parts of the Church should be in persecution at once, either to fulfil the Scripture statements, or to justify the use of the Psalms. It suffers in its different portions at different times. We have had our trials before now; and other portions of the Church are now under similar, or rather worse, afflictions. Of course, if we are members of the *one* body of Christ, we must feel for the rest, in whatever part of the world they are, when they are persecuted, and must remember them in our prayers. Nor does it avail to say that we differ from them in faith: what is that to the purpose in a question of love? Either Christianity is shut up in Britain, or not: if it is, Christ has no longer a Catholic Church, and then, certainly, the prophecies are not now fulfilled to us; or it does exist in other lands, and then we are bound to sympathize in the troubles which Christians there undergo for the name of Christ.

2. But, again, in spite of her prosperity for the moment, even in this country, the Church of Christ is in peril, as is obvious. Can we number the tens and hundreds of thousands who shrink from our Church as if antichristian, or who hate her for being Christian, and wish her downfall? Is there no battle between the Church and the world in this country? and no malevolence, no scorn, no unbelief, no calumny; no prospect, or, at least, materials of open persecution, though persecution, through God's mercy, as yet be away? Consider our great towns, and reflect what a scourge in

God's anger they might be upon our many sins, unless
He were most merciful.

3. But, further, if we are not altogether in a position
to use the words of the Psalter, if we are too happy and
secure, in too great abundance and too much honour, to
be able to use them naturally, is it not possible that so
far we really do lack a note of the Church? is there not
a fear lest the world be friends with us, because we are
friends with the world? This is no new or strange
occurrence in the history of the Gospel. It is not peculiar to our age or country; it is the great disease of the
Church in all ages. Whatever corruptions of doctrine
there have been at particular times and places, no corruption has been so great as this practical corruption, which
has existed in its measure in all times and places—the
serving God for the sake of mammon; the loving religion from the love of the world. And as to ourselves, I
fear, it is no declamatory statement to say, that there
never was an age in which it existed more largely, never
an age in which the Church contained so many untrue
members; that is, so many persons who profess themselves her members, when they know little or nothing
about the real meaning of membership, and remain
within her pale for some reasons short of religious and
right ones. For instance, to put one question on the
subject,—How many supporters of Christ's Holy Catholic Church do you think would be left among us, if her
cause were found to be, not the cause of order, as it
happens to be now, but the cause of disorder, as it was
when Christ came and His Apostles preached? It was
the cry of the Jews of Thessalonica against St. Paul and

St. Silas, " These that have turned the world upside down, are come hither also[1]." Is it not as plain as the day, that the mass of persons who support the Church in her legal privileges, do so, not so much because they care for the Kingdom of the Saints, as because they think that the downfall of our civil institutions is involved in her downfall? I do not say that they have *no* love for the Church, but they have a greater love for worldly prosperity. They have just so much more love for the world than for the Church, as would lead them, were the peace of the world and the welfare of the Church at variance with each other, to side with the world against the Church. As it is, they see that the influence of the Gospel is on the side of good order; that it tends to make men contented and obedient subjects; that it keeps the lower orders from outbreaks; that it makes a firm stand against rebellion, sedition, conspiracy, riot, and fanaticism; that it is the best guarantee for the security of private property. It *does* all these benefits; they *are* benefits; and we may rightly be thankful for them. But numbers of professing Churchmen consider them *the* special benefits of Christ's Kingdom, caring little for the unseen and spiritual blessings which are its true and proper gifts. Look round upon our political parties, our literature, our science, our periodical publications : is it not too plain to need a word of proof, that religion is in the main honoured because it tends to make this life happier, and is expedient for the preservation of our persons, property, advantages, and position in the world? Can a greater stigma be placed upon any

---

[1] Acts xvii. 6.

doctrine in the judgment of the community than that it is anti-social, or that it is irksome, gloomy, or inconvenient?

No wonder, then, while we are in the midst of this serious corruption, that the words of inspired Psalmists, which have been the solace of the Church in every age, do not seem real to us. Let us but put off the love of the world, and follow the precepts of our Lord and His Apostles, and then see in a little while *where* we should all find ourselves, and what would be the condition of the Church.

Meanwhile, whether we will believe it or no, the truth remains, that the strength of the Church, as heretofore, does not lie in earthly law, or human countenance, or civil station, but in her proper gifts; in those great gifts which our Lord pronounced to be beatitudes. Blessed are the poor in spirit, the mourners, the meek, the thirsters after righteousness, the merciful, the pure in heart, the peacemakers, the persecuted.

SERMON XIX.

The Apostolical Christian.

" Know ye not, that they which run in a race run all, but one receiveth the prize? so run, that ye may obtain."—I COR. ix. 24.

THERE was one who came running to Christ, and kneeled to Him, yet he did not obtain; for that haste of his and hurry was no type of the inward earnestness with which the true soul goes sedately forward unto salvation. He was one of the many who, in some sort, run the race, yet do not receive the prize, because they run in self-will, or lightness of mind. "If a man strive for masteries, yet is he not crowned, except he strive lawfully." "I have not sent" them, says the Lord by His Prophet, "yet they ran[1]." Many there are, who are not open sinners, who do not deny Christ, who honour Him with their lips—nay, in some sort with their lives—who, like the young man, are religious in a certain sense, and yet obtain not the crown. For they are not of those who, with the blessed Apostle who speaks in the text,

[1] 2 Tim. ii. 5. Jer. xxiii. 21.

T 2

observe the rules of the contest. They have no claim upon the prize, because they run on their own ground, or at their own time; or, in other respects, after their own pleasure. They make a religion for themselves, and they have a private idea what a Christian ought to be; and they never get beyond, even if they attain, the regulation of their lives and conduct upon this self-devised standard of truth. They can never be said to have "finished their course," for, in truth, they have never entered on it. Or they begin it, and turn aside in some other direction, mistaking the path. "Ye did run well," says St. Paul to the Galatians; "who did hinder you that ye should not obey the truth [1]?"

Let us then, with this thought before us, leave for a while our own private judgment of what is pleasing to God and not pleasing, and turn to consider the picture which Scripture gives us of the true Christian life, and then attempt to measure our own life by it. He alone who gives us eternal happiness, has the power of determining the conditions for attaining it. Let us not take it for granted that we shall know them by our own common sense. Let us betake ourselves to Scripture to learn them.

Now it is very certain, that the New Testament abounds in notices, suggestions, and descriptions of the temper and mode of living of the disciples of Christ; that is, as they were characterized at the time when it was written. The idea of a Christian, as set forth in Scripture, is something very definite. We may conceive we have some general notion from Scripture what

[1] Gal. v. 7.

a Jew was, but we know much more what a Christian was. As a Jew had a very peculiar character, as an Englishman has a character all his own, so the Christian, as described in the inspired writings, is like himself, and unlike any one else. He is not like Pharisee, not like Sadducee, not like Herodian, not like Greek, not like Roman, not like Samaritan; but he is like a follower of Christ, and none but him. Now, whether Christians at this day need be like what Christians were in the primitive times, is a further question. I want, in the first place, to consider *what* the primitive Christians were like, as represented in Scripture. As an historical question, as a matter of fact, thus only I would consider the subject; afterwards will be time enough for us to apply it to our own case, and to settle how far it is necessary for men of this day to conform their lives to the pattern given them once for all by inspiration.

Now so far is certain, that this one peculiar Christian character and life, and none but it, is attributed in Scripture to our Lord, to St. John Baptist, to the Apostles, and to Christians generally. Very different is our Lord from St. John Baptist; very different St. John from the Apostles; very different the Apostles from private Christians. John came in the garb of an ascetic, dressed in a garment of camel's hair, and eating locusts and wild honey. Our Lord came eating and drinking; He lived in the world as St. John in the desert. The Apostles were the teachers of grace, as St. John of repentance; and Christians in general were hearers, not preachers; numbers of them besides were

women, and thereby still more unlike Christ and St.
John and the Apostles: and yet on the whole one only
character distinguishes all of them in Scripture; Christ
Himself, and the Baptist, and St. Peter, and St. John,
and St. Paul, and the Christian multitude, men and
women. And now to draw out what that character is;
though, in doing so, I shall say nothing, my brethren,
but what you know well already, and shall be doing
little more than quoting texts of Scripture. And yet
you have heard these texts so often, that perhaps they
fall dead upon your ear, and they leave you as they
found you, impressing no definite image of their meaning upon your minds.

1. Now the first great and obvious characteristic
of a Bible Christian, if I may use that much abused
term, is to be without worldly ties or objects, to be
living in this world, but not for this world. St. Paul
says, "our conversation is in heaven[1]," or in other
words, heaven is our city. We know what it is to be a
citizen of this world; it is to have interests, rights,
privileges, duties, connexions, in some particular town
or state; to depend upon it, and to be bound to defend
it; to be part of it. Now all this the Christian is
in respect to heaven. Heaven is his city, earth is not.
Or, at least, so it was as regards the Christians of Scripture. "Here," as the same Apostle says in another
place, "we have no continuing city, but we seek one
to come[2]." And therefore he adds to the former of
these texts, "from whence also we look for the Saviour,
the Lord Jesus Christ." This is the very definition of

---

[1] Phil. iii. 20.　　　　　　　　[2] Heb. xiii. 14.

a Christian,—one who looks for Christ; not who looks
for gain, or distinction, or power, or pleasure, or comfort,
but who looks " for the Saviour, the Lord Jesus Christ."
This, according to Scripture, is the essential mark, this
is the foundation of a Christian, from which every
thing else follows; whether he is rich or poor, high
or low, is a further matter, which may be considered
apart; but he surely is a primitive Christian, and
he only, who has no aim of this world, who has no
wish to be other in this world than he is; whose
thoughts and aims have relation to the unseen, the
future world; who has lost his taste for this world,
sweet and bitter being the same to him; who fulfils the
same Apostle's exhortation in another Epistle, " Set
your affection on things above, not on things on the
earth, for ye are dead, and your life is hid with Christ
in God. When Christ, who is our life, shall appear,
then shall ye also appear with Him in glory [1]."

Hence it follows, that watching is a special mark of
the Scripture Christian, as our Lord so emphatically sets
before us: "Watch therefore, for ye know not what
hour your Lord doth come. . . . Be ye also ready, for
in such an hour as ye think not the Son of man
cometh [2]." "At midnight there was a cry made,
Behold, the bridegroom cometh, go ye out to meet Him.
. . . Watch therefore, for ye know neither the day nor
the hour wherein the Son of man cometh [3]." "Watch
ye therefore, for ye know not when the Master of the
house cometh, at even, or at midnight, or at the cock-
crowing, or in the morning; lest coming suddenly he

---

[1] Col. iii. 2—4.   [2] Matt. xxiv. 42. 44.   [3] Matt. xxv. 6. 13.

find you sleeping; and what I say unto you, I say unto all, Watch [1]." And St. Peter, who once suffered for lack of watching, repeats the lesson: "The end of all things is at hand: be ye therefore sober, and watch unto prayer [2]."

And accordingly, prayer, as St. Peter enjoins in the last text, is another characteristic of Christians as described in Scripture. They knew not what hour their Lord would come, and therefore they watched and prayed in every hour, lest they should enter into temptation. "They were continually in the temple praising and blessing God [3]." "These all continued with one accord in prayer and supplication with the women [4]." "They, continuing daily with one accord in the temple, and breaking bread from house to house, did eat their meat with gladness and singleness of heart [5]." "They were all with one accord in one place [6]," at "the third hour of the day." Again, "Peter and John went up together into the temple at the hour of prayer, being the ninth hour [7]." "Cornelius, . . . a devout man, . . . which gave much alms to the people, and prayed to God alway," saw "in a vision evidently about the ninth hour of the day an angel of God [8];" and he says himself, "I was fasting until this hour, and at the ninth hour I prayed in my house." "Peter went up upon the house-top to pray about the sixth hour." "At midnight Paul and Silas prayed, and sang praises unto God [9]." "And they all brought us on our way,

---

[1] Mark xiii. 35—37.　　[2] 1 Pet. iv. 7.　　[3] Luke xxiv. 53.
[4] Acts i. 14.　　[5] Acts ii. 46.　　[6] Acts ii. 1.
[7] Acts iii. 1.　　[8] Acts x. 1—3.　　[9] Acts xvi. 25.

with wives and children, till we were out of the city; and we kneeled down on the shore, and prayed[1]." This habit of prayer then, recurrent prayer, morning, noon, and night, is one discriminating point in Scripture Christianity, as arising from the text with which I began, " our conversation is in heaven."

In a word, there was no barrier, no cloud, no earthly object, interposed between the soul of the primitive Christian and its Saviour and Redeemer. Christ was in his heart, and therefore all that came from his heart, his thoughts, words, and actions, savoured of Christ. The Lord was his light, and therefore he shone with the illumination. For, " The light of the body is the eye: if therefore thine eye be single, thy whole body shall be full of light. But if thine eye be evil, thy whole body shall be full of darkness[2]." And, " Out of the abundance of the heart the mouth speaketh. A good man out of the good treasure of the heart bringeth forth good things: and an evil man out of the evil treasure, bringeth forth evil things[3]." Or, as Christ says elsewhere, " Cleanse first that which is within the cup and platter, that the outside of them may be clean also[4]." Observe this well, my brethren; religion, you see, begins with the heart, but it does not end with the heart. It begins with the conversion of the heart from earth to heaven, the stripping off and casting away all worldly aims; but it does not end there; it did not end there in the Christians whom Scripture describes, whom our Lord's precepts formed: it drew up all the

[1] Acts xxi. 5.
[2] Matt. vi. 22, 23.
[3] Matt. xii. 34, 35.
[4] Matt. xxiii. 26.

faculties of the soul, all the members of the body, to
Him who was in their heart.   Let us then now go on
to see in what that inward Christianity issued; what
Christians then, in that early time, looked like outwardly, who were citizens of heaven within.

2. Christians, then, were a simple, innocent, grave,
humble, patient, meek, and loving body, without earthly
advantages or worldly influence, as every page of the
New Testament shows us.   A description of them is
given in the beginning of the Acts : " The multitude of
them that believed were of one heart and of one soul ;
neither said any of them that ought of the things which
he possessed was his own, but they had all things
common. . . . Neither was there any among them that
lacked : for as many as were possessors of lands or
houses sold them, and brought the prices of the things
that were sold, and laid them down at the Apostles'
feet : and distribution was made unto every man according as he had need [1]."

Such, of course, was the natural consequence of a deep
conviction of the nothingness of this world, and the all-
importance of the other.   Those who understood that
they were " fellow-citizens with the saints, and of the
household of God," could not but show it in their
actions.   In circumstances like theirs they would have
been using idle words, had they said that their conversation was in heaven, yet had gone on eating, and drinking,
and conversing like children of men.   But here our
Lord's words may well take the place of ours.   Consider, then, how solemnly He had warned them.

[1] Acts iv. 32—35.

"As the days of Noe were, so shall also the coming of the Son of man be. For as in the days that were before the flood, they were eating and drinking, marrying and giving in marriage, until the day that Noe entered into the ark, and knew not until the flood came, and took them all away; so shall also the coming of the Son of man be [1]." "They did eat, they drank, they married wives, they were given in marriage, until the day that Noe entered into the ark, and the flood came, and destroyed them all. Likewise also as it was in the days of Lot; they did eat, they drank, they bought, they sold, they planted, they builded; but the same day that Lot went out of Sodom, it rained fire and brimstone from heaven, and destroyed them all [2]." Again, "They all with one consent began to make excuse. The first said unto him, I have bought a piece of ground, and I must needs go and see it : I pray thee have me excused. And another said, I have bought five yoke of oxen, and I go to prove them : I pray thee have me excused. And another said, I have married a wife, and therefore I cannot come [3]." Again, "There was a certain rich man, which was clothed in purple and fine linen, and fared sumptuously every day [4]." Again, "Take heed and beware of covetousness. . . . The ground of a certain rich man brought forth plentifully ; . . and he said . . . I will say to my soul, Soul, thou hast much goods laid up for many years ; take thine ease, eat, drink, and be merry. But God said unto him, Thou fool, this night thy soul shall be required of thee." Again, "Sell that ye have,

<hr />

[1] Matt. xxiv. 37—39.
[2] Luke xvii. 27—29.
[3] Luke xiv. 18—20.
[4] Luke xvi. 19.

and give alms: provide yourselves bags which wax not old, a treasure in the heavens that faileth not, where no thief approacheth, neither moth corrupteth; for where your treasure is, there will your heart be also. Let your loins be girded about, and your lights burning[1]." Again, "How hardly shall they that have riches enter into the kingdom of God[2]!" Again, "Take no thought, saying, What shall we eat? or, What shall we drink? or, Wherewithal shall we be clothed[3]?" And hence St. Paul, after the pattern of his Lord and Saviour, is careful to remind us that "the time is short[4];"—we are labourers in the eleventh hour of the day. "The time is short; it remaineth that both they that have wives be as though they had none; and they that weep, as though they wept not; and they that rejoice, as though they rejoiced not; and they that buy, as though they possessed not; and they that use this world, as not abusing it, for the fashion of this world passeth away." And again, "No man that warreth entangleth himself with the affairs of this life; that he may please him who hath chosen him to be a soldier[5]."

This separation from the world which marked the Christian character as drawn by Christ and His Apostles, is displayed in a variety of details scattered up and down the sacred volume. "Love not the world, neither the things that are in the world[6]," says St. John. "Be not conformed to this world, but be ye transformed by the renewing of your mind[7]," says St.

---

[1] Luke xii. 15—20. 33—35.   [2] Mark x. 23.   [3] Matt. vi. 31.
[4] 1 Cor. vii. 29.   [5] 2 Tim. ii. 4.   [6] 1 John ii. 15.
[7] Rom. xii. 2.

Paul. Again, of himself, "By the Cross of Christ" . . .
"the world is crucified unto me, and I unto the world [1]."
The first Christians were separated from their earthly
kindred and friends. "Henceforth," says he, "know we
no man after the flesh; yea, though we have known
Christ after the flesh, yet now henceforth know we Him
no more. Therefore, if any man be in Christ, he is a
new creature: old things are passed away, behold all
things are become new [2]." Or, in our Lord's words,
"He that loveth father or mother more than Me, is not
worthy of Me; and he that loveth son or daughter more
than Me, is not worthy of Me [3]." They parted with
property: "Every one that hath forsaken houses, . . .
or lands, for My Name's sake, shall receive an hundredfold, and shall inherit everlasting life [4]." They put off
from them things personal: "Provide neither gold, nor
silver, nor brass, in your purses, nor scrip for your
journey, neither two coats, neither shoes, nor yet staves:
for the workman is worthy of his meat [5]." They sacrificed to Christ their dearest wishes and objects, things
nearer and closer to them than the very garments they
had on them: "If thy hand or thy foot offend thee,"
says our Lord, in figurative language, "cut them off,
and cast them from thee; it is better for thee to enter
into life halt or maimed, rather than having two hands
or two feet to be cast into everlasting fire. And if thine
eye offend thee, pluck it out, and cast it from thee: it is
better for thee to enter into life with one eye, rather
than having two eyes to be cast into hell fire [6]." They

[1] Gal. vi. 14.   [2] 2 Cor. v. 16, 17.   [3] Matt. x. 37.
[4] Matt. xix. 29.   [5] Matt. x. 9, 10.   [6] Matt. xviii. 8, 9.

forfeited the common sympathy of humanity, and were cruelly used, or rather, hunted down, as some separate race of beings less than man : " Ye shall be hated of all men for My Name's sake. . . . The disciple is not above his Master, nor the servant above his Lord. . . . If they have called the Master of the house Beelzebub, how much more shall they call them of his household [1] !"

This, to speak briefly on a great subject, is the picture of a Christian as drawn in the New Testament. Christians are those who profess to have the love of the truth in their hearts ; and when Christ asks them whether they so love Him as to be able to drink of His cup, and partake of His Baptism, they answer, " We are able," and their profession issues in a wonderful fulfilment. They love God and they give up the world.

3. And here we are brought to a third and last characteristic of the Christianity of the New Testament, which necessarily follows from the other two. If the first disciples so unreservedly gave up the world, and if, secondly, they were so strictly and promptly taken at their word, what do you think would follow, if they were true men and not hypocrites ? this—they would rejoice to be so taken. This, then, is the third chief grace of primitive Christianity—joy in all its forms ; not only a pure heart, not only a clean hand, but, thirdly, a cheerful countenance. I say joy in all its forms, for in true joyfulness many graces are included ; joyful people are loving ; joyful people are forgiving ; joyful people are munificent. Joy, if it be Christian joy, the refined joy of the mortified and persecuted, makes men peaceful,

[1] Matt. x. 22. 24, 25.

serene, thankful, gentle, affectionate, sweet-tempered, pleasant, hopeful; it is graceful, tender, touching, winning. All this were the Christians of the New Testament, for they had obtained what they desired. They had desired to sacrifice the kingdom of the world and all its pomps for the love of Christ, whom they had seen, whom they loved, in whom they believed, in whom they delighted; and when their wish was granted, they could but "rejoice in that day, and leap for joy, for, behold, their reward was great in heaven[1]:" blessed were they, thrice blessed, because they in their lifetime had evil things[2], and their consolation was to come here-after.

Such, I say, was the joy of the first disciples of Christ, to whom it was granted to suffer shame and to undergo toil for His Name's sake; and such holy, gentle graces were the fruit of this joy, as every part of the Gospels and Epistles shows us. "We glory in tribulations," says St. Paul, "knowing that tribulation worketh patience, and patience experience, and experience hope, and hope maketh not ashamed, because the love of God is shed abroad in our hearts by the Holy Ghost which is given unto us[3]." Again, "Even unto this present hour we both hunger and thirst, and are naked, and are buffeted, and have no certain dwelling-place, and labour working with our own hands: being reviled, we bless; being persecuted, we suffer it; being defamed, we intreat; we are made as the filth of the earth, and are the off-scouring of all things unto this day[4]." How is the

---

[1] Luke vi. 23.　　　　　　[2] Luke xvi. 25.
[3] Rom. v. 3—5.　　　　　 [4] 1 Cor. iv. 11—13.

very same character set before us in the Beatitudes, so
holy, so tender, so serene, so amiable! " Blessed are the
poor in spirit, for theirs is the kingdom of heaven ;
blessed are they that mourn, for they shall be comforted ;
blessed are the meek, they which do hunger and thirst
after righteousness, the merciful, the pure in heart, the
peace-makers, they which are persecuted for righteousness' sake [1]." And again, " Let your communication be
yea, yea, nay, nay ; for whatsoever is more than these
cometh of evil [2]." " I say unto you, That ye resist not
evil ; but whosoever shall smite thee on thy right cheek,
turn to him the other also :" " love your enemies, bless
them that curse you, do good to them that hate you, and
pray for them which despitefully use you and persecute
you ; that ye may be the children of your Father which
is in heaven." Again, " Judge not, that ye be not
judged ; . . . and why beholdest thou the mote that is
in thy brother's eye, but considerest not the beam that
is in thine own eye [3] ?" And again, " In your patience
possess ye your souls [4]." Again, " If I then, your Lord
and Master, have washed your feet, ye also ought to
wash one another's feet [5]." Again, " By this shall all
men know that ye are My disciples, if ye have love one
to another." And again, " Peace I leave with you, My
peace I give unto you, not as the world giveth, give I
unto you. Let not your heart be troubled, neither let it
be afraid [6]." Or again, consider the special prayer which
the Lord Himself taught us, as a pattern of all prayer,
and see how it corresponds to that one idea of a Christian

---

[1] Matt. v. 3—10.　　[2] Matt. v. 37.　　[3] Matt. vii. 1, 3.
[4] Luke xxi. 19.　　[5] John xiii. 14.　　[6] John xiv. 27

which I have been drawing out. It consists of seven petitions; three have reference to Almighty God, four to the petitioners; and could any form of words be put together which so well could be called the Prayer of the Pilgrim? We often hear it said, that the true way of serving God is to serve man, as if religion consisted merely in acting well our part in life, not in direct faith, obedience, and worship: how different is the spirit of this prayer! Evil round about him, enemies and persecutors in his path, temptation in prospect, help for the day, sin to be expiated, God's will in his heart, God's Name on his lips, God's kingdom in his hopes: this is the view it gives us of a Christian. What simplicity! what grandeur! and what definiteness! how one and the same, how consistent with all that we read of him elsewhere in Scripture!.

Alas! my brethren, so it is, when you have subjects like this dwelt upon, too many of you are impatient of them, and wish to hurry past them, and are eager to be reminded by the preacher in the same breath with his presenting them—nay, you remind yourselves—that you of this day can have no immediate interest in them,—that times are changed. Times *are* changed, I grant; but without going on to the question of the obligation now of such a profession of the Gospel as I have been describing, do persuade yourselves, I entreat you, to contemplate the picture. Do not shut your eyes, do not revolt from it, do not fret under it, but look at it. Bear to look at the Christianity of the Bible; bear to contemplate the idea of a Christian, traced by inspiration, without gloss, or comment, or tradition of man. Bear

[S. D.]   U

to hear read to you a number of texts; texts which might be multiplied sevenfold; texts which can be confronted by no others; which are no partial selections, but a specimen of the whole of the New Testament. Before you go forward to the question, "How do they affect us, must we obey them, or why need we not?" prevail on yourselves to realize the idea of a Scriptural Christian, and the fact that the first Christians really answered to it. Granting you have to apply and modify the pattern given you, before you can use it yourselves, which I am not denying, yet after all, your pattern it is; you have no other pattern of a Christian any where. No other view of Christianity is given you in Scripture. If Scripture is used, you must begin with accepting that pattern; how can you apply what you will not study? Study what a Bible Christian is; be silent over it; pray for grace to comprehend it, to accept it.

And next ask yourselves this question, and be honest in your answer. This model of a Christian, though not commanding your literal imitation, still is it not the very model which has been fulfilled in others in every age since the New Testament was written? You will ask me in whom? I am loth to say; I have reason to ask you to be honest and candid; for so it is, as if from consciousness of the fact, and dislike to have it urged upon us, we and our forefathers have been accustomed to scorn and ridicule these faithful, obedient persons, and, in our Saviour's very words, to "cast out their *name* as evil, for the Son of man's sake." But, if the truth must be spoken, what are the humble monk, and the holy nun, and other regulars, as they are called, but

Christians after the very pattern given us in Scripture?
What have they done but this—perpetuate in the world
the Christianity of the Bible? Did our Saviour come
on earth suddenly, as He will one day visit it, in whom
would He see the features of the Christians whom He and
His Apostles left behind them, but in them? Who but
these give up home and friends, wealth and ease, good
name and liberty of will, for the kingdom of heaven?
Where shall we find the image of St. Paul, or St. Peter,
or St. John, or of Mary the mother of Mark, or of
Philip's daughters, but in those who, whether they
remain in seclusion, or are sent over the earth, have
calm faces, and sweet plaintive voices, and spare frames,
and gentle manners, and hearts weaned from the world,
and wills subdued; and for their meekness meet with
insult, and for their purity with slander, and for their
gravity with suspicion, and for their courage with
cruelty; yet meet with Christ every where—Christ,
their all-sufficient, everlasting portion, to make up to
them, both here and hereafter, all they suffer, all they
dare, for His Name's sake?

And, lastly, apply this pattern to yourselves; for
there only will you have power to apply it rightly.
You know very well, most of us know it too well, that
such precepts and examples do not directly apply to
every one of us. We are not severally bound to give up
the world by so literal a surrender. The case of Ananias
and Sapphira is enough to show us this. Their sin lay
in professing to do what they need not have done; in
making pretence of a voluntary renunciation which they
did not execute. They kept back part of the price of

the land which they made a show of giving up: and St. Peter urged it against them. "Whiles it remained, was it not thine own? and after it was sold, was it not in thine own power?" A most awful warning to every one, not to affect greater sanctity or self-denial than he attempts; but a proof withal, that those great surrenders which Scripture speaks of, are not incumbent on all Christians. They could not be voluntary if they were duties; they could not be meritorious if they were not voluntary. But though they are not duties to all, they may be duties to you; and though they are voluntary, you may have a call to them. It may be your duty to follow after merit. And whether it is you cannot learn, till first you have fairly surrendered your mind to the contemplation of that Christianity which Scripture delineates. After all, it may prove to be your duty to remain as others, and you may serve Him best and most acceptably in a secular life. But you cannot tell till you inquire; enough do we hear of private judgment in matters of doctrine; alas! that we will not exercise it where it is to a certain extent allowable and religious; in points, not public and ecclesiastical and eternal and independent of ourselves, but personal,—in the choice of life, in matters of duty!

SERMON XX.

Wisdom and Innocence.

"Behold, I send you forth as sheep in the midst of wolves; be ye there-fore wise as serpents, and harmless as doves."—MATT. x. 16.

SHEEP are defenceless, wolves are strong and fierce. How prompt, how frightful, how resistless, how decisive, would be the attack of a troop of wolves on a few straggling sheep which fell in with them! and how lively, then, is the image which our Lord uses to express the treatment which His followers were to receive from the world! He Himself was the great Exemplar of all such sufferings. When He was in the hands of His enemies, surrounded by a mad multitude, gazed on by relentless enemies, jeered at, struck, hurried along, tormented by rude soldiers, and at length nailed to the cross, what was He emphatically but a sheep among wolves? "He is brought as a lamb to the slaughter, and as a sheep before her shearers is dumb, so He openeth not His mouth." And what He foretold of His followers, that the Psalmist had declared of them at an earlier time, and His Apostle applies it to them on its fulfilment. "As it is written," says St. Paul, "For Thy sake we are killed all the day long; we are accounted as sheep for the slaughter [1]." Such was the Church of Christ in its beginnings, and such has it been in every age in proportion to its purity. The purer it has been, the more defenceless; whenever it has been pure, it has, in one way or another, been defenceless. The less worldly it has been, and the more it has cultivated its proper gifts, and the less it has relied upon sword and bow, chariots and horses, and arm of man, the more it has been exposed to ill-usage; the more it has invited oppression, the more it has irritated the proud and powerful. This, I say, is exemplified in every age. Seasons of peace, indeed, have been vouchsafed to it from the first, and in the most fearful times; but not an age of peace. A reign of temporal peace it can hardly enjoy, except under the reign of corruption, and in an age of faithlessness. Peace and rest are future.

Now, then, what is it natural to suppose will be the conduct of those who are helpless and persecuted, as the Holy Spouse of Christ? Pain and hardship and disrepute are pleasant to no man; and though they are to be gloried in when they are undergone, yet they will rather, if possible, be shunned or averted. Such avoidance is sanctioned, nay, commanded, by our Lord. When trials are inevitable, we must cheerfully bear them; but when they can be avoided without sin, we ought to prevent them. But how were Christians to prevent them when they might not fight? I answer,

[1] Rom. viii. 36.

they were allowed the arms, that is, the arts, of the
defenceless. Even the inferior animals will teach us
how wonderfully the Creator has compensated to the
weak their want of strength, by giving them other
qualities which may avail in their struggle with the
strong. They have the gift of fleetness; or they have
a certain make and colour; or certain habits of living;
or some natural cunning, which enables them either
to elude or even to destroy their enemies. Brute force
is countervailed by flight, brute passion by prudence
and artifice. Instances of a similar kind occur in our
own race. Those nations which are destitute of material
force, have recourse to the arts of the unwarlike; they
are fraudulent and crafty; they dissemble, negotiate,
procrastinate, evading what they cannot resist, and
wearing out what they cannot crush. Thus is it with
a captive, effeminate race, under the rule of the strong
and haughty. So is it with slaves; so is it with
ill-used and oppressed children; who learn to be
cowardly and deceitful towards their tyrants. So is
it with the subjects of a despot, who encounter his axe
or bowstring with the secret influence of intrigue and
conspiracy, the dagger and the poisoned cup. They
exercise the unalienable right of self-defence by such
methods as they best may; only, since human nature is
unscrupulous, guilt or innocence is all the same to
them, if it works their purpose.

Now, our Lord and Saviour did not forbid us the
exercise of that instinct of self-defence which is born
with us. He did not forbid us to defend ourselves, but
He forbad certain *modes* of defence. All sinful means,

of course, He forbad, as is plain without mentioning. But, besides these, He forbad us what is not sinful, but allowable by nature, though not in that more excellent and perfect way which He taught—He forbad us to defend ourselves by force, to return blow for blow. " Ye have heard," He says, " that it hath been said, An eye for an eye, and a tooth for a tooth ; but I say unto you, That ye resist not evil : but whosoever shall smite thee on thy right cheek, turn to him the other also. And if any man will sue thee at the law, and take away thy coat, let him have thy cloke also. And whosoever shall compel thee to go a mile, go with him twain." Thus the servants of Christ are forbidden to defend themselves by violence ; but they are not forbidden other means ; direct means are not allowed them, but others are even commanded. For instance, *foresight ;* " beware of men [1] :" *avoidance,* " when they persecute you in this city, flee ye into another :" *prudence and skill,* as in the text, " be ye wise as serpents."

Here we are reminded of the awful history with which the sacred volume opens. In the beginning, " the serpent was more subtle than any beast of the field which the Lord God had made." First, observe then, our Lord in the text sanctions that very reference which I have been making to the instincts and powers of the inferior animals, and puts them forth as our example. As we are to learn industry from the ant, and reliance on Him from the ravens, so the dove is our pattern of innocence, and the serpent our pattern of wisdom. But, moreover, considering that the serpent was chosen by

[1] Matt. x. 17.

the Enemy of mankind, as the instrument of his temptations in Paradise, it is very remarkable that Christ
should choose it as the pattern of wisdom for His
followers. It is as if He appealed to the whole world of
sin, and to the bad arts by which the feeble gain
advantages here over the strong. It is as if He set
before us the craft, the treachery, the perfidy of the
captive and the slave, and bade us extract a lesson even
from so great an evil. It is as if the more we are
forbidden violence, the more we are exhorted to prudence; as if it were our bounden duty to rival the
wicked in endowments of mind, and to excel them in
their exercise. And He makes a reference of this very
kind in one of His parables, where "the lord commended the unjust steward, because he had done wisely;
for the children of this world are in their generation
wiser than the children of light." "Be ye wise as
serpents," He said; then, knowing how dangerous such
wisdom is, especially in times of temptation, if a severe
conscientiousness is not awake, He added, "and harmless as doves." "Behold, I send you forth as sheep in
the midst of wolves; be ye therefore wise as serpents,
and harmless as doves."

It needs very little knowledge of the history of the
Church, to understand how remarkably this exhortation
to wisdom has been fulfilled in it. If there be one
reproach more than another which has been cast upon
it, it is that of fraud and cunning—cast upon it, even
from St. Paul's day, whose word was accused of being
" yea and nay [1];" and himself of " walking in craftiness,

[1] 2 Cor. i. 17.

and handling the word of God deceitfully [1];" of being
a "deceiver," though he was "true [2];" of "terrifying
by letters [3];" and of "being crafty," and "catching"
his converts "with guile [4]." Nay, cast upon it in the
person of our Lord, who was called "a deceiver," and
said to "deceive the people." Priestcraft has ever been
considered the badge, and its imputation is a kind
of note of the Church; and in part, indeed, truly,
because the presence of powerful enemies, and the sense
of their own weakness, has sometimes tempted Christians to the abuse, instead of the use of Christian
wisdom, to be wise without being harmless; but partly—
nay, for the most part—not truly, but slanderously, and
merely because the world called their wisdom craft, when
it was found to be a match for its own numbers and
power. Christians were called crafty, because "they were,
in fact, so strong, though professing to be weak." And
next, in mere consistency, they were called hypocritical,
because "they were, forsooth, so crafty, professing to be
innocent." And thus whereas they have ever, in accordance with our Lord's words, been wise and harmless,
they have ever been called instead crafty and hypocritical. The words "craft" and "hypocrisy" are but
the version of "wisdom" and "harmlessness," in the
language of the world.

It is remarkable, however, that not only is harmlessness the corrective of wisdom, securing it against the
corruption of craft and deceit, as stated in the text;
but innocence, simplicity, implicit obedience to God,

---

[1] 2 Cor. iv. 2.　　　　[2] 2 Cor. vi. 8.
[3] 2 Cor. x. 9.　　　　[4] 2 Cor. xii. 16.

tranquillity of mind, contentment, these and the like virtues are themselves a sort of wisdom ;—I mean, they produce the same results as wisdom, because God works for those who do not work for themselves ; and thus Christians especially incur the charge of craft at the hands of the world, because they pretend to so little, yet effect so much. This circumstance admits dwelling on.

By innocence, or harmlessness, is meant simplicity in act, purity in motive, honesty in aim ; acting conscientiously and religiously, according to the matter in hand, without caring for consequences or appearances ; doing what appears one's duty, and being obedient for obedience' sake, and leaving the event to God. This is to be innocent as the dove ; yet this conduct is the truest wisdom ; and this conduct accordingly has pre-eminently the appearance of craft.

It appears to be craft, and is wisdom, in many ways.

1. First : sobriety, self-restraint, control of word and feeling, which religious men exercise, have about them an appearance of being artificial, because they are not natural ; and of being artful, because artificial. I do not deny there is something very engaging in a frank and unpremeditating manner ; some persons have it more than others ; in some persons it is a great grace. But it must be recollected that I am speaking of times of persecution and oppression to Christians, such as the text foretells ; and then surely frankness will become nothing else than indignation at the oppressor, and vehemence of speech, if it is permitted. Accordingly, as persons have deep feelings, so they will find the necessity of self-control, lest they should say what they

ought not. All this stands to reason, without enlarging upon it. And to this must be added, that those who would be holy and blameless, the sons of God, find so much in the world to unsettle and defile them, that they are necessarily forced upon a strict self-restraint, lest they should receive injury from such intercourse with it as is unavoidable; and this self-restraint is the first thing which makes holy persons seem wanting in openness and manliness.

2. Next let it be considered that the world, the gross, carnal, unbelieving world, is blind to the peculiar feelings, objects, hopes, fears, affections of religious people. It cannot understand them. Religious men are a mystery to it; and, being a mystery, they will be called by the world, in mere self-defence, mysterious, dark, subtle, designing; and that the more, because, as living to God, they are at no pains to justify themselves to the world, or to open their hearts, or account to it for their conduct. The world will impute motives, either because it cannot find any, or because it simply will not believe those motives to be the real ones which are such, and are avowed as such. It cannot believe that men will deliberately sacrifice this life to the next; and when they profess to do so, it thinks that of necessity there must be something behind which they do not divulge. And, again, all the reasons which religious men allege, seem to the world unreal, and all the feelings fantastical and strained; and this strengthens it in its idea that it has not fathomed them, and that there is some secret to be found out. And indeed it has not fathomed them, and there is a secret; but it is the power of Divine grace,

their state of heart, which is the secret; not their motives or their ends, which the world is told to the full. Here is a second reason why the dove seems but a serpent. Christians give up worldly advantages; they sacrifice rank or wealth; they prefer obscurity to station; they do penance rather than live delicately; and the world says, " Here are effects without causes sufficient for them; here is craft."

3. Further, let this be considered. The precept given us is, that " we resist not evil ;" that we yield to worldly authority, and " give place unto wrath." This the early Christians did in an especial way. But it is very difficult to make the world understand the difference between an outward obedience, and an interior assent. When the Christians obeyed the heathen magistrate in all things not sinful, it was not that they thought the heathen right; they knew them to be idolaters. There are a multitude of cases, and very various, where it is our duty to obey those who nevertheless have no power over our belief or conviction. When, however, religious men outwardly conform, on the score of duty, to " the powers that be," the world is easily led into the mistake that they have renounced their opinions as well as submitted their actions; and it feels or affects surprise, to learn that their opinions remain; and this it considers or calls an inconsistency, or a duplicity. It argues that they are breaking promise, cherishing what they disown, or resuming what they professed to abandon. And thus the very fact that they are so harmless, so inoffensive, that they do so much in the way of compliance, becomes a ground of complaint against them,

that they do not do more—that they do not do more than they have a right to do. They yield outwardly; to assent inwardly would be to betray the faith; yet they are called deceitful and double-dealing, because they do as much as they can, and not more than they may.

4. Again : the cheerfulness, contentment, and readiness with which religious men resign their cause into God's hands, and are well-pleased that the world should seem to triumph over them, have still further an appearance of craft and deceit. For why should they be so satisfied to give up their wishes, unless they knew something which others did not know, or were really gaining while they seemed to lose? Other men make a great clamour and lamentation over their idols; there is no mistaking that they have lost them, and that they have no hope. But Christians resign themselves. They are silent; silence itself is suspicious—even silence is mystery. Why do they not speak out? why do they not show a natural, an honest indignation? The submitting to calumny is a proof that it is too true. They would set themselves right, if they could. Still more strange and suspicious is the confidence which religious men show, in spite of apparent weakness, that their cause will triumph. The boldness, decisiveness, calmness of speech, which are necessarily the result of Christian faith and hope, lead the world to the surmise of some hidden reliance, some secret support, to account for them ; as if God's word, when received and dwelt on, were not a greater encouragement to the lonely combatant than any word of man, however powerful, or any conspiracy, however far-spreading.

5. And still stronger is this delusion on the part of the world, when the event justifies the confidence of religious men. The truest wisdom is to stand still and trust in God, and to the world it is also the strongest evidence of craft. God fights for those who do not fight for themselves; such is the great truth, such is the gracious rule, which is declared and exemplified in the Gospel: "Dearly beloved, avenge not yourselves," says St. Paul, "but rather give place unto wrath, for it is written, Vengeance is Mine, I will repay, saith the Lord[1]." Do nothing, and you have done every thing. The less you do, the more God will do for you. The more you submit to the violence of the world, the more powerfully will He rise against the world, who is irresistible. The less you ward off the world's blows from you, the more heavy will be His blows upon the world, if not in your cause, at least in His own. When, then, the world at length becomes sensible that it is faring ill, and receiving more harm than it inflicts, yet is unwilling to humble itself under the mighty hand of God, what is left but to attribute its failure to the power of those who seem to be weak? that is, to their craft, who pretend to be weak when really they are strong.

6. To this must be added, that the truth has in itself the gift of spreading, without instruments; it makes its way in the world, under God's blessing, by its own persuasiveness and excellence; "So is the kingdom of God," says our Lord, "as if a man should cast seed into the ground, and should sleep, and rise night and day,

[1] Rom. xii. 19.

and the seed should spring and grow up, he *knoweth not how*[1]." The Word, when once uttered, runs its course. He who speaks it has done his work in uttering it, and cannot recall it if he would. It runs its course; it prospers in the thing whereunto God sends it. It seizes many souls at once, and subdues them to the obedience of faith. Now when bystanders see these effects and see no cause, for they will not believe that the Word itself is the cause, which is to them a dead-letter—when it sees many minds moved in one way in many places, it imputes to secret management that uniformity which is nothing but the echo of the One Living and True Word.

7. And of course all this happens to the surprise of Christians as well as of the world; they can but marvel and praise God, but cannot account for it more than the world. " When the Lord turned again the captivity of Sion," says the Psalmist, " then were we like unto them that dream[2]." Or as the Prophet says of the Church, " Thine heart shall fear and be enlarged ; because the abundance of the sea shall be converted unto thee, the forces of the Gentiles shall come unto thee[3]," and here again the Christian's true wisdom looks like craft. It is true wisdom to leave the event to God; but when they are prospered, it looks like deceit to show surprise, and to disclaim the work themselves. Moreover, meekness, gentleness, patience, and love, have in themselves a strong power to melt the heart of those who witness them. Cheerful suffering, too, leads spectators to sympathy, till, perhaps, a reaction takes place in the minds

---

[1] Mark iv. 26, 27.   [2] Ps. cxxvi. 1.   [3] Isa. lx. 5.

of men, and they are converted by the sight, and glorify
their Father which is in heaven. But it is easy to
insinuate, when men are malevolent, that those who
triumph through meekness have affected the meekness
to secure the triumph.

8. Here a very large subject opens upon us, to which
I shall but allude. Those who surrender themselves to
Christ in implicit faith are graciously taken into His
service; and, " as men under authority," they do great
things without knowing it, by the Wisdom of their
Divine Master. They act on conscience, perhaps in
despondency, and without foresight; but what is obedience in them, has a purpose with God, and they are
successful, when they do but mean to be dutiful. But
what duplicity does the world think it, to speak of conscience, or honour, or propriety, or delicacy, or to give
other tokens of personal motives, when the event seems
to show that a calculation of results has been the
actuating principle at bottom ! It is God who designs,
but His servants seem designing; and that the more,
should it so happen that they really do themselves catch
glimpses of their own position in His providential course.
For then what they do from the heart, approves itself
to their reason, and they are able to recognize the expedience of obedience.

How frequently is this remark in point in the history—
nay, in the very constitution of the Church ! Jacob, for
instance, is thought worldly-wise in his dealings with
Laban, whereas he was a " plain man," simply obedient
to the Angel who " spake unto him in a dream," who
took care of his worldly interests for him, and protected

[S. D.]   x

him against his avaricious kinsman. Moses, again, is sometimes called sagacious and shrewd in his measures or his laws, as if wise acts might not come from the Source of wisdom, and provisions were proved to be human, when they could be shown to be advisable. And so, again, in the Christian Church, bishops have been called hypocritical in submitting and yet opposing themselves to the civil power, in a matter of plain duty, if a popular movement was the consequence; and then hypocritical again, if they did their best to repress it. And in like manner, theological doctrines or ecclesiastical usages are styled politic if they are but salutary; as if the Lord of the Church, who has willed her sovereignty, might not effect it by secondary causes. What, for instance, though we grant that sacramental confession and the celibacy of the clergy do tend to consolidate the body politic in the relation of rulers and subjects, or, in other words, to aggrandize the priesthood? for how can the Church be one body without such relation, and why should not He, who has decreed that there should be unity, take measures to secure it? Marks of design are not elsewhere assumed as disproofs of His interference. Why should not the Creator, who has given us the feeling of hunger that we may eat and not die, and sentiments of compassion and benevolence for the welfare of our brethren, when He would form a more integral power than mankind had yet seen, adopt adequate means, and use His old world to create a new one? and why must His human instruments set out with a purpose, because they accomplish one? Nothing is safe in Revelation on such an interpretation. As the expedience of its provisions is made an objection to their honesty, so the beauty of its facts becomes an argument against their truth. The narratives in the Gospels have lately been viewed as mythical representations from their very perfection; as if a Divine work could not be most beautiful on the one hand and most expedient on the other.

The reason is this: men do not like to hear of the interposition of Providence in the affairs of the world; and they invidiously ascribe ability and skill to His agents, to escape the thought of an Infinite Wisdom and an Almighty Power. They will be unjust to their brethren, that they may not be just to Him; they will be wanton in their imputations, rather than humble themselves to a confession.

But for us, let us glory in what they disown; let us beg of our Divine Lord to take to Him His great power, and manifest Himself more and more, and reign both in our hearts and in the world. Let us beg of Him to stand by us in trouble, and guide us on our dangerous way. May He, as of old, choose "the foolish things of the world to confound the wise, and the weak things of the world to confound the things which are mighty"! May He support us all the day long, till the shades lengthen, and the evening comes, and the busy world is hushed, and the fever of life is over, and our work is done! Then in His mercy may He give us a safe lodging, and a holy rest, and peace at the last!

SERMON XXI.

Invisible Presence of Christ.

" The kingdom of God cometh not with observation ; neither shall they say, Lo here! or, Lo there! for, behold, the kingdom of God is within you."—LUKE xvii. 20, 21.

WHAT our Lord announced came to pass. The Kingdom of God came; it filled the world; it took possession of the high places of the earth; but it came without observation. All other kingdoms which have come, have sounded a trumpet before them, and have challenged attention. They have come out with a

---

[1] The four following Sermons, on the safety of continuance in our communion, are not addressed, 1, either to those who happily are without doubts on the subject, 2, or to those who have no right to be in doubt about it. Doubts are often the punishment of existing neglect of duty. Persons who make no efforts after strictness of life, who do not live by rule, who do not attempt to know themselves, to correct their faults, to keep out of temptation, to resist evil, and to deny their wills, must not be surprised if they are unsettled and restless, and have no encouragement to seek an intellectual remedy for difficulties which may be assigned to grave moral deficiencies. That there are such persons, the author makes no question at all; at the same time, he is bound to add that he is not alluding to any with whom he is personally acquainted, though of most of these more of course might fairly be required than they have hitherto effected. On the other hand, where persons are in no perplexity on the subject, the discussion contained in these Sermons may be, for

sword, and with a spear, and with a shield. They have been the ravenous beast from the north; the swift eagle, or the swarming locusts. "A fire devoured before them, and behind them a flame burned. The appearance of them has been as the appearance of horsemen, and as horsemen, so did they run; . . . and the sound of their wings was as the sound of chariots of many horses running to battle [1]." Such has been the coming of earthly power; and a Day will be, when that also will have a fulfilment, and find its antitype in the history of heaven; for when our Lord comes again, He too will come with a shout, " with the voice of the Archangel, and with the trump of God." This will be with observation; so will He end, but so did He not begin, His Church upon earth; for it had been foretold, "He shall not strive, nor cry, neither shall any man hear His voice in the streets; a bruised reed shall He not break, and smoking flax shall He not quench, till He send forth judgment unto victory [2]."

And that noiseless, unostentatious coming was rendered still more secret, because, in spite of His own assurances, men would not believe that it would be secret. The Pharisees asked for a sign from heaven. They would not believe He could come, unless He came with a show; they looked out for a temporal prince, with a sword of earth; and thus, through the unbelief of men, He was "as a thief in the night," and He was

---

that very reason, simply of a disturbing character, and should be read with the caution exercised in opening the work of a Christian Apologist, who is obliged to state painful objections, or to make extreme admissions. in the process of refuting his opponents.

[1] Joel ii. 3, 4. Rev. ix.   [2] Matt. xii. 19, 20.

come and in possession before they well understood that He was coming.

"The kingdom of God," says the Divine Speaker, "cometh not with observation; neither shall they say, Lo here! or, Lo there! *for* the kingdom of God is within you." He tells us why He was not observed; it was that He came, not as the world cometh, not by an influence from without, but by an inward power; not subduing the outward man through the senses, but touching the secret heart. Kingdoms of this world spread in space and time; they begin from a point, and they travel onwards, and range around. Their course may be traced: first they secure this territory, then they compass that. Of course the Kingdom of Christ also, as being in this world, has an outward shape like this world, though it be not of this world; and, as viewed with the eyes of this world, it has an aspect of growth and development like other kingdoms; but after all this is not the true process of its rise and establishment. It came by an inward and secret presence; by outward instruments, indeed, but with effects far higher than those instruments, and really by God's own agency. He who is Omnipresent and Omniscient, touched many hearts at once in many places; they forthwith, one and all, spoke one language, not learning it one from the other, but taught by Him the Song of the Lamb; or if in one sense by man's teaching too, yet catching and mastering it supernaturally, almost before the words were spoken. Men broke out all at once in His praises, in the east and in the west, in the north and in the south; and the perplexed world searched about in vain whence came that concord of sweet and holy sounds. Upon the first voice of the preacher, upon a hint, upon a mere whisper in the air, a deep response came from many lips, a deep, full, and ready harmony of many voices, one and all proclaiming Christ. For the Spirit of the Lord had descended and filled the earth; and there were thrilling hearts, and tremulous pulses, and eager eyes in every place. It was a time of visitation, when the weak become strong, and the last become first. It was the triumph of faith, which saith not, "Who shall ascend into heaven? or, Who shall descend into the deep? but what saith it? The word is nigh thee, even in thy mouth and in thy heart; that is, the word of faith which we preach." And thus, as Nineveh and Babylon were surprised of old by the army of the enemy, so was the world then surprised by Him who "rode upon a white horse, and was called Faithful and True;" and as it befell Egypt, that there was not a house where there was not one dead, so now, on this more gracious visitation, there was not a house where there was not one alive. For God had come down among them, and was everywhere; the Lord of Angels was walking the earth; He was diffusing His Presence, and multiplying His Image; and in this sense, as well as that in which He spoke the words, "a man's foes were those of his own household." The despised, the hated influence, insinuated itself every where; the leaven spread, and none could stay it; and in the most unfavourable places, in the family of the haughty senator and fierce soldier, amid the superstitions of

idolatry, and the debasement of slavery, the noblest and
ablest and the fairest, as well as the brutish and the
ignorant, one and all, by a secret charm, became the
prey of the Church, and the bondsmen of Christ. And
thus a great and wide-spreading kingdom came into
existence all at once, like spring after winter, from
within.

Now if you ask me how this was done, or in what
way the grace of Almighty God dealt with the spirits
He had created, the answer is ready: Man is not
sufficient for his own happiness; he is not happy except
the Presence of God be with him.   When he was
created, God breathed into him that supernatural life of
the Spirit which is his true happiness: and when he fell,
he lost the divine gift, and with it his happiness also.
Ever since he has been unhappy; ever since he has a
void within him which needs filling, and he knows not
how to fill it.   He scarcely realizes his own need: only
his actions show that he feels it, for he is ever restless
when he is not dull and insensible, seeking in one thing
or another that blessing which he has lost.   Multitudes,
indeed, there are, whose minds have never been opened;
and multitudes who stupify and deaden their minds, till
they lose their natural hunger and thirst: but, whether
aware of their need or not, whether made restless by it
or not, still all men have it, and the Gospel supplies it;
and then, even if they did not recognize their want by
nature, they at length learn it by its supply.   This,
then, is the secret of the triumph of Christ's Kingdom.
Soldiers of this world receive their bounty-money on
enlisting.   They take it, and become the servants of an

earthly prince: shall not they, much more, be faithful, yea, unto the death, who have received the earnest of the true riches, who have been fed with the hidden manna, who have "tasted the good word of God, and the powers of the world to come," and "the graciousness of the Lord," and "the peace which passeth all understanding"? It is the Presence of Christ which makes us members of Christ: "neither shall they say, Lo here! and Lo there! for the kingdom of God is within us." Others marvel; others try to analyze what it is which does the work; they imagine all manner of human causes, because they cannot see, and do not feel, and will not believe the inward influence; and they impute to some caprice or waywardness of mind, or to the force of novelty, or to some mysterious insidious persuasives, or to some concealed enemy, or to some dark and subtle plotting, and they view with alarm, and they fain would baffle, what is really the keen, vivid, constraining glance of Christ's countenance. "The Lord turned and looked upon Peter;" and "as the lightning cometh out of the east, and shineth even unto the west, so also is the Presence of the Son of man." It is come, it is gone, it has done its work, its abiding work, before men see it.

And what took place in the first years of His Kingdom, when it was brought into being, holds good, in its measure, of all times of the Church; whether before the Law, or under the Law, or in this late and dark age, when Christians have divided into parties, and fight against each other. For on Jacob, as he slept, the Presence of God descended, and when he woke, he said,

"Surely the Lord is in this place, and I knew it not;" and he added, as having his mind opened to new thoughts by the manifestation, "If God will be with me, and will keep me in this way that I go, ... then shall the Lord be my God[1]." And Moses also asked for this great gift, and obtained it. He said, "See, Thou sayest unto me, Bring up this people, and Thou hast not let me know whom Thou wilt send with me. Yet Thou hast said, I know thee by name, and thou hast also found grace in My sight. . . . . And He said, My Presence shall go with thee, and I will give thee rest. And he said unto Him, If Thy Presence go not with me, carry us not up hence. . . . . And the Lord said unto Moses, I will do this thing also which thou hast spoken, for thou hast found grace in My sight, and I know thee by name[2]." And in like manner the Prophet tells us, with reference to all the people, "In all their affliction He was afflicted, and the Angel of His Presence saved them; in His love and in His pity He redeemed them, and He bare them, and carried them all the days of old[3]."

Much more is this personal gift fulfilled in these latter days, which are days of the Gospel, though they be degenerate days. What is described in the text had been foretold in the Prophets. "Behold the days come, saith the Lord, that I will make a new covenant with the house of Israel, and with the house of Judah; not according to the covenant that I made with their fathers in the day that I took them by the hand to

[1] Gen. xxviii. 15—21.   [2] Exod. xxxiii. 12—17.
[3] Isa. lviii. 9.

bring them out of the land of Egypt; . . . but this shall be the covenant that I will make with the house of Israel. After those days, saith the Lord, I will put My law in their inward parts, and write it in their hearts, and will be their God, and they shall be My people. And they shall teach no more every man his neighbour, and every man his brother, saying, Know the Lord : for they shall all know Me, from the least of them unto the greatest of them, saith the Lord; for I will forgive their iniquity, and I will remember their sin no more." And again, "All thy children shall be taught of the Lord, and great shall be the peace of thy children." And the Apostles, after the fulfilment of the promise, in like manner, "Ye have an unction from the Holy One, and ye know all things;" "He that believeth on the Son of God hath the witness in himself." And again, "The Spirit Itself beareth witness with our spirit, that we are the children of God[1]."

I said just now, that there are multitudes who neither feel their need, nor believe in the supply; they have never thought upon religious subjects, or they have stupified their conscience by sensuality or by covetous-ness. And I also said, that those whose minds have been roused and opened, perceive their need, or at least feel it, though unconsciously, and if it be not supplied, become restless in consequence. And now I add, and a solemn thought it is, that numbers among ourselves, though we profess the Gospel, are in that restless state, ever seeking, never finding! Look around you, my

---

[1] Jer. xxxi. 31—34. Isa. liv. 13. 1 John ii. 20; v. 10. Rom. viii. 16.

brethren, on every side: what, on the whole, is the religion of England? it is restlessness. Look round, I say, and answer, why it is that there is so much change, so much strife, so many parties and sects, so many creeds? because men are unsatisfied and restless; and why restless, with every one his psalm, his doctrine, his tongue, his revelation, his interpretation? they are restless because they have not found. Alas! so it is, in this country called Christian, vast numbers have gained little from religion, beyond a thirst after what they have not, a thirst for their true peace, and the fever and restlessness of thirst. It has not yet brought them into the Presence of Christ, in which "is fulness of joy" and "pleasure for evermore." Had they been fed with the bread of life, and tasted of the honeycomb, their eyes, like Jonathan's, had been enlightened, to acknowledge the Saviour of men; but having no such real apprehension of things unseen, they have still to seek, and are at the mercy of every rumour from without, which purports to bring tidings of Him, and of the place of His abode. "By night on my bed I sought Him whom my soul loveth. I sought Him, but I found Him not. I will rise now, and go about the city in the streets, and in the broad ways I will seek Him whom my soul loveth; I sought Him, but I found Him not." "I sought Him, but I could not find Him; I called Him, but He gave me no answer. The watchmen that went about the city found me; they smote me, they wounded me; the keepers of the walls took away my veil from me[1]." Mary wept because they

[1] Cant. iii. 1, 2; v. 6, 7.

had taken away her Lord, and she knew not where they had laid Him. She was in trouble because she sought Him, yet in vain. Poor wanderers, helpless and ill-fated generation, who understand that Christ is on earth, yet do but seek Him in the desert or in the secret chambers,—Lo here! and Lo there! O sad and pitiable spectacle, when the people of Christ wander on the hills as "sheep which have no shepherd;" and instead of seeking Him in His ancient haunts and His appointed home, busy themselves in human schemes, follow strange guides, are taken captive by new opinions, become the sport of chance, or of the humour of the hour, or the victims of self-will, are full of anxiety, and perplexity, and jealousy, and alarm, "tossed to and fro, and carried about by every wind of doctrine, by the sleight of men, and cunning craftiness whereby they lie in wait to deceive;"—and all because they do not seek the "one body" and the "one Spirit," and the "one hope of their calling," the "one Lord, one faith, one baptism, one God and Father of all," and find rest for their souls! O how different from that Apostolic state, when "all that believed were together and had all things common; and . . . continuing daily with one accord in the temple, and breaking bread from house to house, did eat their meat with gladness and singleness of heart, praising God, and having favour with all the people"! and whence was this outward order, which we have lost? it was because of that inward Gift, which, being One, made them all one, according to our Saviour's prayer, "The glory which Thou gavest Me, I have given them; that they may be one, even as We are

One; I in them and Thou in Me, that they may be made perfect in one[1]."

How great a blessing is it, my brethren, at all times, but especially in an age like this, that the tokens of Christ are not only without us, but more properly within us! I say in this age especially, because it is an age in which the outward signs of Christ's Presence have well nigh deserted us. Christ, in mercy to all who seek Him, has been accustomed in all ages, in anticipation of His true inward witness, to hold forth certain plain and general tokens of His Presence, to show the world where He is to be found. These are for beginners; or for those who are not yet beginners, that they *may* begin, and may thus be led on by such experience of His grace, to discern those holier and better notes of which He speaks in the text. Since then, in this our age, He has in judgment obscured the visible and public notes of His Kingdom among us, what a mercy is it to us that He has not deprived us of such as are personal and private! Alas! how few even of serious men could remain peaceful and steadfast, or be secure about themselves, that they would not run any whither, if they judged merely by what is seen! "We see not our tokens; there is not one prophet more; no, not one is there among us that understandeth any more." "Thou makest us to be rebuked of our neighbours, to be laughed to scorn and had in derision of them that are round about us; Thou makest us to be a by-word among the heathen, and that the people shake their heads at us. My confusion is daily before me, and the

---

[1] Eph. iv. 5, 6. Acts ii. 44—47. John xvii. 22, 23.

shame of my face hath covered me; for the voice of the slanderer and blasphemer, for the enemy and avenger [1]." Who among us does not at this day participate in this ancient trial? for who would account that to be the Church of God in which we are, if he went merely by sight? who has not cause to appeal, and who may not appeal, and who will not find an answer when he appeals, to the notes of that Kingdom, which abides, as it came, "without observation," and which proclaims not "Lo here! or Lo there!" because it is a Kingdom of God which is "within us"? Yes, I say; who among us may not, if he will, lead such a life as to have these secret and truer tokens to rest his faith on, so as to be sure, and certain, and convinced, that the Church which baptized us has still the Presence of Christ, and therefore is within the bounds of His Kingdom, and is the gate to His eternal favour?

When, then, we are overwhelmed, as we well may be, at the confusion of all things around us, as Psalmists and Prophets have been before us, let us turn to the thought of that gift which Psalmists and Prophets had not as we may have, and which is personal and incommunicable and unspeakable, but known to religious men. What are signs and tokens of any kind whatever, but the way *to* Christ? what need of *them*, should it so be, through His mercy, that we have found Him? Who asks his way when he has got to his destination? why seek the shadow, if we already have the substance? why seek Him elsewhere, if we have reason to trust we have found Him here? why turn from Him, if we are already

[1] Ps. lxxiv. 10; xliv. 14—17.

in His Presence ? If so be we have " tasted that the
Lord is gracious," what need we more ? When the
women met Christ after His resurrection, "they came
and held Him by the feet and worshipped Him."
Magdalen would have done the like, but He forbade
it. The two disciples, when " He made as though He
would have gone farther," "constrained Him." When
Jacob wrestled with the Angel, he would not refrain
even at His word, but said, " I will not let Thee go,
except Thou bless me." " I held Him, and would not
let Him go," says the Bride, "until I had brought
Him into my mother's house, and into the chamber of
her that conceived me." What want we *more* than His
Presence ? Andrew "findeth his own brother Simon,
and saith unto Him, We have *found* the Messias."
What can we need beyond finding Him ? Can we gain
more than Him any where? shall we be thankful, shall
we be dutiful, shall we be believing, if we leave Him ?
The holy women would not let Him go ; can we be
certain, if we once loose our hold of Him, that we
shall ever regain it ? shall we not rather, in that case,
be of the number of those, who, though they saw His
mighty works, came to Him, and " besought Him that
He would depart out of their coasts" ?

But you will, perhaps, ask, " Is there no chance of
Christ ever leaving a home where once He was ? and
if His Presence leaves it, must not we leave it also?"
Yes, verily ; did He leave His home, we must follow
Him ; who doubts it ? But let me ask, Does He commonly leave without tokens that He is leaving ? and
if we have tokens that He is still with us, we have

sufficient tokens that He has not yet left us. Doubtless
there was a time when even from Jerusalem, the Holy
City, it was a duty to depart; but our Lord gave a
sign when it was to be. "When ye shall see the
abomination of desolation stand in the Holy Place, then
let them which be in Judæa flee unto the mountains;"
and when the time came, other signs were added. The
Lord had come upon the Jewish people with miracles;
and with miracles He left them. He foretold and
brought to pass "fearful sights, and great signs from
heaven." Strange portents happened in the fated city,
and the voice of Angels was heard in the Temple, saying
one to another, thereby to guide God's people, "Let us
depart hence." Such, too, was the command when the
people came out of Egypt: "Fear ye not, stand still,
and see the salvation of the Lord. The Lord shall fight
for you, and ye shall hold your peace."

Let, then, the disorder in religious matters which
now prevails among us, only lead each of us to ask
himself this plain question, whether he may not have
more tokens, real and intimate, that Christ is with
himself and his brethren in our ordinances, than he has
evidence in the present absence or mutilation of the
truth, whatever it is, that Christ is not with him.
Christ may be at a distance from others, yet may be
with him. The word runs, "According to thy faith, be
it done unto thee." If, then, "there is any consolation
in Christ, if any fellowship of the Spirit, if any bowels
and mercies;" if you have gained any good thing, not
merely in, but through your Church; if you have come
to Service, and been favoured with the peace or the

[S. D.]   Y

illumination you needed; or if you can recollect times when you visited holy places, and certainly gained there a manifestation such as the world could not give; or if sermons have come to you with power, and have been blessed to your spiritual good; or if your soul has been, as it were, transfigured within you, when you came to the Most Holy Sacrament; or if Lent and Passiontide brought to you what you had not before; or if at Ordinations you have been partakers of an indescribable influence, and almost savour of grace, though you realized it not at the time; or if strange providences, and almost supernatural coincidences have hung about the Church's Ordinances; if mercies or judgments have descended through them upon yourselves, or upon those about you; or if you have experience of death-beds, and know how full of hope the children of our Church can die;—O! pause ere you doubt that we have a Divine Presence among us still, and have not to seek it. Let us enjoy what we still have, though the world deride us;—though our brethren tell us that in their and our Sacraments we have not what we think we have; though they tell us it is all a dream, and rudely bid us seek elsewhere: no, they do not need to seek who have already found; we need other arguments before we seek what, through God's mercy, we hope to enjoy where we are. "The lot is fallen unto me in a fair ground; yea, I have a goodly heritage;" why should not we enjoy the hidden Kingdom of Christ, though others may not have faith to see it? And we will cling to the Church in which we are, not for its own sake, but because we humbly trust that Christ is in it; and while

He is in it, we will abide in it. He shall leave before
we do. He shall lead, and we will but follow; we will
not go before Him; we will not turn away from Him,
we will ever turn towards Him. We will but ask
ourselves this single question, "*Is* He here?" for "with
Him is the well of life," and justifying grace, and
Divine favour. "Therefore, my brethren, dearly beloved
and longed for, my joy and crown, so stand fast in the
Lord, my dearly beloved. Rejoice in the Lord alway;
and again I say, Rejoice. Let your moderation be
known unto all men; the Lord is at hand. Be careful
for nothing : but in every thing by prayer and supplication, with thanksgiving, let your requests be made
known unto God. And the peace of God, which passeth
all understanding, shall keep your hearts and minds,
through Christ Jesus."

SERMON XXII.

Outward and Inward Notes of the Church.

" I know whom I have believed, and am persuaded that He is able to keep that which I have committed unto Him against that day."—2 TIM. i. 12.

IT is not to be supposed that any of us, in this fallen time, should be able to use these words of the great Apostle as he used them. God who made us, has given to each of us his own place. Some He places in heathen countries, some in Christian ; some in the full light and grace of the Gospel, others amid shadows; some He visits almost with sensible tokens of His presence, others He barely supports with the hope and surmise of it. Some He leads forward only by intimations, and, as it were, whispers; as the old Saints, who "went out, not knowing whither they went;" and "died in faith, not receiving the promise." And others, like St. Paul, have before now been granted visions of the third heaven, that full and intimate Presence of Christ, which enables the Apostle to say, in the words of the text, "I know whom I have believed, and am persuaded that He is able to keep that which I have committed unto Him against that day."

Yet in spite of these great differences in God's dealings with man and man, there is this one thing the same in all cases, that He *has* dealt with each. I mean that religion is a personal, private, and individual matter, that it consists in a communion between God and the soul, and that its true evidences belong to the soul that believes, are its property, and not something common to it and the whole world. God vouchsafes to speak to us one by one, to manifest Himself to us one by one, to lead us forward one by one; He gives us something to rely upon which others do not experience, which we cannot convey to others, which we can but use for ourselves.

Now that there is much in Scripture agreeable to this statement, no one I suppose will deny; but this question arises, which is worth considering, whether the Gospel Dispensation does not, even more than the Law, in one respect modify it, or even run counter to it and reverse it? For if there be a distinction of the Gospel plainly laid down in Scripture, it is that it is a social religion, and addresses individuals as parts of a whole. And, being social, it must have all things in common, and its evidences and tokens in the number. And, further, if it is social, it must be a public religion, "a city set upon a hill;" and its evidences will be in a measure public. Nay, further, its great note, as announced by the Prophets, is not only that it is social, that it is public, but that it is both social and public in the very highest sense, because it is Catholic, universal every where; and this note is insisted on as something special in itself, of a nature to dazzle and subdue the mind, like a miracle, or like the sun's light in the heavens. It was to be the

characteristic gift of the Christian Church, that she herself was to be a great public evidence of her mission,
that she was to be her own evidence. Her very look,
her bearing, her voice, were to be her credentials. As
Adam had sovereignty over brute animals on his
creation, or as the second Adam, her Lord and Maker,
"spake as one having authority, and not as the Scribes,"
so she was to win or to awe the souls of men generally;
not this one or that, but all, though variously, by the
manifest royalty of her very presence. She received
this gift from her Lord in the beginning—to claim and
command obedience when she spoke, because she spoke;
and that not from any thing special in the mind of the
hearer, but from the voice and tone of the speaker.

Never must we disguise this great truth. "The
labour of Egypt, and the merchandize of Ethiopia and
of the Sabeans, men of stature, shall come over unto
thee, and they shall be thine, they shall come after thee,
in chains they shall come over; and they shall fall down
unto thee; they shall make supplication unto thee, saying, Surely God is in thee, and there is none else, there
is no God." Again, "I will pour My Spirit upon thy
seed, and My blessing upon thine offspring; and they
shall spring up as among the grass, as willows by the
water-courses. One shall say, I am the Lord's, . . .
and another shall subscribe with his hand unto the Lord,
and surname himself by the name of Israel." Again:
"Enlarge the place of thy tent, and let them stretch
forth the curtains of thine habitations; spare not,
lengthen thy cords, and strengthen thy stakes." And
again: "No weapon that is formed against thee shall

prosper, and every tongue that shall rise against thee in judgment thou shalt condemn." And again: "The nation and kingdom that will not serve thee shall perish, yea, those nations shall be utterly wasted." And again: "The sun shall be no more thy light by day, neither for brightness shall the moon give light unto thee; but the Lord shall be unto thee an everlasting light, and thy God thy glory." And, as if the Church were to "declare the glory of God" more perfectly than the natural heavens, and to bear witness to her own origin without evidence beyond herself, we are told, "Behold, I create new heavens and a new earth; and the former shall not be remembered, nor come into mind. But be ye glad and rejoice for ever in that which I create; for, behold, I create Jerusalem a rejoicing, and her people a joy[1]."

These of course are but a few out of the multitude of passages in the Prophet Isaiah, descriptive of the Christian Church; they speak of tokens outward, visible, common to all; and yet, in spite of these, St. Paul in the text, when about to die, and contemplating the judgment, speaks, not of them, of an evidence not outward, not visible, not common, but inward, private, incommunicable. "I know," he says, "whom I have believed." I bear about me "the marks of the Lord Jesus" in my own person; I have assurance that He has "stood by me," because He has "strengthened me;" His tabernacle is not only "with men," but "the grace of Christ tabernacles upon me." In other words (could we doubt it?), in his instance the general had become particular; the external had flowed into his secret soul;

[1] Isa. xlv. 14; xliv. 3—5; liv. 2. 17; lx. 12. 19; lxv. 17, 18.

the universal gift had been appropriated; the visible glory had kindled a light in his own breast; and thus, just as we need not read a friend's writing when we hear his voice, so, though Christ had gone forth into the wide world, and had been lifted up aloft to draw men to Him, and had lodged among them the power and the presence of His Atonement, yet the blessed Apostle needed not seek Him abroad, who had graciously condescended to " come under his roof," and manifest Himself unto him.

Now this is a distinction very necessary in all ages of the Church, for different reasons: when her outward glory is great, by way of turning our attention to our own hearts, and our personal responsibility; and when it is obscured, in order to keep our faith from failing, and to revive our hope; at all times, to hinder our being engrossed by what is external to the loss of what is inward in religion.

I observe, then, this: that the public notes of the Church, which are the common property of all men, are rather a sign to unbelievers than to the faithful, and to the world than to Christians; and a sign to members of the Church in proportion as they are without, and till they gain those truer and more precious tokens, to which the external notes lead, and by which they are practically superseded. This I conceive to be the Scripture doctrine concerning them, in the very passages which promise them to us.

For instance: " This people have I formed for Myself; they shall *show forth* My praise;" that is, they are an external evidence to the world of God's mighty power. Again, more explicitly: " *The Gentiles* shall come to

thy light, and kings to the brightness of thy rising:
. . . . the sons of *the strangers* shall build thy walls,
and their kings shall minister unto thee." Again:
"The Lord hath made bare His Holy Arm *in the eyes of
all the nations;* and *all the ends of the earth* shall see
the salvation of our God." Again: "Behold, I have
taken out of thine hand the cup of trembling, . . . but
I will put it into the hand of *them that afflict thee."*
And again: "Lift up thine eyes round about, and
behold: all these gather themselves together and *come
to thee,* . . . that thou mayest say to the *prisoners,* Go
forth; to *them that are in darkness,* Show yourselves."
Once more: "From the rising of the sun even unto the
going down of the same My Name shall be great *among
the Gentiles*[1]." You see the external glory of the
Church is shown towards strangers and Gentiles, that
they may join her; to prisoners, for their release; to
enemies, for their conversion; to oppressors, for their
punishment. I do not mean to say, that nothing is
implied of such a manifestation being still a support and
comfort to those who *have* joined her, who *have* been
released, who *are* converts, who *have* been punished and
repented; such a result of it is expressed by the holy
Baptist, when he, as standing without the Church,
though a destined member of it, and as it were contemplating the sacred building at the gate, while he was yet
only entering it, says, "He that hath the Bride is the
Bridegroom; but the friend of the Bridegroom, which
standeth and heareth Him, rejoiceth greatly because of
the Bridegroom's voice; this my joy therefore is ful-

[1] Isa. xliii. 21; lx. 3. 10; lii. 10; li. 22. 23; xlix. 18. 9. Mal. i. 11.

filled [1]." But granting this, we shall find, nevertheless, that the special promise to the children of the Church, considered as such, is of a different kind. They first see her glory from without; next they taste her good gifts from within. "All thy children," runs the promise to the Christian Church, not merely shall see thy glory, but, "all thy children shall be *taught of the Lord*, and great shall be the peace of thy children." Again: "Thy people shall be all righteous." Again: "I will put My Law in their inward parts, and write it in their hearts; and will be their God, and they shall be My people. And they shall teach no more every man his neighbour, and every man his brother, saying, Know the Lord; for they shall all know Me, from the least of them unto the greatest of them [2]." You see it was their very gift, as Christians, to know the Lord personally, individually, inwardly; and hence the Apostle says in the text, "I *know* whom I have believed, and am persuaded that He is able to keep that which I have committed unto Him against that day."

What is told us in the New Testament is to the same purpose. For instance: consider the very precept of Christ, which binds us together in one body, and observe the reason it gives for doing so. "A new commandment I give unto you, that ye love one another; as I have loved you, that ye also love one another; *by this shall all men know* that ye are My disciples, if ye have love one to another." You see it was to be a sign to the world, not to the Church herself. Still more clearly is this implied in our Lord's intercessory prayer:

[1] John iii. 29.   [2] Isa. liv. 13; lx. 21.   Jer. xxxi. 33. 34.

" As Thou, Father, art in Me, and I in Thee, that they also may be one in Us, that the *world may believe* that Thou hast sent Me." You see, unity was for the sake of the world; He repeats it: "I in them, and Thou in Me, that they may be perfect in one, and *that the world may know* that Thou hast sent Me, and hast loved them, as Thou hast loved Me." The visibility of the Church was rather for her proclaiming the truth, than for her dispensing grace. Again: "Ye are the *light of the world;* a city that is set on a hill cannot be hid. . . . Let your light *so shine before men,* that they may see your good works, and *glorify your Father* which is in heaven." And we see our Saviour's precepts and prayers actually fulfilled in the first days of His Church: "And they continued steadfastly in the Apostles' doctrine and fellowship, and in breaking of bread, and in prayers;" and what was the consequence? "and *fear came upon every soul.*" But let us proceed with the passage: "They continuing daily with one accord in the temple, and breaking bread from house to house, did eat their meat with gladness and singleness of heart, praising God;"—and what followed?—"and *having favour with all the people.*" And again, observe the result of this unanimity: "And the Lord *added to the Church* daily such as should be saved¹."

On the other hand, that there are other and higher gifts for Christians themselves, flowing indeed from the Church, according to a Divine appointment, and her notes, but private notes, conformably with the foregoing

¹ John xiii. 34, 35; xvii. 21. 23. Matt. v. 14. 16. Acts ii. 42, 43. 46, 47.

passages from the Prophets, is told us in many places of
the New Testament. The Prophets had spoken of a
"feast of fat things;" of "wine and milk;" of the
Lord "guiding us continually, and satisfying our soul
in drought, and making our bones fat;" of our "light
rising in obscurity, and our darkness being as the
noon-day [1];" and in accordance, St. John tells us, "Ye
have an unction from the Holy One, and ye know all
things; . . . the anointing which ye have received
of Him abideth in you, and ye need not that any man
teach you." And St. Paul: "Ye were sealed with
that Holy Spirit of promise, which is the earnest of our
inheritance;" and he prays that "Christ may dwell in"
his brethren's "hearts by faith, that they, being rooted
and grounded in love, might be able to comprehend
with all saints what is the breadth, and length, and
depth, and height, and to know the love of Christ,
which passeth knowledge, that they might be filled with
all the fulness of God." And our Lord Himself says,
"To him that overcometh, will I give to eat of the
hidden manna, and will give him a white stone, and in
the stone a new name written, which no man knoweth,
saving he that receiveth it [2]."

It seems plain then, and it is a great source of
comfort at a time like this, when the public notes
of the Church shine so faintly and feebly among us,
to have cause to believe, that her private tokens are
the true portion of Christians; that her private tokens
were meant to guide them; and that if these are vouch-

[1] Isa. xxv. 6; lv. 1; lviii. 10, 11.
[2] 1 John ii. 20. 27.   Eph. i. 13, 14; iii. 17—19.   Rev. ii. 17.

safed to us, they are God's guides to us, and signs of His Presence, and that we need not look out for others.

Nay, further, as I suggested when I began, not only children of the Church, but even those who are seeking and have not found, are often guided to judge from Scripture, by personal and private intimations, and not merely by that manifested glory of His Kingdom which is the symbol of His Presence to the world. Surely much is said in the Old Testament to the point here. Abraham and the Patriarchs, Moses, Gideon, David, Solomon, Jonah, Nehemiah, Esther, and many others, are instances of what I mean, in their respective measures, according to their particular dispensation. They were guided, even in a system of miracles, by other miracles and providences, personal and particular, as is very certain. They were not left, though seekers, to the general evidence, though miraculous. Again, in the New Testament, the wise men are directed by a star; the shepherds, by the Angelic Host; Cornelius, by a vision; Saul, by the visible presence of our Lord: and though the very sight of the Church be such, as by her ordinary and general attributes to draw many out of the world into herself (according to the text already cited, which, after speaking of her excellent order in her first days, adds, "The Lord *added* to the Church daily such as should be saved"), yet even where she converts by her outward notes, you will find that there is a something of a personal nature combined with them when they are addressed to individuals. For instance: St. Paul, speaking of the prophesying or preaching of the Apostolic age, says, "If . . . there come in one that believeth not, or one unlearned, he is convinced of all, he is judged of all ; and *thus are the secrets of his heart made manifest*, and so falling down on his face, he will worship God ; and report that God is in you of a truth." He is converted, you see, by a token addressed to himself personally ; viz. the knowledge bestowed upon the Church of his secret heart. And so, again, the Samaritan woman, after experiencing our Lord's supernatural knowledge, says, "Come see a man which told me all things that ever I did : is not this the Christ?" And Nathanael, when our Lord spoke of his having been under the fig-tree, said, "Rabbi, Thou art the Son of God ; Thou art the King of Israel." And the Apostles : "Now are we sure that Thou knowest all things, and needest not that any man should ask Thee ; by this we believe that Thou camest forth from God [1]." The exercise of His Omniscience was, in these instances, displayed towards themselves.

On the whole, then, I repeat, the distinction surely cannot be questioned, which I have been drawing out. Man needs recovery ; his conscience tells him so : the Sacraments and Ordinances of the Church promise him what he needs ; the great question which arises in his mind is, what guarantee has he that the Church has a right to promise it ? or that what professes to be the Church is the Church ? I answer, that, before he partakes those Sacraments, he will be attracted to the Church by her public notes ; but when he once has tasted the good word, and in proportion as he

[1] 1 Cor. xiv. 24, 25. John iv. 29 ; i. 49 ; xvi. 30.

is partaker of it, that word itself in its inward power, in its power upon himself, will keep him firm in his allegiance to her.

Now it is plain how this doctrine applies to these times, and to us. Alas! I cannot deny that the outward notes of the Church are partly gone from us, and partly going[1]; and a most fearful judgment it is. " Behold . . . the stars of heaven and the constellations thereof shall not give their light; the sun shall be darkened in his going forth, and the moon shall not cause her light to shine." "I will cause the sun to go down at noon, and I will darken the earth in the clear day. And I will turn your feasts into mourning, and all your songs into lamentation." "All the bright lights of heaven will I make dark over them, and set darkness upon thy land, saith the Lord God[2]." This in good measure has fallen upon us. The Church of God is under eclipse among us. Where is our unity, for which Christ prayed? where our charity, which He enjoined? where the faith once delivered, when each has his own doctrine? where our visibility, which was to be a light to the world? where that awful worship, which struck fear into every soul? And what is the consequence? " We grope for the wall like the blind, and we grope as if we had no eyes; we stumble at noonday as

---

[1] An allusion was here intended to the then recent appointment (1841) of an Anglican Bishop at Jerusalem, which has had a most grievous effect in weakening the argument for our Church's Catholicity, and in shaking the belief in it of individuals. May that measure utterly fail and come to nought, and be as though it had never been!

[2] Isa. xiii. 10. Amos viii. 9, 10. Ezek. xxxii. 8.

in the night; we are in desolate places as dead men[1]."
And as the Jews shortly before their own rejection had
two dark tokens—the one, a bitter contempt of the
whole world, and the other, multiplied divisions and
furious quarrels at home—so we English, as if some
abomination of desolation were coming on us also, scorn
almost all Christianity but our own; and yet have, not
one, but a hundred gospels among ourselves, and each of
them with its own hot defenders, till our very note and
symbol is discord, and we wrangle and denounce, and
call it life; but peace we know not, nor faith, nor love.
And this being so, what a temptation is it to those who
read and understand the word of God, who perceive
what it enjoins and promises, and also feel keenly what
we are—what a temptation is it to many such to be
impatient under this visitation! Who indeed is there at
all, who lets himself dwell upon the thought of it, but
must at times be deeply troubled at it? and who can be
startled, not I, if a person here or there, painfully
sensitive of this fearful eclipse of the Sun of Truth, and
hoping, if that be possible, to find something better
elsewhere; and either not having cherished, or neglecting to look for those truer tokens of Christ's presence in
the Church, which are personal to himself, leaves us for
some other communion? Alas! and we, instead of
being led to reflect on our own share in his act, instead
of dwelling on our own sin, are eloquent about his; instead of confessing our own most unchristian divisions,
can but cry out against his dividing from us; instead of
repenting of our own profaneness which has shocked

---

[1] Isa. lix. 10.

him, protest against his superstition; instead of calling
to mind the lying and slandering, the false witness, the
rejoicing in evil, the ungenerousness and unfairness
which abound among us, our low standard of duty and
scanty measures of holiness, our love of the world and
our dislike of the Cross; instead of acknowledging that
our brother has left us because we have left God, that
we have lost him because we have lost our claim to keep
him; we, forsooth, think we "do well to be angry,"
and can but enlarge on his impatience, or obstinacy, or
wilfulness, or infatuation. Or if we are alarmed, as well
as indignant, we dream of foes and traitors among us,
when the foe and the traitor is within us; and we look
any where but there; and we wonder, to be sure, that
we cannot find what it implies so much address to conceal; and we are restless till we have traced the guilt
some whither, to any one but ourselves,—like the
Prophet beating his ass because she saw, what from him
was hidden, the Angel with a drawn sword. "Thou
hypocrite; first cast out the beam out of thine own eye,
and then shalt thou see clearly to cast out the mote out
of thy brother's eye." "Ye blind guides, which strain
at a gnat and swallow a camel!" "Thou satest and
spakest against thy brother, yea, and hast slandered
thine own mother's son." "Thou which teachest
another, teachest thou not thyself? . . . thou that makest
thy boast of the law, through breaking the law dis-
honourest thou God? for the Name of God is blas-
phemed among the Gentiles through you, as it is
written [1]."

[1] Matt. vii. 5; xxiii. 24. Ps. l. 20. Rom. ii. 21. 23, 24.

For me, with these convictions, never will I shrink, through God's help, at fitting times, and in my place, from warning my brethren of that so great sin of the day, their disregard of the grievous judgment under which we lie. If it was promised to the Church that she should be " the pillar and ground of the truth," that her " teachers should not be removed into a corner any more," but that her " ears should hear a voice behind her, saying, This is the way, walk ye in it;" and if, to us in this country, she is not such as this, surely we have forfeited something, surely are under a judgment; and if we are under a judgment, how inexpressibly it must offend Almighty God, that we do not " humble ourselves under His mighty hand " ! This being so, it is a very light thing indeed for one whose eyes are in his measure opened to see it, to find himself opposed for speaking plainly about it; and, even though opposed, it must be more difficult for him to keep silence *than* to speak.

And he speaks with the more freedom, because, as has been said already, the public notes of the Church are not her only tokens, and a failure or deficiency in them here or there, is no argument that the Presence of Christ is away. Such a misfortune must, indeed, ever diminish her external power in the places where it is found, but not her influence at home ; it may stint her growth, and obstruct her propagation; but her present fruit may remain on her, notwithstanding, with a firm hold. For, after all, what really and practically attaches any one to the Church, is not any outward display of magnificence or greatness, but the experience of her benefits upon himself. These private and special evidences of the Divine Presence I may have another opportunity of enlarging upon; meanwhile I will mention a personal consideration of another kind, which, though abstractedly of less influence, yet, under the circumstances in which it comes to us, surely ought to be considered not a slight argument for a Christian's continuing where Providence originally placed him, in spite of the scandals which surround him.

It is this: in various parts of our Church, various persons, who do not know each other, and who gained their religious views in various ways, men and women, have, in consequence of the miserable confusions of the time, been tempted to look out for the True Church elsewhere. They have been tempted to do so; but yet when they proceeded on, and came towards, or upon, or over the border, they have, one by one, though separate from each other, felt as it were a nameless feeling within them, forbidding and stopping them. Now did this take place in the instance of one person only, one might impute it to some accident of his particular condition; he has been imbued with early prejudices; or he has dear ties of friends, relatives, or admirers, to detain him; or he has committed himself to statements which he is ashamed to falsify by his actions; or he shrinks from throwing himself upon strangers and the forlorn dreary life which will be the consequence. Doubtless, there are ten thousand bad motives to hinder our concurrence in the motions of grace; but I think the persons in question, viewed as a whole, have been too honest, too free in mind, too independent and fearless, too distressed and unhappy, too acute and far-seeing, too religious, too enthusiastic, too many, to admit of this account of their common feeling. This feeling has been something singular and distinctive, and of so cogent an influence, that, where individuals *have* left us, the step has commonly been taken in a moment of excitement, or of weakness, or in a time of sickness, or under misapprehension, or with manifest eccentricity of conduct, or in deliberate disobedience to the feeling in question, as if that feeling were a human charm, or spell of earth, which it was a duty to break at all risks, and which, if one man broke, others would break also [1].

---

[1] Such conversions to the Church of Rome as have occurred among us, are, for the most part, subsequent to March, 1841; from which date our Church has, in various ways, and through various of her organs, taken a side, and that the Protestant side, in a number of questions of the day. The authorities who were parties to the condemnation of No. 90 of the "Tracts for the Times," by that interposition, released the author, in his own feelings, of the main weight of a great responsibility; the responsibility, which up to that time attached to him, of inculcating religious views which, however primitive, however necessary for our Church, however sanctioned by her writers, tended, without a strong safeguard, towards the theology of Rome. .Till then, whatever happened amiss in the spread of Catholic doctrine, might be supposed to flow as a direct result from that one cause which alone seemed in operation, the advocacy of patristical theology; and of its advocates the remedy and correction of all irregularities in the direction of Rome might fairly be demanded. But the state of the case was changed, when persons in station interfered with the work, and took the matter into their own hands. In saying this, the author has no wish at all to rid himself of such responsibility as really belongs to him. That in the course of his exposition of Anglican principles, statements or views were evolved which have become a disposing cause of certain tendencies to Rome, now existing, he does not deny; but theological principles and doctrines have little influence on the mind holding them, without the stimulus of external circumstances. Many a man might have held an abstract theory about the Catholic Church to which it was difficult to adjust our own, might have admitted a suspicion, or even painful doubts

It may be added, that this attachment to our own communion is almost peculiar to ourselves among the religious professions of this age and country. Men of other communions seem not to possess this secret instinct, attaching them to the body to which they belong; but they can change about from sect to sect, or form new ones, without any scruple or misgiving. The feeling in question is ours, not theirs; and therefore is the more deserving of deference, as something definite, real, and special. And let it be borne in mind, that even if an individual who is tempted to leave us has no experience of the feeling himself, yet the mere fact that others around us bear witness to it, should weigh with himself, and he should guide himself, at least for a while, by the direction thus given to his brethren.

Let us beware of turning a deaf ear to what may prove to be a Divine token; let us not do despite to a Divine privilege. Angels are our guardians; Angels surely stand in our way, in mercy, not in wrath; Angels warn us back. Let us obey the warning. When St. Peter was fleeing from Rome, shortly before his martyrdom, Jesus Christ met him at the gate, as if entering the city; and the Apostle understood that he was to return. When

---

about the latter, yet never have been impelled onwards, had our rulers preserved the quiescence of former years; but it is the corroboration of a present, living, and energetic heterodoxy, which realizes and makes them practical; it has been the recent speeches and acts of authorities, who had so long been tolerant of Protestant error, which have given to inquiry and to theory its force and its edge. Such toleration of Catholic doctrine may have been impossible or wrong; that is another question, with which private persons have no right to interfere; still it may be a fact, that the want of it has been the cause of recent secessions.

the Christians were to flee from Jerusalem, Angels went first, crying one to another, "Let us depart hence." Let us fear to go before, or to fall behind, the pillar of the cloud in the wilderness, the Presence of "God and the Lord Jesus Christ, and the elect Angels."

SERMON XXIII.

Grounds for Steadfastness in our Religious Profession.

"Now we believe, not because of thy saying; for we have heard Him ourselves, and know that this is indeed the Christ, the Saviour of the world."—JOHN iv. 42.

RELIGIOUS persons are sometimes taunted with having only what is called an hereditary religion; with believing what they believe, and practising what they practise, because they have been taught so to do, without any reasons of their own. Now it may very possibly happen that they have no reasons to *produce*, that they do not *know* their own reasons, that they have never analyzed what passes through their minds, and causes their impressions and convictions; but that is no proof that they have no reasons; and in truth they have always, whether they recognize them or not, very good reasons. It does not make a man more religious that he knows *why* and *how* he became so; many a man, doubtless, was converted by the Apostles' miracles, who could not draw out accurately into words the process through which his thoughts went, and who, had he

tried so to do, would have done himself injustice, and
exposed himself to the criticism of the practised dis-
putant. And so, again, in this day, when our disci-
pleship is confessedly, in the first instance, the act of
others not our own (for we were baptized and taught in
our first years without ourselves having a will in the
matter) ; though in this sense our religion may be
called hereditary, yet, for all that, it may be much more
than hereditary, when we have lived long enough to
have made trial of it, and that, although we have not
the skill to bring out into words the details and the
result of that trial, or to show in a clear logical form
that we have this or that good reason for believing.

I am speaking of religious men ; for doubtless it is
true of others, that good grounds they have none for
their religious profession ; they may, indeed, have got
together some reasons from books, and may make a
show with them ; but they have none of their own.
And if they produce ever so many, still, I repeat, it is
because they have been taught them. They have been
taught the truths, and taught the reasons ; but the
reasons are their own as little as the truths ; the
reasons are hereditary or traditionary as well as the
truths : they have no root in themselves ; they have
nothing within them connecting the reasons with, and
grafting them upon, the divine doctrines. And be they
ever so intellectual and acute, ever so able to investigate,
and argue, and reflect upon themselves, this will avail
them nothing. What avails the form of searching,
when there is nothing to find ? What avail scientific
forms, when we have no subject matter to work upon ?

But so it is, from the circumstance that these sensual, gross-hearted, indevout, or insincere persons are often men of education and ability, they show to advantage in the world, talk loudly and largely, are powerful controversialists, are considered bulwarks of the truth, and cast into the shade humble and religious men, who have not their gifts. But he who has the truth within him, though he cannot evolve it out of his heart in shape and proportions for another's inspection, is blessed beyond all comparison above him, who has much to say, and says what is true, but says it not from himself, but by rote, and could say quite as well just the reverse, did it so happen that he mistook it for truth. His, indeed, is in the worst sense mere hereditary religion, though he will commonly think himself of all men the least in danger of it; and will be among the foremost to impute it to religious men instead, who feel what they cannot express.

Surely, as the only true religion is that which is seated within us, a matter, not of words, but of things, so the only satisfactory test of religion is something within us. If religion be a personal matter, its reasons also should be personal. Wherever it is present, in the world or in the heart, it produces an effect, and that effect is its evidence. When we view it as set up in the world, it has its external proofs, when as set up in our hearts, it has its internal; and that, whether we are able to elicit them ourselves, and put them into shape, or not. Nay, with some little limitation and explanation, it might be said, that the very fact of a religion taking root within us, is a proof, so far, that it is true. If it

were not true, it would not take root. Religious men
have, in their own religiousness, an evidence of the
truth of their religion. That religion is true which has
power, and so far as it has power; nothing but what is
divine can renew the heart. And this is the secret
reason *why* religious men believe, whether they are ade-
quately conscious of it or no, whether they can put it
into words or no; viz. their past experience that the
doctrine which they hold is a reality in their minds, not
a mere opinion, and has come to them, "not in word,
but in power." And in this sense the presence of
religion in us is its own evidence. I am not at all
denying the use of either of those arguments for religion
which are external to us, or of the practice of drawing
out our reasons into form; but still so it is, we go by
external reasons, before we have, or so far as we have
not, inward ones; and we rest upon our logical proofs
only when we get perplexed with objections, or are in
doubt, or otherwise troubled in mind; or, again, we
betake ourselves to the external evidence, or to argu-
mentative processes, not as a matter of personal interest,
but from a desire to gaze upon God's great work more
intently, and to adore God's wisdom more worthily.

This, surely, is what may be called the common-sense
view of the subject. We wander from one form of religion to another, when we have not found its power; if
we have found it, then we not only remain where we
are, but we are shocked at the very notion of a change;
and in proportion as we have found, are we contented
and zealous adherents of our present position. I do not
say that all who wander are seeking, nor that all who

are contented with their state, have found; nor, again,
that all who, in their degree, have found, remain contented; else there were no such sin as unthankfulness.
Nor do I mean that all who fail to find are justified in
wandering, as if waiting were not necessary, or as if
youth, or the consciousness of faults on our part, would
not account for our having as yet received so little
personal benefit from our religion. Nor, after all, do I
mean to imply that no conceivable circumstances can
arise when this rule is allowably broken: unless a voice
from without may, in certain cases, supersede the feeling from within, Nathanael would not have been converted, nor Apollos. But still it holds good, that a
man's real reason for attachment to his own religious
communion, why he believes it to be true, why he is
eager in its defence, why he feels indignant at being
invited to abandon it, is not any series of historical or
philosophical arguments, not any thing merely beautiful in its system, or supernatural, but what it has
done for him and others; his confidence in it as a means
by which men may be brought nearer to God, and may
become better and happier. Would you know why holy
men believe even in an age of miracles? Hear St. Poly-
carp's words, when the heathen magistrate urged him
to blaspheme Christ: "Eighty and six years," said he,
"have I served Him, and *He hath never wronged me;*
and how can I blaspheme my King, who hath saved
me?" Or, as St. Paul said, "I know whom I have
believed." It is these inward effects (I speak of the
matter of fact), according to the degree in which they
are realized, which guarantee to a man the divinity of

his form of religion, which make him willing to risk his salvation upon it; as is expressed, in another form, by the Samaritans in the text, when they say to their countrywoman, " Now we believe, not because of thy saying, for we have heard Him ourselves, and know that this is indeed the Christ, the Saviour of the world."

You will observe, that neither the blessed Martyr, who had served Christ so long, nor the ignorant Samaritans, who were beginning to acknowledge Him, stated *what* their reasons were, though they had reasons. And, in truth, it is very difficult to draw out our reasons for our religious convictions, and that on many accounts. It is very painful to a man of devout mind to do so; for it implies, or even involves a steadfast and almost curious gaze at God's wonder-working presence within and over him, from which he shrinks, as savouring of a high-minded and critical temper. And much more is it painful, not to say impossible, to put these reasons forth in explicit statements, because they are so very personal and private. Yet, as in order to the relief of his own perplexity, a religious man may at times try to ascertain them, so again for the service of others he will try, as best he may, to state them.

If then we are asked for " a reason of the hope that is in us," why we are content, or rather thankful, to be in that Church in which God's Providence has placed us, would not the reasons be some or other of these, or rather all of them, and a number of others besides, which these may suggest, deeper than they?

1. I suppose a religious man is conscious that God

has been with him, and given him whatever he has of good within him. He knows quite enough of himself to know how fallen he is from original righteousness, and he has a conviction, which nothing can shake, that without the aid of his Lord and Saviour, he can do nothing aright. I do not say he need recollect any definite season when he turned to God and gave up the service of sin and Satan; but in one sense every season, every year is such a time of turning. I mean, he ever has experience, just as if he had hitherto been living to the world, of a continual conversion; he is ever taking advantage of holy seasons and new providences, and beginning again. The elements of sin are still alive within him; they still tempt and influence him, and threaten when they do no more; and it is only by a continual fight against them that he prevails; and what shall persuade him that his power to fight is his own, and not from above? And this conviction of a Divine Presence with him is stronger according to the length of time during which he has served God, and to his advance in holiness. The multitude of men—nay, a great number of those who think themselves religious—do not aim at holiness, and do not advance in holiness; but consider what a great evidence it is that God is with us, so far as we have it. Religious men, really such, cannot but recollect in the course of years, that they have become very different from what they were. I say "in the course of years:" this it is, among other things, which makes young persons less settled in their religion. They have not given it a trial; they have not had time to do so; but in the course of years a religious person finds that a mysterious unseen influence has been upon him and has changed him. He is indeed very different from what he was. His tastes, his views, his judgments are different. You will say that time changes a man as a matter of course; advancing age, outward circumstances, trials, experience of life. It is true; and yet I think a religious man would feel it little less than sacrilege, and almost blasphemy, to impute the improvement in his heart and conduct, in his moral being, with which he has been favoured in a certain sufficient period, to outward or merely natural causes. He will be unable to force himself to do so: that is to say, he has a conviction, which it is a point of religion with him not to doubt, which it is a sin to deny, that God has been with him. And this is of course a ground of hope to him that God will be with him still; and if he, at any time, fall into religious perplexity, it may serve to comfort him to think of it.

2. And I suppose that every religious person is conscious of this, that he never has so profited by God's grace as he might have done; that he has never fathomed God's mercies towards him; that God is present with him to an extent, with a fulness, in a depth, which he knows not; that, whatever other reasons there may be for his parting company with us, at least he need not go elsewhere for more grace, for the power to be better than he is. When he has exhausted what is offered him here, then will be the time for looking about him and providing for his necessity: but as yet he has sufficient for his day.

3. Again, every religious man may be expected to

have experience more or less of wonderful providences,
which he cannot speak about to others, but which make
it certain to him that, in spite of his own unworthiness,
God is with him. We are told in Scripture to " cast all
our care upon Him, for He careth for us ;" to " ask and
we shall receive [1] ;" and surely what Jacob felt and said,
will in its degree—nay, rather more abundantly—be
fulfilled in our case. " I am not worthy of the least of
all the mercies, and of all the truth which Thou hast
showed unto Thy servant." " God, before whom my
fathers Abraham and Isaac did walk, the God which fed
me all my life long unto this day, the Angel which
redeemed me from all evil [2]." Is it not, I may say,
most touching and affecting to read in patriarchal
history things which are fulfilled in us at this latter
time?—but He is the Lord, He changes not. You
may see what He is to us, by what Jacob tells us He
was to him. Scripture gives certain specimens or
criteria, what it is to have God with us, to be guided by
God, as in the history of Jacob or of David. Now
consider Jacob's life and confessions, or consider David's
overflowings of heart in the Psalms—are they not in
our measure ours also? is there not a sympathy of
heart, is there not a concordant testimony as to God's
providences in the ancient Saints and in ourselves?
Well, then, are we not therefore in their case? do not
we stand with them ? have not *we* the God of Jacob for
our help, and is not David's Lord and David's hope ours
also? We are under just the sort of guidance they

[1] 1 Pet. v. 7. Matt. vii. 7, 8.
[2] Gen. xxxii. 10; xlviii. 15, 16.

were under : why should we break away from it? It
has wrought upon us in and through that form of
religion, those doctrines, those Ordinances, those Sacraments, those teachers, under which we find ourselves;
what want we more?

4. It is impossible to speak, without the risk of
misconception, on the subject of answers to prayer;
I mean, this is just one of those sacred matters upon
which one man deceives himself, and another does not.
A man will tell you, as an excuse for his following the
wildest and most pernicious errors, that he has con-
sulted God, that God has answered him, and that he is
obeying God. What can you say in reply? Nothing.
You think, and think rightly, that the man is deceiving
himself; but you cannot show to his own satisfaction,
or that of others, that he has not as much right as
another to believe that God has revealed to him His
will. Yet, because some men are presumptuous and
mistaken in this most sacred subject, this does not show
that another may not judge rightly. In dreams, in
delirium, in madness, men think they see and hear what
they do not; yet, for all that, do not men, awake and
in their senses, see and hear? And, in like manner,
religious men are right in thinking their prayers
answered, and half-religious men are wrong; and the
real answers which religious men receive are an evidence
to them, whereas the apparent answers made to half-
religious men are no evidence; because in the case of
religious men such tokens are in addition to those other
tokens arising from their habitual obedience and subjection to Christ, but in enthusiasts they are the very

foundation of their faith, which conscience, sense of duty, love of truth, and the Divine Law, ought to be. But let us turn from such as make much of the lesser and secondary tokens of God's favour to the disparagement of the greater, to those who are possessed of the greater and lesser also, who strive to please God in their hearts and lives, and are in many ways rewarded. We are told, that " the effectual fervent prayer of a righteous man availeth much;" now, of course, the more fully he realizes that God is thus mercifully dealing with him, the less he will like to speak about it; and this is one reason why the pretenders whom one meets in the world have not the real insight into the course of Providence which they think they have, viz. because they talk of it so freely. Were the privileges of which they boast what they think they are, they would not speak of them. Religious men, on the contrary, are very reserved, if only that they dare not betray, if we may so speak, God's confidence. This circumstance, however, makes it the more difficult to speak on the subject without unreality; still I suppose it is true that religious men have their prayers answered in a wonderful way, and with sufficient distinctness to be, in addition to other evidences, a ground of confidence to them that God is with them.

5. I might go on to mention a still more solemn subject, viz. the experience which, at least, certain religious persons have, of the awful sacredness of our Sacraments and other Ordinances. If these are attended by the Presence of Christ, surely we have all that a Church can have in the way of privilege and blessing. The

promise runs, "Lo I am with you alway, even unto the end of the world." That is a Church where Christ is present; this is the very definition of the Church. The question sometimes asked is, whether our services, our holy seasons, our rites, our Sacraments, our institutions, really have with them the Presence of Him who thus promised? If so, we are part of the Church; if not, then we are but performers in a sort of scene or pageant, which may be religiously intended, and which God in His mercy may visit, but if He visits, will in visiting go beyond His own promise. But observe, as if to answer to the challenge, and put herself on trial, and to give us a test of her Catholicity, our Church boldly declares of her most solemn ordinance, that he who profanes it, incurs the danger of judgment. She seems, like Moses, or the Prophet from Judah, or Elijah, to put her claim to issue, not so openly, yet as really, upon the fulfilment of a certain specified sign. Now she does not speak to scare away the timid, but to startle and subdue the unbelieving, and withal to assure the wavering and perplexed; and I conceive that in such measure as God wills, and as is known to God, these effects follow. I mean, that we really have proofs among us, though, for the most part, they will be private and personal, from the nature of the case, of clear punishment coming upon profanations of the holy ordinance in question; sometimes very fearful instances, and such as serve, while they awe beholders, to comfort them;—to comfort them, for it is plain, if God be with us for judgment, surely He is with us for mercy also: if He punishes, why is it but for profanation? and how can there be profanation, if there is nothing to be profaned? Surely, He does not manifest His wrath, but where He has first vouchsafed His grace.

6. And, further, much might be said, were not a suggestion sufficient, of the manifestation of Christ which often attends on death-beds for the benefit of survivors. Consider whether, under certain circumstances, an evidence is not thereby given to the reality of our religious principles, and the divine origin of our Church, as great as any note or token of any kind which can be given. What is any note of the Church, but an indication that Christ is invisibly within it? It cannot prove *more* than this; a hundred notes cannot prove more. If so much as this is proved, it is enough, and there are single tokens which, by themselves, suffice to prove it; and such, surely, to those who witness them, are many of the scenes which take place on death-beds. May not we reverently hope, that Almighty God does sometimes vouchsafe to show bystanders then, that our Church, in spite of its manifold disorders, is a safe Church to die in?

7. And, lastly, I might say much on what is a more ordinary evidence, yet perhaps as cogent,—the evidences of sanctity in the living, which we are from time to time vouchsafed. Surely that is a Church visited by the influences of Divine grace, which contains in her pale men so saintly in their lives, so heavenly in their hearts and minds, so self-denying, so obedient, as are vouchsafed to her even in this degenerate time. Is it not safe to trust our souls in their company? is it not

dangerous to part company with them in our journey across the trackless wilderness?

On such subjects as I have been led to treat, whatever be the words made use of, they will be sure not precisely to touch and satisfy the feelings of others, nor even to be adequate to one's own meaning; they must, after all, be poor and unreal. Yet the great use of language is, not to represent, but to suggest and convey thought; and we must bear to use words which we feel to be deficient, if they serve to rouse the mind, and to begin trains of reflection which they do not end. I think there is a truth in such considerations as I have been urging, which will be acknowledged by the serious and thoughtful, though it may be cavilled at and denied by others.

And should any one consider, that the very raising the question of the Catholicity of our Church, entertaining objections to it, and replying to them, is a great irreverence towards her, and inconsiderate and cruel towards hearers who are thus introduced to them, I would have him reflect that his objection strikes very deeply, considering how very frequent have been defences, in Sermons and other religious works, of Revelation altogether. I am not defending the tone of divinity prevalent among us during a century and a half past; but such persons at least as justify the writers of that period, in admitting the possibility of the Gospel being false, on the ground that they were but solving, not raising, a difficulty, cannot blame others who, in a similar necessity, do that towards their Church which these authors have ventured towards their Lord.

And now, in conclusion, I shall take notice of one or two objections to which the foregoing representation may give rise. It may be said, first, to proceed upon an unsound method of reasoning; and next, to be no protection after all to the sacred interests which it professes to advocate.

1. On the one hand, it may be urged that it is very dangerous to guide ourselves by our feelings in religious inquiries, and very unwarrantable to judge of creeds by their effects. If we seek to determine what truth is, what falsehood, by evidence taken from the course of things, then evidence on both sides of the question must be taken into account. Almighty God, it may be said, often seems to be fighting against a man, and to be driving him away from the religion he at present professes, as the Angel resisted Balaam. Providences befall him which he is justified in interpreting as a suggestion to seek God elsewhere; and thus the search after religious truth is made a matter of mere feeling, or imagination. I reply, that I have said nothing to sanction such a proceeding. I have said nothing to lead men to consult the fluctuations of their minds in the passing hour, for information concerning God's will. We all are depressed at one time, and encouraged and revived at another; we have our times of gloom, of disquiet, of doubt, of impatience, of disgust. And further, if we have but lately turned to God at all, we have no real experience whatever of God's dealings with us to which we can appeal; and if we attempt to judge by such personal evidences, we are guided as a matter of necessity by the feeling of the moment. It is also

certain that we are apt to magnify present evils; and
we may easily be led to fancy that any communion, or,
at least, that some communions are more in the light
of day than our own, with less of dimness and of scandal.
And of course we may act according to such feelings
while we are under them, and may consider such a
procedure as an acting from what is within us, not
without us.

All this we certainly may do, but without any sanction
from the doctrine which I have been laying down.   The
simple question is, whether such temporary frames of
mind can be proved to come from God.   Now we cannot
be sure of the divine origin of any suggestion which
comes to us for the first time.   He indeed is always like
Himself, and is Himself, whether He comes once or
many times; but to our limited faculties, the Tempter
is able to represent Christ so closely at first sight, that
Christ alone can enable us to detect the difference; and
He generally grants the knowledge by careful waiting
on Him and examination, not at once.   Now when we
look back on the course of our whole lives, we secure
two advantages : first, the absence of present excitement,
and next, a sufficient extent of time to make our remarks
upon.   And, moreover, what we must look for is proof
of improvement in our heart and life, and not mere
comfort or transport.   And, again, we should look for
plain external facts, however private and secret, not for
mere emotions, to determine whether or not God is
with us.   Now all these conditions being observed, the
inquirer being a consistent Christian, and that for years,
and the motions and works of holiness being taken as

the sign of Christ's presence, and calmness and sobriety
having their due place in his inquiry, I really do not
think that, however he might determine, we could justly
find fault with the process, or throw the blame of his
error, if he made one, upon it; nor, again, that it would
often happen that a son of our Church would not find
evidence that Christ is with us still, in spite of our
many sins and great corruptions.

And let no one say, that to judge of the religious
communion in which we find ourselves, by its fruits, is
worldly-wise and unbelieving. To judge of *doctrines*
indeed in this way, is presumptuous, because these are
divine revelations, and are commonly mysteries, and are
to be received on faith, whatever comes of them. But
it is otherwise with religious bodies; they are to be
tested and judged of by their visible effects,—our Lord
saying expressly of the false prophets, "Ye shall *know*
them *by their fruits;*" and St. Paul, "There must be
also heresies among you, that they which are approved
may be made manifest among you;" and St. John,
"They went out, that they might be *made manifest* that
they were not all of us;" and Gamaliel, "If this counsel
or this work be of men, it will *come to nought;*" and
the Psalmist, "I went by, and lo, *he was gone;*" and
the Prophet, "Let all the nations be gathered together,
and let the people be assembled; . . . let them bring
forth their witnesses that they may be justified, or let
them hear and say, It is truth. *Ye are My witnesses,*
saith the Lord, and My servant whom I have chosen;"
and again, "Produce your cause, saith the Lord; bring
forth your strong reasons, saith the King of Jacob. Let

them bring them forth, and show us what shall happen,
. . . that we may know that ye are gods; yea, *do good
or do evil*, that we may be dismayed, and behold it
together¹." And if the outward notes of the Church
are thus matter for our judgment, surely its inward power
may be religiously inquired into also.

2. But now, in the next place, it may perhaps be
asked, whether there never was an instance when it
was a person's duty to leave the communion in which
he finds himself; and if so, whether what I have been
saying about private tokens of grace would not apply
to his case as well as ours. If it serves to keep religious
persons in the Church, it will equally well serve to keep
religious persons in dissent. Abraham, it may be urged,
was doubtless under God's Providence, even in Chaldea,
yet he had to quit his country; and the Jews were
under God's Providence, yet they were commanded to
quit the Law for the Gospel. Nor can we doubt that
the merciful Hand of God has before now dealt with
man in those far-spreading communions, though heretical, which have so long existed in the East; yet it is a
duty to leave them for the One True Church. And as
little can we doubt that the secret influence of Christ
operates at this day in the large dissenting bodies which
exist here and in another continent; and yet we think
it right to invite their members to Catholic communion,
though they surely might in like manner appeal to their
experience of God's Providences, and turn a deaf ear to
our call.

¹ Matt. vii. 16. 1 Cor. xi. 19. 1 John ii. 19. Acts v. 38. Ps.
xxxvii. 37. Isa. xliii. 9, 10; xli. 21—23.

I answer, that there seem to be two reasons which may lead a man to leave the communion in which he was born: first, some clear indisputable command of God to leave it, and secondly, some plain experience that God does not acknowledge it. The Ethiopian eunuch *came* to Jerusalem to *seek* Him; and the Christians *left* Jerusalem to *obey* Him. If Almighty God moves away from us, or if we are away from God, in either case we must go forward at all risks, and " forget our own people and our father's house." But consider what great signs have generally been attendant upon the calls of God. What prophecies, what miracles, what portents, what judgments were displayed to convince the Jews that Judaism was at an end! Consider what plain tokens of God's wrath rested on those ancient heresies which I have spoken of, especially the perishable nature of certain of them; how they began from the first swiftly to " draw to an end, and had no sign of virtue to show," so that they left the world almost before men had time to leave them, or at least to leave them was but to be beforehand with them. And as to heathen religions, consider what plain contrariety to the first laws of all true faith and morality is involved in many of their first principles; how they sin against sincerity, purity, and mercy. Here then are abundant indications afforded to the thoughtful and honest inquirer, who is born in such religious body as is in question, that the Divine Presence does not go with it, as a body.

And then, as to the various forms of religion of this day, let this be considered, that we call their members to join us indeed, but we do not call them really to *quit* any thing, for in truth they have nothing to quit; they profess they have nothing to quit. The Jews had a Church; even heretics and schismatics profess to have Churches, and often are possessed of a succession from the Apostles; but the religious sects around us profess to be nothing more than mere voluntary assemblies of men, each complete in himself, each a Church to himself, bound together by no Divine bond, but merely at their own will. Whatever might have been professed in their origin, such is the belief of their members now: so far from believing that Christ's Presence is with their own communion as such, they consider this ascription of grace to a corporate body, this belief that ordination is a Divine act and by an Apostolical succession, this doctrine of a priesthood under the Gospel—for all these are but aspects of one and the same great truth—alas! they consider it the beginning of all error and evil in religion, and make it accordingly a first principle, the principle of their own religious existence, the essence of their faith, to deny it. Accordingly, they take no religious account whatever of the bodies to which they happen to belong, nor of the rites and ordinances which they use, except as a matter of order, more commonly of taste and liking. They are, it is most certain, indifferent to their particular communion, as a communion; eager to exalt themselves above it; sensitive of the appearance of subjection to it; proud of insubordination; jealous of forms and ordinances; destitute of any definite creed; willing to fraternize with any who will but profess a like disbelief of the doctrine of a Church; ready to change, because it is really no change, whenever it

occurs to them, and is open to them; nay, familiar in
many cases to the use of two or three religious communions at once. Surely they may be called upon to
change to the Church, who by their very principle may
change about to any thing else; surely they have not
found, who profess to be ever seeking; surely they may
be taught something new, who have nothing old, or
rather, nothing to lose at all; surely they may be made
loyal to the Church, who are not the willing servants,
or the loyal subjects, or the dear children of any other
sovereign and parent. This is the great distinction
between our Church and all these bodies round about
her. A great multitude of our people, to say the least,
feel and know that the Church in herself, and considered
as a Church, is a great blessing. They are convinced
that Christ is in her; that she is here that favoured
spiritual body which is present in many places, one
and the same all over the earth, perfect and entire here
and there and every where, as if she were nowhere else,
and called in Scripture, "the Bride, the Lamb's wife."
They do not merely dislike other forms of worship, but
they love and revere hers. They are witnesses to themselves—yes, and to each other—that Christ is in them of
a truth. But it is seldom indeed that a member of a
seceding body is zealous for that body; he is zealous
for what he considers the Gospel, that is, at the utmost
for what he would call a doctrine,—though that means,
if we may so speak, *his own particular* doctrine, which
is, properly speaking, no *doctrine* at all, in any accurate
sense of the word, but an opinion, his own private
opinion; he is zealous for what he thinks to be the

message which Christ brought from heaven, whatever
it be, and that, whether any other person in the whole
world agrees with him or not, not for that communion
external to himself, to which he happens to belong. He
has not found Christ *in* that communion. He confesses
that, in his judgment, religion is but a solitary matter;
he thinks he has found the truth, but not in his sect or
party, but in himself merely; so as to be lodged in
himself, and to go with him wherever he goes, whether
he stays in it or leaves it. In calling him away then
from his particular communion into our own Church, I
am calling on him to violate no principle of obedience,
no sentiment of reverence or loyalty, for he has none;
I am but using his private judgment in behalf of the
Church, as he has hitherto used it in opposition to it.
In leaving his present sect, he does injury to no dutiful
feeling; in leaving it he is leaving nothing valuable;
he was of value to it, not it to him. I am calling him
to a great idea which it never before entered into his
mind to conceive, to a something over and above what
he has at present; to what is distinct, for what is vague
and confused, to what is real and living, for what is
nominal,—to a visible body with invisible privileges,—
to God dwelling in very deed upon earth, the King of
Saints upon the holy hill of Zion, Him who inhabiteth
eternity abiding invisibly, not in buildings made with
hands, but in a chosen company, which He both formed
at the first and has continued ever since. This awful
and great sight is a new thing to the inquirer in
question; he did not know there was such a one any
where; we invite him to turn aside and see: but we

turn him merely from the wilderness which lies around him, from nothing else. We are not unsettling his mind, we find it unsettled; we are not showing disrespect to his present communion, it has never been reverenced even by himself; his personal religious experience was not built upon and united to its rules and ordinances; ours is united to those of our Church. They who call us to quit our Church, must first refute our long experience of her benefits; but he has had no such experience of benefits at all. We have personal tokens, not only that we are in grace, but that this great blessing is given through our sacraments; he not only does not profess the like, but protests against such a profession. In resting then our allegiance to our Church on her private and secret notes, not on her public ones, I am giving no advantage to disputers and heretics of this day in their warfare against her.

However, so much I will grant, and will not grudge it,—that if there be persons born in dissent, and filially attached to their own communion, and "fearing God and working righteousness in it," in them, we may humbly trust, is fulfilled St. Peter's saying, that "in every nation," such men are "accepted with Him." I am far indeed from wishing rudely to disengage such persons from the sect in which they find themselves, if they are zealous for it, little as I may think it part of the true Church. We must not do evil that good may come; sudden changes are in themselves an evil, though they are unavoidable when the truth is preached to many at once, and in the conflict of the Church and the world. St. Paul's conversion, it is true, was sudden;

but then it was miraculous also: yet no one would call miracles the ordinary or the appointed means of Divine teaching. Such persons then as I am speaking of, I would humbly leave in God's hands, to work His blessed will in them; whether to lead them forward through their present creed into a purer one, or, if such be His inscrutable pleasure, to save them, though not through it, yet in it, by a mercy overflowing the bounds of His revealed covenant [1].

That time will never come in this world, when the strife of tongues and the alienation of hearts shall cease; but let us at least beseech the Prince of Peace, that times of refreshing may come from the presence of the Lord; that He would vouchsafe to hide us for a little moment under the shadow of His wings, until this tyranny be overpast, in anticipation of that blessed time when "they shall not hurt nor destroy in all His holy mountain, for the earth shall be full of the knowledge of the Lord, as the waters cover the sea [2]."

[1] Nothing that is here said about uncovenanted mercies must be taken to imply that individuals ought to be satisfied in remaining external to the Catholic Church, when they are once *convinced* of the fact; but mere impressions, impulses, fancies, frames of mind, logical deductions, or the blindness which follows on religious carelessness, may easily be mistaken for convictions. It is a duty, then, to doubt about what appear to be such—nay, to resist them, and often for a very long time; and under this painful and weary trial, though not under other circumstances, surely the mind may religiously dwell on the thought of God's extraordinary dispensations of grace, as a relief of its apprehensions.

[2] Isa. xi. 9.

𝔈lijah the 𝔓rophet of the 𝔏atter 𝔇ays.

" And, behold, the Lord passed by, and a great and strong wind rent the mountains, and brake in pieces the rocks before the Lord ; but the Lord was not in the wind : and after the wind an earthquake ; but the Lord was not in the earthquake : and after the earthquake a fire ; but the Lord was not in the fire : and after the fire, a still small voice."—I KINGS xix. 11, 12.

ST. JAMES reminds to " take the Prophets, who have spoken in the name of the Lord, for an example of suffering affliction and of patience." And he presently adds, " Elias was a man subject to like passions as we are ; and he prayed earnestly that it might not rain, and it rained not on the earth by the space of three years and six months. And he prayed again, and the heaven gave rain, and the earth brought forth her fruit[1]."

Elijah was the foremost, and in one sense the beginning of the Prophets ; and, whereas he is so prominent in the Old Testament, he is not less prominent in the New ; for he has come to the Church, as if over again, in the person of St. John the Baptist, of whom it was

[1] James v. 10. 17. 18.

prophesied before his birth, that he should go before our Lord, "in the spirit and power of Elias," to "turn the heart of the fathers to the children, and the heart of the children to their fathers;" and whom we twice commemorate in the course of the year;—at one time praying that "after his example we may constantly speak the truth, boldly rebuke vice, and patiently suffer for the truth's sake;" at the other, that, as he was sent as a messenger, to prepare Christ's way, so the ministers and stewards of His mysteries may so turn "the hearts of the disobedient to the wisdom of the just, that at His second coming we may be found an acceptable people in His sight."

As then St. John is a great saint in the Christian Church, and though not united to her communion in this world, and but a "friend of the Bridegroom," took his rank in it upon his martyrdom; so may we say that, with St. John, Elias also, at least "in spirit and power," and as a pattern, is received into her catalogue of saints, and becomes one of her "burning and shining lights." Nay, if it be true, as has very generally been thought, that the prophecy about his coming was not exhausted in the Baptist, but that Elijah is still to come in his own person at the end of the world, then more awfully still, and in a special manner above all other of the ancient saints, is Elijah connected with the Church of Christ, though the fire from heaven and the slaughter of the idolaters belong exclusively to the Elder Covenant. "Behold, I will send you Elijah the Prophet, before the coming of the great and dreadful day of the Lord;" and whereas, in one sense, all days resemble that last day, whereas Christ is ever coming, the love of many ever failing, and iniquity ever abounding (because there is ever distress of nations with perplexity, and rumours of Christ in the desert and in the secret chambers, "Lo here! and Lo there!"), in this respect Elias is ever entering upon his mission, and in his power and spirit the ministers of Christ must ever labour. And in truth he has not been forgotten, nor his Carmel, as the history of the Christian Church bears witness.

Let us then, in this disordered, dreary time, when the heaven above us is so dark, and its stars so hidden—let us, as shepherds keeping watch over their flock by night, and soon to be visited by their Lord, consider whether the history of Elijah will not supply us with as clear and satisfactory rules how we ought to "walk in these dangerous days," as might have been anticipated from the place which the Prophet holds in the Christian Church. And if so it be, as we trust it is, that among us the truths of religion are not so fearfully depraved as they were in the kingdom of Ahab, then this consideration will, as we shall find, make the argument only so much the stronger which is deducible from it, and the pattern which Elijah sets us only the more binding.

Now I need hardly say what great Prophets were Elijah and those that followed him,—such as Elisha, Micaiah, and the sons of the Prophets; especially Elisha; so much so, that their miracles almost anticipate our Lord's, as a sort of harbinger and first-fruits of His mighty works, and a type of His doctrines. Was there not some great grace shed in those schools, in which the

loaves were multiplied, the oil failed not, fire came down
from heaven, lepers were cleansed, the dead were raised,
and one was taken up into heaven without death, and
another, after death, by the very contact of his bones,
restored life to the dead? Was there not great grace
there, where future events were predicted and the secrets
of the heart read from afar? Was there not grace there
almost of the Gospel, where we find the Gentiles visited,
Sacraments shadowed forth, and the resurrection and
immortality of the flesh begun? Whatever be meant
by "the spirit and power of Elias," though the gift of
physical miracles be not included in it, as the Baptist's
history leads us to think, yet it cannot but be something
great; it must at least have a secret inward greatness, if
its outward manifestations at the first were so extraordinary.

Now there is this remarkable fact concerning Elijah
and his brethren, that he, who on the Mount of Trans-
figuration spake with Moses about their common Lord's
passion, was not in communion with the Church of
Moses in his lifetime, did not worship at the Temple,
was cut off from them with whom was "the adoption,
and the glory, and the covenants, and the giving of the
Law, and the service of God, and the promises; whose
were the fathers, and of whom as concerning the flesh
Christ came, who is over all, God blessed for ever[1]."
A most remarkable fact certainly, which, while it gives
us great comfort, as regards those religious bodies at
this day who are deprived of the ordinary channels of
grace, is not without its element of encouragement even

[1] Rom. ix. 4, 5.

for us, who, though not without the Apostolical line and
the possession of the Sacraments, are separated from the
great body of the Church. Now let us dwell on this
fact.

It is indeed a most remarkable and gracious providence, that these great Prophets, Elijah and the rest,
should have been vouchsafed to revolted Israel; nay,
and that they themselves, as their history shows, should
have made no effort to set right what had gone so
wrong; nay, should not even themselves have paid that
honour to the Mosaic worship which had been enjoined
upon all the descendants of Israel. You will say that
they wrought miracles; doubtless; but that beforehand
was a reason rather why they should have enforced a
still stricter obedience to the Law, not a reason for their
being silent about it. Hear what Moses had said to
them : "When ye go over Jordan, and dwell in the land
which the Lord your God giveth you to inherit, and
when He giveth you rest from all your enemies round
about, so that ye dwell in safety; then there shall be
a place which *the Lord your God shall choose* to cause
His Name to dwell there. Thither shall ye bring all
that I command you; your burnt offerings, and your
sacrifices, your tithes, and the heave offering of your
hand, and all your choice vows which ye vow unto the
Lord." "Three times in the year all thy males shall
appear before the Lord God." "What thing soever I
command you, observe to do it: thou shalt not add
thereto, nor diminish from it [1]." If, then, God sent a
Prophet with the power of miracles, this was a reason

---

[1] Deut. xii. 10, 11.   Exod. xxiii. 17.   Deut. xii. 32.

why the Prophet should be especially rigid in his observance of the Law of the Master who sent him. God
sends His Prophets to keep the Law, not to break it.
He indeed who gave it might recall it; and a Prophet
might be His instrument in recalling it, or in modi-
fying, or in developing it; but while the Law continued, surely it was to be "magnified and made
honourable," not disregarded. Consider our Saviour's
example, and you will acknowledge what I say. He
came with greater miracles; He was Giver and Lord of
the Law; and moreover, He actually came to supersede
it; yet how reverently did He treat, how dutifully did
He obey, His own ordinances! He went up to the
Temple continually, and bade His hearers obey those
who sat in Moses' seat; He sent those whom He cured
to the Priests; He paid the Temple tribute; He did
not destroy, till He had gained (so to say) a right to
destroy, in that He had fulfilled. Not till He could
say, "It is finished," did the veil of the Temple rend in
twain. Miracles, then, and a Prophet's office, are no
warrant at all, as the conduct of the Holiest shows us,
for the neglect of God's Law. Why then did He
dispense with obedience in the instance of Elijah? why
do we not hear of Elijah's going up to Jerusalem three
times a year? why did he not do honour to the Priests,
and to the Temple service? Even in the last age of the
Jewish Church, our Lord said to the Samaritan woman,
"Salvation is of the Jews [1];" and yet Elijah and Elisha,
and their brethren, acquiesce in the disorders which
surround them; and rather strive to make the best of

[1] John iv. 22.

things as they are, than to bring back a rule of religion which had passed away.

Of course they acted at God's bidding. He can dispense with His laws when He pleases, as well as abrogate them; He did at that time dispense with them, as He abrogated them afterwards; but the strange circumstance is, that He *should* dispense with them. Yet observe what the matter of fact was: He raised up Elijah for a certain definite work, and for that alone, neither more nor less. First, the Prophet executed the Divine sentence upon Baal's priests, in his own person; next, he was bidden to anoint Jehu for the same work, —a purpose which Elisha brought to effect. But he did no more; to this his mission was limited. How different from our usual way of viewing things! We are accustomed to say that nothing is done, unless all is done; but God's thoughts are not our thoughts, neither our ways His ways. He raises up Prophets and gifts them with miraculous power, to do a half work; not to heal the division of the kingdoms, but to destroy idolatry; not to restore outward unity, but to repress inward unbelief; not to retrace the steps of the wanderers, but to keep them from wandering still farther.

What makes this providence stranger still, is, that a return to the Temple service might, in this particular instance, have seemed the very remedy of their idolatrous excesses. The kingdom of Israel had been set up in idolatry; the ten tribes had become idolatrous *by* leaving the Temple, and they would have ceased to be idolatrous by returning again to it. The real removal of error is the exhibition of the truth. Truth *supplants* error;

make sure of truth, and error is at an end : yet Elijah acted otherwise; he suffered the people to remain where they were; he tried to reform them *in* that state.

Now why this was so ordered we do not know; whether it be, that when once a people goes wrong, it cannot retrace its steps; or whether there was so much evil at that time in Judah also, that to have attempted a reunion would have been putting a piece of new cloth into an old garment, and had it been effected, would have been an hollow, unreal triumph; or whether such good works have a sort of natural march, and the nearer work must first be done, and then that which is farther removed, and men must undo their sins in the order in which they committed them, and thus, as neglect of the Temple was the sin of Jeroboam, and Baal-worship the sin of Ahab, so they must ascend back again from Ahab to Jeroboam; but, whatever was the reason, so it was, that Elijah and Elisha kept the people shut up under that system, if it might so be called, in which they found them, and sought rather to teach them their duty, than to restore to them their privileges. So had it been with the Israelites in the wilderness, when, after listening to the evil report of the promised land, and murmuring, they were condemned to wander outside its borders, yet not abandoned by the pillar of the cloud, and on their presumptuously attempting to fight the enemy and force a passage, were beaten back, and taught to exhaust the dreary days of the years of their pilgrimage in patience. So was it with Balaam, who, when he tempted God, was bidden to go with the enemies of Israel, yet with God's anger on him because he went. So was it with holy David, who cheerfully waited out the full term of years during which he was to be a wanderer on the mountains, and to cry, "When shall I come to appear before the presence of God?" So was it not with **Jeroboam**, but so should it have been, who lost patience, **and** did not wait for the promise, but seized the kingdom before the destined time, and thereby lost that communion with Jerusalem which Elijah did not attempt to restore. So was it with well-beloved **Daniel**, who in a heathen court led a saint's life, and was visited by Angels, when he could but look towards the Temple. Well then might the schools of the Prophets also be an "example of suffering affliction and of patience;" well might they be content not to go over Jordan, but to die in the wilderness; well might they feed their people with the mere elements of truth, with "milk not with strong meat," while they but obscurely signified Gospel doctrine; for there was envying and strife and division among them, and they were carnal, and were not able to bear the food of men and **Angels.** So the patient Prophets were satisfied with enforcing, not ecclesiastical duties, but <u>the Ten Commandments;</u> teaching the First and the Second to the multitudes on Carmel by the judgment on Baal's priests; and the Third to those who bade the "man of God" come down from the mountain, and were thereupon smitten with fire from heaven; and the Fifth to the little children who cried out "Bald head;" and the Sixth and the Seventh and the Ninth, in the judgments on her who murdered Naboth, and whose whoredoms were so many; and the Eighth and the Tenth

' on Ahab, who coveted the vineyard and also took
possession;—not sending the Shunammite to Jerusalem,
nor eager for a proselyte in Naaman, yet making the
heathen fear the Name of God, and proving to them
that there was a Prophet in Israel.

Yes, surely, the Ten Commandments were the appropriate theme of a Prophet's preaching in that day; and
Elijah would seem best to be renewing communion with
Moses, if he went back to that elementary lesson, so
solemnly impressed upon the favoured Lawgiver in the
wilderness;—what time in his solitary fast he heard the
Lord pass by before him, and a Voice proclaimed, "The
Lord, the Lord God, merciful and gracious, longsuffering, and abundant in goodness and truth, keeping
mercy for thousands, forgiving iniquity and transgres-
sion and sin, and that will by no means clear the
guilty [1]." And therefore when, at the season of which
the text speaks, the Prophet had to flee for his life for
fear of Jezebel, and in his heart thought that his mission
had failed, he sought not the kingdom of David, he
honoured not the precept of unity, he had no heart for
that outward glory of holier times; he passed by Jerusalem, he passed on, along a forlorn and barren way,
into that old desert in which the children of Israel did
wander, till he came to Horeb the Mount of God [2]. He
fled to Antiquity, and would not stop short of it, and so
he heard the words of comfort which reconciled him to
his work and to its issue. He went in weariness and
despondency, for "the children of Israel had forsaken
God's covenant, thrown down His altars, and slain His

---

[1] Exod. xxxiv. 6, 7.　　　　　[2] Vide Mal. iv. 4, 5

Prophets," and Elijah alone was left; and he wished to die, for he was not better than his fathers. But when he came to Horeb, his gracious Master, the wonder-working God, taught him by the mighty acts recorded in the text, that He was to be found, not in public, but in private, by notes and tokens personal and secret; according to the words of a later prophecy, " I dwell in the high and holy place, with him also that is of a contrite and humble spirit, to revive the spirit of the humble, and to revive the heart of the contrite ones;" or in those of our Lord Himself, " Neither shall ye say, Lo here! or Lo there! for the kingdom of God is within you [1]."

First, there was a great and strong Wind, which rent the mountains, and brake in pieces the rocks; and next an Earthquake; and then a Fire. What is the Wind, but that "rushing, mighty wind" that was heard on the day of Pentecost? and what the Earthquake, but that " shaking of the place where " the Apostles "were assembled together" when they had prayed? and what the Fire, but the " cloven tongues, like as of fire," which " sat upon each of them"? And the strong Wind went forth into all the world, and swept it clean of idols, and breathed life into the dead bones, and made them live. And the Earthquake followed, and the kingdoms of men were cleared away, and the gold and silver and brass and iron fell down shattered and " broken to pieces together, and became like the chaff of the summer threshing-floors," till " the wind carried them away, that no place was found for them." And then came the

[1] Isa. lvii. 15. Luke xvii. 21

Fire, when the light of the Church burnt keen and manifest, like the flame of fire in the bush, attracting to it, by its shining, all who passed by. And now has come a time of Silence, like Elijah's time, when the love of many has waxed cold, and truth and antiquity are given up. Surely, then, it is merciful to read in this vision, granted to the Prophet of the latter days, that after all God was not in the Wind, not in the Earthquake, not in the Fire, though He wrought through them; but that His Living and True Word, our Hope and our Salvation, "the engrafted Word, which is able to save our souls," is "a still small Voice;" and that even in that miserable time, when an idol was openly worshipped, God had yet reserved unto Him a remnant, and yet had work for Elijah. "Go, return on thy way to the wilderness of Damascus, and when thou comest, anoint Hazael to be king over Syria; and Jehu the son of Nimshi shalt thou anoint to be king over Israel; and Elisha, the son of Shaphat of Abel-meholah, shalt thou anoint to be prophet in thy room. . . . Yet I have left Me seven thousand in Israel, all the knees which have not bowed to Baal, and every mouth which hath not kissed him."

Let us, then, think it enough, with the Prophets of old, to be patient, to pray, and to wait. "The effectual fervent prayer of a righteous man availeth much. . . . The prayer of faith shall save the sick, and the Lord shall raise him up. . . . Be patient, therefore, brethren, unto the coming of the Lord. Behold, the husbandman waiteth for the precious fruit of the earth, and hath long patience for it, until he

receive the early and latter rain." A Prophet of God
was satisfied, in silence, though with a full heart, to
build the altar of God of twelve stones, in remembrance
of the number of the tribes of the sons of Jacob, on the
barren top of Carmel, and to do no more. He was
satisfied to minister to the widow and fatherless, though
it were only, if so be, to bring their sin to remembrance.
He was satisfied to do his work in his day, though the
only fruit of it were, that Jehoram should talk with
Gehazi of all the great things which Elisha had done.
He was satisfied with the reverence and affection of the
Shunammite in private, while the world at large was
scoffing at him. Let us, in like manner, feel certain, as
well we may, that however great are the disorders of
this present age, and though the unbelieving seek and
find not, yet that to the humble and lowly, the earnest-
minded and pure in heart, the Lord God of Elijah still
reveals Himself. The Presence of Christ is still among
us, in spite of our many sins and the sins of our people.
"The spirit and power of Elias" should now especially
be with us, because the notes of his day are among us.
What is the token of his coming but a backsliding age?
what are the notes of that Man of God, but dimness
and confusion, the threatenings of evil, the scattering of
the faithful, and the defection of the powerful? "In
the way of Thy judgments, O Lord, have we waited for
Thee; the desire of our soul is to Thy Name, and to the
remembrance of Thee. With my soul have I desired
Thee in the night, yea with my spirit within me will
I seek Thee early." "Although the fig-tree shall not
blossom, neither shall fruit be in the vines; the labour

of the olive shall fail, and the fields shall yield no meat; the flock shall be cut off from the fold, and there shall be no herd in the stalls; yet I will rejoice in the Lord, I will joy in the God of my salvation[1]."

What want we then but faith in our Church? with faith we can do every thing; without faith we can do nothing. If we have a secret misgiving about her, all is lost; we lose our nerve, our powers, our position, our hope. A cold despondency and sickness of mind, a niggardness and peevishness of spirit, a cowardice and a sluggishness, envelope us, penetrate us, stifle us. Let it not be so with us; let us be of good heart; let us accept her as God's gift and our portion; let us imitate him, who, when he was "by the bank of Jordan, . . . took the mantle of Elijah, that fell from him, and smote the waters, and said, Where is the Lord God of Elijah[2]?" She is like the mantle of Elijah, a relic from Him who is gone up on high.

[1] Isa. xxvi. 8, 9.   Hab. iii. 17, 18.   [2] 2 Kings ii. 13, 14.

SERMON XXV.

ꜰꜰꜱꜱ in Captivity.

(PREACHED ON THE ANNIVERSARY OF THE CONSECRATION
OF A CHAPEL.)

*" The fast of the fourth month, and the fast of the fifth, and the fast of
the seventh, and the fast of the tenth, shall be to the house of Judah
joy and gladness, and cheerful feasts ; therefore love the truth and
peace."*—ZECH. viii. **19.**

WHEN we reflect upon the present state of the Holy
Church throughout the world, so different from
that which was promised to her in prophecy, the doubt
is apt to suggest itself to us, whether it is right to
rejoice when there is so much to mourn over and to
fear. Is it right to keep holiday, when the Spouse of
Christ is in bondage, and the iron almost enters into her
soul? We know what prophecy promises us, a holy
Church set upon a hill; an imperial Church, far-spreading among the nations, loving truth and peace, binding
together all hearts in charity, and uttering the words of
God from inspired lips; a Kingdom of Heaven upon
earth, that is at unity within itself, peace within its
walls and plenteousness within its palaces; "a glorious

Church, not having spot or wrinkle or any such thing, but holy and without blemish." And, alas! what do we see? We see the Kingdom of God to all appearance broken into fragments—authority in abeyance—separate portions in insurrection—brother armed against brother—truth, a matter not of faith but of controversy. And looking at our own portion of the heavenly heritage, we see heresies of the most deadly character around us and within us; we see error stalking abroad in the light of day and over the length of the land unrebuked—nay, invading high places; while the maintainers of Christian truth are afraid to speak, lest it should offend those to whom it is a duty to defer. We see discipline utterly thrown down, the sacraments and ordinances of grace open to those who cannot come without profaning them and getting harm from them. Works of penance almost unthought of; the world and the Church mixed together; and those who discern and mourn over all this looked upon with aversion, because they will not prophesy smooth things and speak peace where there is no peace. On us have fallen the times described by the Psalmist when he laments, "Thou hast broken the covenant of Thy servant, and cast his crown to the ground. Thou hast overthrown all his hedges and broken down his strongholds. . . Thou hast put out his glory and cast his throne down to the ground. The days of his youth hast Thou shortened, and covered him with dishonour." The days of age have come on us, "the evil days" "when thou shalt say, I have no pleasure in them [1]," the days when the Bridegroom has

[1] Eccles. xii. 1.

been taken away, and when men should fast;—how then in the day of our fast can we find pleasure and keep festival?

What profit is the full gathering and the concourse of men, when all the families of Israel that remain should rather mourn, "every family apart and their wives apart"? Music is for the merry; Darius put away his instruments of music when the Prophet was lost to him. The father of the family had music and dancing, and killed the fatted calf, when the wanderer came home. Tobit in captivity attempted to eat the bread of joyfulness on the feast of Pentecost, and was suddenly reduced to "eat his meat in heaviness," remembering the prophecy of Amos, as he said, "Your feasts shall be turned into mourning, and all your mirth into lamentation." Flowers are for the innocent and gay; how suit they with the dark prison and the fretting chain? Harmony in form and colour, the high arch and the rich window, what have these in common with the fallen and the polluted? Beauty for ashes, the oil of joy for mourning, the garment of praise for the spirit of heaviness,—these surely should be reserved for the year of Jubilee, and when the season of redemption draweth near. This is what may be said, not without plausibility.

Nay, not said plausibly but felt acutely; so acutely felt, as to hinder the mind from taking part in the rejoicing to which it is invited. When men discern duly the forlorn state in which the Spouse of Christ at present lies, how can they have the heart to rejoice? "The ark and Israel and Judah abide in tents," said

Uriah, "and the servants of my lord are encamped in the open fields; shall I then go into mine house to eat and to drink? . . . as thou livest, and as thy soul liveth, I will not do this thing." The desponding soul falls back when it makes the effort; it is not equal to the ceremonial which comes natural to light hearts, and at best but coldly obeys what they anticipate without being bidden. What is to be done with this dull, dispirited, wearied, forlorn, foreboding heart of ours? "By the waters of Babylon we sat down and wept, when we remembered thee, O Sion. As for our harps, we hanged them up upon the trees that are therein. For they that led us away captive required of us then a song, and melody in our heaviness,—Sing us one of the songs of Sion. How shall we sing the Lord's song in a strange land?"

Yet, since there is some danger of over-sensitiveness in this matter, it may be useful here to make some remarks upon it.

This then must be ever kept in mind, when such thoughts arise within us, that cheerfulness and lightness of heart are not only privileges, but duties. Cheerfulness is a great Christian duty. Whatever be our circumstances, within or without, though "without be fightings and within be fears," yet the Apostle's words are express, "Rejoice in the Lord *always*." That sorrow, that solicitude, that fear, that repentance, is not Christian which has not its portion of Christian joy; for "God is greater than our hearts," and no evil, past or future, within or without, is equal to this saying, that Christ has died and reconciled the world unto

Himself. We are ever in His Presence, be we cast
down, or be we exalted; and "in His Presence is the
fulness of joy." "Let the brother of low degree rejoice
in that he is exalted, but the rich in that he is made
low[1]." "He that is called in the Lord, being a servant,
is the Lord's freeman; likewise also he that is called,
being free, is Christ's servant[2]." Whether we eat or
drink, or whatever we do, to His glory must we do all,
and if to His glory, to our great joy; for His service
is perfect freedom : and what are the very Angels in
heaven but His ministers? Nothing is evil but separation from Him; while we are allowed to visit His
Temple, we cannot but "enter into His gates with
gladness and thanksgiving, and into His courts with
praise." "Is any," then, "among us afflicted? let him
pray; is any merry? let him sing psalms."

Such even was the conduct of the devout Israelites,
who had no promise such as we have, of a continual
Divine Presence, which is our spiritual life,—which is
the life of our very sorrow, if it be godly, the life of our
repentance, our fear, our self-chastisement; and in
which we must rejoice, because through it we repent,
are in fear, and afflict ourselves. Even Jews, we see,
attempted to rejoice in captivity, though it was prophesied against them, "I will turn your feasts into
mourning, and all your songs into lamentation[3];"
whereas the very reverse is graciously assured in the
text to the Gospel Church, that her times of humiliation
should be times of rejoicing. "The fast of the fourth
month, and the fast of the fifth, and the fast of the

[1] James i. 9, 10.   [2] 1 Cor. vii. 22.   [3] Amos viii. 10.

seventh, and the fast of the tenth, shall be to the house
of Judah joy and gladness and cheerful feasts; therefore
love the truth and peace."

What did Hezekiah and Josiah in those mournful
times when wrath hung over the chosen people? In
the Paschal Feast held by the former king, he prayed,
"The good Lord pardon every one that prepareth his
heart to seek God, the Lord God of his fathers, though
he be not cleansed according to the purification of the
sanctuary." And the children of Israel kept the feast
seven days with great gladness, and the Levites and
priests praised the Lord with loud instruments, and
Hezekiah spake comfortably to the Levites,—so that
"there was great joy in Jerusalem; for since the time
of Solomon . . . there was not the like in Jerusalem."
And of Josiah's passover it is said, "There was no
passover like to that kept in Israel, from the days of
Samuel the Prophet."

Again, what could be more miserable and forlorn
than the state of the Jews when they returned from
captivity? yet, in spite of the ruins among which they
dwelt, God *had* shown them mercy, and thereby given
them hope; He had begun to be gracious to them, and
though they had no heart for the work of rebuilding the
Temple, when so many things were against them, and
the new fabric would for certain be so poor and unworthy at the best, yet it was their duty to look to the
future and rejoice. "Thus speaketh the Lord of hosts,
saying, This people say, The time is not come, the time
that the Lord's house should be built[1]." And He

[1] Haggai i. 2.

added for their encouragement, "According to the word
that I covenanted with you when ye came out of Egypt,
so My Spirit *remaineth* among you : fear ye not[1]."
And still more appositely, as we read elsewhere, "Nehemiah and Ezra the priest the scribe, and the Levites
that taught the people, said unto all the people, This
day is holy unto the Lord your God; mourn not, nor
weep. For all the people wept, when they heard the
words of the Law. Then he said unto them, Go your
way, eat the fat, and drink the sweet, and send portions
unto them for whom nothing is prepared : for this day
is holy unto our Lord; neither be ye sorry, for the joy
of the Lord is your strength[2]." The sacred narrative
proceeds; "So the Levites stilled all the people, saying,
Hold your peace, for the day is holy; neither be ye
grieved. And all the people went their way to eat, and
to drink, and to send portions, and to make great mirth,
because they had understood the words that were declared unto them." And after this they proceeded to
keep the feast of tabernacles, with "olive branches and
pine branches, and myrtle branches, and palm branches,
and branches of thick trees, to make booths, as it is
written. . . . And all the congregation of them that
were come again out of the captivity made booths, and
sat under the booths; for since the days of Joshua the
son of Nun, unto that day, had not the children of
Israel done so. And there was very great gladness."

We have a still more remarkable and solemn instance
of the duty of keeping festival and rejoicing even in the
darkest day, in our Lord's own history. If there was

[1] Haggai ii. 5.   [2] Neh. viii. 9, 10.

a season in which gloom was allowable, it was on the
days and hours before His Passion: but He who came
to bring joy on earth and not sorrow; who came eating
and drinking, because He was the true Bread from
heaven; who changed the water into wine at a marriage
feast, and fed the hungry thousands in the wilderness;
even in that awful time when His spirit fainted within
Him, when, as He testified, His "soul was troubled,"
and He was led to cry, "Father, save Me from this
hour," and more solemnly and secretly, "If it be
possible, let this cup pass from Me;" He, our great
Exemplar, kept the feast—nay, anticipated it, as if
though He Himself was to be the very Paschal Lamb,
still He was not thereby excused from sharing in the
typical rite.   "With desire" did He "desire to eat
that passover" with His disciples before He suffered.
And a few days before it, He took part in a public and
(as it were) triumphant pageant, as though the bitter-
ness of death had been already passed.   He came to
Bethany, where He had raised Lazarus; and there they
made Him a supper; and Mary took the precious
ointment and poured it on His head, and anointed His
feet, and the house was filled with the fragrance.   And
next the people took branches of palm-trees, and went
forth to meet Him, and strewed their garments in the
way, and cried, " Hosanna, Blessed is the King of Israel,
that cometh in the Name of the Lord!"

To rejoice, then, and to keep festival, is a Christian
duty, under all circumstances.   Indeed, is not this
plain, by considering the obligation, yet the nature, of
that chief Gospel Ordinance which we celebrate to-day?

There is an ordinance which we are bound to observe always till the Lord come: is it an ordinance of humiliation and self-abasement, or is it a feast? The Holy Eucharist is a Feast; we cannot help feasting, we cannot elude our destiny of joy and thanksgiving, if we would be Christians.

As I have already remarked, the same rule is to be observed even in the instance of personal penitence, which is on no account to be separated from the duty of Christian cheerfulness. Penitents are as little at liberty to release themselves from Christian joy as from Christian love; love alone can make repentance available; and where there is love, there joy must be present also. The true penance is not to put away God's blessings, but to add chastisements. As Adam did not lose the flowers of Eden on his fall, but thorns and thistles sprung up around them; and he still had bread, but was forced to eat it in the sweat of his face; and as the Israelites ate their Paschal lamb with bitter herbs; so in like manner we show our repentance, not in rejecting what God gives, but in adding what sin deserves.

And I will add, that there is much which is expedient as well as dutiful in this simple adherence to the plain formularies of Christian devotion and practice, even under circumstances unsuitable to them. For if these observances are inconsistent with our actual state, they will force themselves upon our minds as a mockery, and thus suggest to us of what we ought to be, and make us discontented with what we are. Our Lord gives us a pattern of this in His very Prayer, in which we ask that our trespasses may be forgiven, *as* we forgive them that trespass against us; words which are quite out of place, or rather words which will do us harm, if we are not what Christians should be in spirit, but remember injuries and cherish malice. And thus, in like manner, when we profess to hold the Apostolic faith, *yet* take up with modern notions of Gospel truth, what is this but a great inconsistency?—yet a profitable one withal, if through God's grace the profession of what is ancient at length overcomes our attachment to what is novel and unauthorized. And, again, what can be more incongruous than for the run of Christians of this age to call themselves Catholics? yet their calling themselves so may be the first step to their becoming so. And how little fitted are we to discharge ecclesiastical censures, or to enforce ecclesiastical discipline, or to live by rule! yet, by attempting to do so, we may learn our wants, and seek the supply of them. And how unlike are the best among us to the Saints and Martyrs of old time; to St. Cyprian, or St. Basil, or St. Ambrose, or St. Leo! and what an utter mockery it is to couple their names with modern names, and to compare their words with our words, as is sometimes done! yet, if true love be the tie that binds us to them, since they most certainly cannot move towards us, we through God's mercy perchance may be drawn to them. And in like manner, poor and mean and unworthy as may be our attempts at a ceremonial on days such as this, yet we trust He will accept it, as He did her offering, who did " what she could," and will vouchsafe to bless it and to make it a means of teaching us a deeper reverence and a more constraining love, and will draw us on into the very bosom of Catholic sanctity and the very heart of Catholic affection, by observances and usages which in themselves are little worth, and excite the jeer or the criticism of the worldly or the profane. In a word, if we claim to *be* the Church, let us act *like* the Church, and we shall *become* the Church. Here, as in other matters, to doubt is to fail, and to go forward is to succeed.

One danger there is,—that of our attempting one of these aspects or constituent portions of the Christian character while we neglect the other. To attempt Apostolical Christianity at all, we must attempt it all. It is a whole, and cannot be divided; and to attempt one aspect of it only, is to attempt something else which looks like it, instead of it. "All is not gold that glitters," as the proverb goes; and all is not Catholic and Apostolic which affects what is high and beautiful, and speaks to the imagination. Religion has two sides, a severe side, and a beautiful; and we shall be sure to swerve from the narrow way which leads to life, if we indulge ourselves in what is beautiful, while we put aside what is severe.

I have a hope, my brethren, that we are not committing this fault; for to be aware of the danger is one special preservative against it, in the case of those who wish to do what is right. Had we no other memento of the duty of combining strictness of life with our attention to external religion, this very day would remind us of it, occurring as it does in so close a connexion with the Ember-week. We commemorate the dedication of this Chapel to God's service, either,

as in this year, in the *midst* of the fast[1], or, as on other
years, just *after* it. If, in the words of the text, our
fasts issue in cheerful feasts, still this is only saying, in
other words, that our feasts spring out of fasts.

And there are other reasons why we should be preserved (through God's mercy) from the temptation of
indulging in (what may be called) the luxuries of religious worship; still there is great cause to fear that
others are not equally out of danger. It were well, if
others had more of that despondency and trouble of mind
about the state of the Church, which I described when I
began; it might preserve them from a very hurtful
excess. Too many men at this time are for raising a
high superstructure ere they have laid a deep foundation. They shrink from sowing in tears, though they
would fain reap in joy. The austere doctrines of the
Gospel they turn from them, like him who said, "Be
it far from Thee, Lord: this shall not be unto Thee[2];"
—they stumble at the doctrine of post-baptismal sin;
and what part of their creed can be profitable to them,
if this is neglected? They are slow to admit that our
times are like those of backsliding Israel, or treacherous
Judah; and how can they attempt to mend them, if
they see them not as God sees them? They scoff at
the ascetic life of the Saints as an extravagance or
corruption; or they slur over their austerities, as if they
were an accident of their religion peculiar to *their* times;
and they would live like the world, yet worship like
the Angels. These things being so, misgivings of mind
arise of necessity about the present growing attention,

[1] Thursday, Sept. 22, 1842.   [2] Matt. xvi. 22.

which is seen on all sides of us, to church architecture and
church decoration; not as if all this were not right in
itself, but lest we should be too fast about it; lest it
be disjoined in the case of the multitude from real
seriousness, from deep repentance, from strict conscientiousness, from inward sanctity, from godly fear
and awe. There are other things to be done first.
However, we can but leave the issue to God's Providence; and pray Him, who seems at present engaged
in a great work among us, to overrule all our mistakes
to His glory, and to the welfare of the Catholic Church,
and to our salvation.

Let us recollect this for our own profit; that, if it is
our ambition to follow the Christians of the first ages,
as they followed the Apostles, and the Apostles followed
Christ, they had the discomfort of this world without
its compensating gifts. No high cathedrals, no de-
corated altars, no white-robed priests, no choirs for
sacred psalmody,—nothing of the order, majesty, and
beauty of devotional services had they; but they *had*
trials, afflictions, solitariness, contempt, ill-usage. They
were "in weariness and painfulness, in watchings often,
in hunger and thirst, in fastings often, in cold and
nakedness." If we have only the enjoyment and none
of the pain, and they only the pain and none of the
enjoyment, in what does our Christianity resemble
theirs? what are the tokens of identity between us?
why do we not call theirs one religion and ours
another? What points in common are there between
the easy religion of this day, and the religion of St.
Athanasius, or St. Chrysostom? How do the two agree,

except that the name of Christianity is given to both of them?

O may we be wiser than to be satisfied with an untrue profession and a mere shadow of the Gospel! May God raise our hearts on high to seek first His kingdom and His righteousness, that all other things may be added to us! My brethren, let what is inward be chief with you, and what is outward be subordinate! Think nothing preferable to a knowledge of yourselves, true repentance, a resolve to live to God, to die to the world, deep humility, hatred of sin, and of yourselves as you are sinners, a clear and habitual view of the coming judgment. Let this be first; and secondly, labour for the unity of the Church; let the peace of Jerusalem and the edification of the body of Christ be an object of prayer, close upon that of your own personal salvation. Pray that a Divine Influence may touch the hearts of men, and that in spite of themselves, while they wonder at themselves, not to say while others wonder at them, they may confess and preach those Catholic truths which at present they scorn or revile; that so at length the language of the prophecy from which the text is taken, and which has been read in the course of the Service, may be fulfilled to us; "I am returned unto Zion, and will dwell in the midst of Jerusalem," and "the seed shall be prosperous, the vine shall give her fruit, and the ground shall give her increase, and the heavens shall give their dew;" and "many people and strong nations shall come to seek the Lord of Hosts in Jerusalem, and to pray before the Lord."

SERMON XXVI.

The Parting of Friends.

(PREACHED ON THE ANNIVERSARY OF THE CONSECRATION
OF A CHAPEL.)

" Man goeth forth to his work and to his labour until the evening."—
Ps. civ. 23.

WHEN the Son of Man, the First-born of the creation of God, came to the evening of His mortal
life, He parted with His disciples at a feast. He had
borne "the burden and heat of the day;" yet, when
"wearied with His journey," He had but stopped at the
well's side, and asked a draught of water for His thirst;
for He had "meat to eat which" others "knew not of."
His meat was "to do the will of Him that sent Him,
and to finish His work;" "I must work the works of
Him that sent Me," said He, "while it is day; the
night cometh, when no man can work[1]." Thus passed
the season of His ministry; and if at any time He
feasted with Pharisee or publican, it was in order that
He might do the work of God more strenuously. But
"when the even was come He sat down with the

---

[1] John iv. 6. 34; ix. 4.

Twelve." " And He said unto them, With desire have
I desired to eat this Passover with you, before I suffer [1]."
He was about to suffer more than man had ever suffered
or shall suffer.   But there is nothing gloomy, churlish,
violent, or selfish in His grief; it is tender, affectionate,
social.   He calls His friends around Him, though He
was as Job among the ashes; He bids them stay by
Him, and see Him suffer; He desires their sympathy;
He takes refuge in their love.   He first feasted them,
and sung a hymn with them, and washed their feet; and
when His long trial began, He beheld them and kept
them in His presence, till they in terror shrank from it.
Yet, on St. Mary and St. John, His Virgin Mother and
His Virgin Disciple, who remained, His eyes still rested;
and in St. Peter, who was denying Him in the distance,
His sudden glance wrought a deep repentance.   O
wonderful pattern, the type of all trial and of all duty
under it, while the Church endures.

   We indeed to-day have no need of so high a lesson
and so august a comfort.   We have no pain, no grief
which calls for it; yet, considering it has been brought
before us in this morning's service [2], we are naturally
drawn to think of it, though it be infinitely above us,
under certain circumstances of this season and the
present time.   For now are the shades of evening falling
upon the earth, and the year's labour is coming to its
end.   In Septuagesima the labourers were sent into the
vineyard; in Sexagesima the sower went forth to sow;—
that time is over; "the harvest is passed, the summer is
ended [3]," the vintage is gathered.   We have kept the

[1] Matt. xxvi. 20.   Luke xxii. 15.   [2] Sept. 25, 1843.   [3] Jer. viii. 20.

Ember-days for the fruits of the earth, in self-abasement, as being unworthy even of the least of God's mercies; and now we are offering up of its corn and wine as a propitiation, and are eating and drinking of them with thanksgiving.

"All things come of Thee, and of Thine own have we given Thee[1]." If we have had the rain in its season, and the sun shining in its strength, and the fertile ground, it is of Thee. We give back to Thee what came from Thee. "When Thou givest it them, they gather it, and when Thou openest Thy hand, they are filled with good. When Thou hidest Thy face, they are troubled; when Thou takest away their breath, they die, and are turned again to their dust. When Thou lettest Thy breath go forth, they shall be made, and Thou shalt renew the face of the earth[2]." He gives, He takes away. "Shall we receive good at the hand of God, and shall we not receive evil[3]?" May He not "do what He will with His own[4]?" May not His sun set as it has risen? and must it not set, if it is to rise again? and must not darkness come first, if there is ever to be morning? and must not the sky be blacker, before it can be brighter? And cannot He, who can do all things, cause a light to arise even in the darkness? "I have thought upon Thy Name, O Lord, in the night season, and have kept Thy Law;" "Thou also shalt light my candle, the Lord my God shall make my darkness to be light;" or as the Prophet speaks, "At the evening time it shall be light[5]."

"All things come of Thee," says holy David, "for we

---

[1] 1 Chron. xxix. 14.　　[2] Ps. civ. 28—30.　　[3] Job ii. 10.
　　　[4] Matt. xx. 15.　　　　[5] Zech. xiv. 7.

are strangers before Thee and sojourners, as were all our
fathers; our days on the earth are as a shadow, and there
is none abiding[1]." All is vanity, vanity of vanities, and
vexation of spirit. "What profit hath a man of all his
labour which he taketh under the sun? One generation
passeth away, and another generation cometh; but the
earth abideth for ever; the sun also ariseth, and the sun
goeth down; . . . all things are full of labour, man cannot
utter it; . . . that which is crooked cannot be made
straight, and that which is wanting cannot be num-
bered[2]." "To every thing there is a season, and a time
to every purpose under heaven; a time to be born and a
time to die; a time to plant and a time to pluck up that
which is planted; a time to kill and a time to heal; a
time to break down and a time to build up; . . . a time
to get and a time to lose; a time to keep and a time to
cast away[3]." And time, and matter, and motion, and
force, and the will of man, how vain are they all, except
as instruments of the grace of God, blessing them and
working with them! How vain are all our pains, our
thought, our care, unless God uses them, unless God has
inspired them! how worse than fruitless are they, unless
directed to His glory, and given back to the Giver!

"Of Thine own have we given Thee," says the royal
Psalmist, after he had collected materials for the Temple.
Because "the work was great," and "the palace, not for
man, but for the Lord God," therefore he "prepared with all
his might for the house of his God," gold, and silver, and
brass, and iron, and wood, "onyx stones, and stones to be
set, glistering stones, and of divers colours, and all man-

[1] 1 Chron. xxix. 15.   [2] Eccles. i. 3 - 15.   [3] Eccles. iii. 1—6.

ner of precious stones, and marble stones in abundance[1]." And "the people rejoiced, for that they offered willingly; . . . and David the king also rejoiced with great joy." We too, at this season, year by year, have been allowed in our measure, according to our work and our faith, to rejoice in God's Presence, for this sacred building which He has given us to worship Him in. It was a glad time when we first met here,—many of us now present recollect it; nor did our rejoicing cease, but was renewed every autumn, as the day came round. It has been "a day of gladness and feasting, and a good day, and of sending portions one to another[2]." We have kept the feast heretofore with merry hearts; we have kept it seven full years unto "a perfect end;" now let us keep it, even though in haste, and with bitter herbs, and with loins girded, and with a staff in our hand, as they who have "no continuing city, but seek one to come[3]."

So was it with Jacob, when with his staff he passed over that Jordan. He too kept feast before he set out upon his dreary way. He received a father's blessing, and then was sent afar; he left his mother, never to see her face or hear her voice again. He parted with all that his heart loved, and turned his face towards a strange land. He went with the doubt, whether he should have bread to eat, or raiment to put on. He came to "the people of the East," and served a hard master twenty years. "In the day the drought consumed him, and the frost by night; and his sleep departed from his eyes[4]." O little did he think, when father and mother had forsaken

---

[1] 1 Chron. xxix. 1, 2. 9.   [2] Esther ix. 19.

[3] Heb. xiii. 14.   [4] Gen. xxxi. 40.

him, and at Bethel he lay down to sleep on the desolate
ground, because the sun was set and even had come, that
there was the house of God and the gate of heaven, that
the Lord was in that place, and would thence go forward
with him whithersoever he went, till He brought him
back to that river in "two bands," who was then cross-
ing it forlorn and solitary!

So had it been with Ishmael; though the feast was
not to him a blessing, yet he feasted in his father's tent,
and then was sent away. That tender father, who, when
a son was promised him of Sarah, cried out to his
Almighty Protector, " O that Ishmael might live before
Thee[1]!"—he it was, who, under a divine direction, the
day after the feast, "rose up early in the morning, and
took bread, and a bottle of water, and gave it unto Hagar,
putting it on her shoulder, and the child, and sent her
away. And she departed, and wandered in the wilderness of Beersheba[2]." And little thought that fierce
child, when for feasting came thirst and weariness and
wandering in the desert, that this was not the end of
Ishmael, but the beginning. And little did Hagar read
his coming fortunes, when "the water was spent in the
bottle, and she cast the child under one of the shrubs, and
she went and sat her down over against him a good way
off; . . . for she said, Let me not see the death of the
child. And she sat over against him, and lift up her
voice, and wept."

So had it been with Naomi, though she was not quit-
ting, but returning to her home, and going, not to a land
of famine, but of plenty. In a time of distress, she had

---

[1] Gen. xvii. 18.   [2] Gen. xxi. 14.

left her country, and found friends and made relatives among the enemies of her people. And when her husband and her children died, Moabitish women, who had once been the stumbling-block of Israel, became the support and comfort of her widowhood. Time had been when, at the call of the daughters of Moab, the chosen people had partaken their sacrifices, and "bowed down to their gods. And Israel joined himself unto Baal-peor, and the anger of the Lord was kindled against Israel." Centuries had since passed away, and now of Moabites was Naomi mother; and to their land had she given her heart, when the call of duty summoned her back to Bethlehem. "She had heard in the country of Moab, how that the Lord had visited His people in giving them bread. Wherefore she went forth out of the place where she was, and her two daughters-in-law with her, and they went on the way to return unto the land of Judah[1]."

Forlorn widow, great was the struggle in her bosom, whether shall she do?—leave behind her the two heathen women, in widowhood and weakness like herself, her sole stay, the shadows of departed blessings? or shall she selfishly take them as fellow-sufferers, who could not be protectors? Shall she seek sympathy where she cannot gain help? shall she deprive them of a home, when she has none to supply? So she said, "Go, return each to her mother's house: the Lord deal kindly with you, as ye have dealt with the dead and with me!" Perplexed Naomi, torn with contrary feelings; which tried her the more,—Orpah who left her, or Ruth who remained? Orpah who was a pain, or Ruth who was a charge?

[1] Ruth i. 6—8. 14, 15

"'They lifted up their voice and wept again; and Orpah kissed her mother-in-law, but Ruth clave unto her. And she said, Behold, thy sister-in-law is gone back unto her people and unto her gods; return thou after thy sister-in-law. And Ruth said, Entreat me not to leave thee, or to return from following after thee: for whither thou goest, I will go; and where thou lodgest, I will lodge: thy people shall be my people, and thy God my God. Where thou diest, will I die, and there will I be buried; the Lord do so to me, and more also, if aught but death part thee and me[1]."

Orpah kissed Naomi, and went back to the world. There was sorrow in the parting, but Naomi's sorrow was more for Orpah's sake than for her own. Pain there would be, but it was the pain of a wound, not the yearning regret of love. It was the pain we feel when friends disappoint us, and fall in our esteem. That kiss of Orpah was no loving token; it was but the hollow profession of those who use smooth words, that they may part company with us with least trouble and discomfort to themselves. Orpah's tears were but the dregs of affection; she clasped her mother-in-law once for all, that she might not cleave to her. Far different were the tears, far different the embrace, which passed between those two religious friends recorded in the book which follows, who loved each other with a true love unfeigned, but whose lives ran in different courses. If Naomi's grief was great when Orpah kissed her, what was David's when he saw the last of him, whose "soul had from the first been knit with his soul," so that "he loved

[1] Ruth i. 14—17.

him as his own soul[1]"? "I am distressed for thee, my brother Jonathan," he says; "very pleasant hast thou been unto me; thy love to me was wonderful, passing the love of women[2]." What woe was upon that "young man," "of a beautiful countenance and goodly to look to," and "cunning in playing, and a mighty valiant man, and a man of war, and prudent in matters[3];" when his devoted affectionate loyal friend, whom these good gifts have gained, looked upon him for the last time! O hard destiny, except that the All-merciful so willed it, that such companions might not walk in the house of God as friends! David must flee to the wilderness, Jonathan must pine in his father's hall; Jonathan must share that stern father's death in battle, and David must ascend the vacant throne. Yet they made a covenant on parting: " Thou shalt not only," said Jonathan, "while yet I live, show me the kindness of the Lord, that I die not; but also thou shalt not cut off thy kindness from my house for ever; no, not when the Lord hath cut off the enemies of David, every one from the face of the earth. . . . And Jonathan caused David to swear again, because he loved him, for he loved him as he loved his own soul." And then, while David hid himself, Jonathan made trial of Saul, how he felt disposed to David; and when he found that "it was determined of his father to slay David," he "arose from the table in fierce anger, and did eat no meat the second day of the month; for he was grieved for David, because his father had done him shame." Then in the morning he went out into the field,

---

[1] 1 Sam. xviii. 1—3.   [2] 2 Sam. i. 26.
[3] 1 Sam. xvi. 12. 18.

where David lay, and the last meeting took place between the two. " David arose out of a place toward the south, and fell on his face to the ground, and bowed himself three times; and they kissed one another, and wept one with another, till David exceeded. And Jonathan said to David, Go in peace, forasmuch as we have sworn both of us in the Name of the Lord, saying, The Lord be between me and thee, and between my seed and thy seed for ever. And he arose and departed; and Jonathan went into the city[1]."

David's affection was given to a single heart; but there is another spoken of in Scripture, who had a thousand friends and loved each as his own soul, and seemed to live a thousand lives in them, and died a thousand deaths when he must quit them : that great Apostle, whose very heart was broken when his brethren wept; who "lived if they stood fast in the Lord;" who "was glad when he was weak and they were strong;" and who was " willing to have imparted unto them his own soul, because they were dear unto him[2]." Yet we read of his bidding farewell to whole Churches, never to see them again. At one time, to the little ones of the flock; " When we had accomplished those days," says the Evangelist, "we departed, and went our way, . . . with wives and children, till we were out of the city; and we kneeled down on the shore and prayed. And when we had taken our leave one of another, we took ship, and they returned home again." At another time, to the rulers of the Church : " And now behold," he says

---

[1] 1 Sam. xx. 14—42.
[2] Acts xxi. 21, 22. 1 Thess. ii. 8; iii. 8. 2 Cor. xiii. 9.

to them, "I know that ye all, among whom I have
gone preaching the kingdom of God, shall see my face no
more.   Wherefore, I take you to record this day, that I
am pure from the blood of all men, for I have not
shunned to declare unto you all the counsel of God. . . .
I have coveted no man's silver, or gold, or apparel ; . . .
I have showed you all things, how that so labouring he
ought to support the weak; and to remember the words
of the Lord Jesus, how he said, It is more blessed to give
than to receive."   And then, when he had finished, " he
kneeled down, and prayed with them all.   And they all
wept sore, and fell on Paul's neck, and kissed him ;
sorrowing most of all for the words which he spake, that
they should see his face no more.   And they accompanied him unto the ship[1]."

There was another time, when he took leave of his
"own son in the faith," Timothy, in words more calm,
and still more impressive, when his end was nigh : "I
am now ready to be offered," he says, "and the time of
my departure is at hand.   I have fought a good fight,
I have finished my course, I have kept the faith.   Henceforth there is laid up for me a crown of righteousness,
which the Lord, the Righteous Judge, shall give me at
that day[2]."

And what are all these instances but memorials and
tokens of the Son of Man, when His work and His
labour were coming to an end?   Like Jacob, like
Ishmael, like Elisha, like the Evangelist whose day is
just passed, He kept feast before His departure; and, like

[1] Acts xxi. 5, 6; xx. 25—27. 33. 35, 36—38.
[2] 2 Tim. iv. 6—8.

David, He was persecuted by the rulers in Israel; and, like Naomi, He was deserted by His friends; and, like Ishmael, He cried out, "I thirst" in a barren and dry land; and at length, like Jacob, He went to sleep with a stone for His pillow, in the evening. And, like St. Paul, He had "finished the work which God gave Him to do," and had "witnessed a good confession;" and, beyond St. Paul, "the Prince of this world had come, and had nothing in Him[1]." "He was in the world, and the world was made by Him, and the world knew Him not. He came unto His own, and His own received Him not[2]." Heavily did He leave, tenderly did He mourn over the country and city which rejected Him. "When He was come near, He beheld the city, and wept over it, saying, If thou hadst known, even thou, at least in this thy day, the things which belong unto thy peace! but now they are hid from thine eyes." And again: "O Jerusalem, Jerusalem, which killest the prophets, and stonest them that are sent unto thee, how often would I have gathered thy children together, as a hen doth gather her brood under her wings, and ye would not! Behold, your house is left unto you desolate[3]."

A lesson surely, and a warning to us all, in every place where He puts His Name, to the end of time; lest we be cold towards His gifts, or unbelieving towards His word, or jealous of His workings, or heartless towards His mercies. . . . O mother of saints! O school of the wise! O nurse of the heroic! of whom went forth, in whom have dwelt, memorable names of old, to spread the

---

[1] 1 Tim. vi. 13.　John xiv. 30.　　[2] John i. 10, 11.
[3] Luke xix. 41, 42; xiii. 34, 35.

truth abroad, or to cherish and illustrate it at home! O
thou, from whom surrounding nations lit their lamps!
O virgin of Israel! wherefore dost thou now sit on the
ground and keep silence, like one of the foolish women
who were without oil on the coming of the Bridegroom?
Where is now the ruler in Sion, and the doctor in the
Temple, and the ascetic on Carmel, and the herald in the
wilderness, and the preacher in the market-place? where
are thy "effectual fervent prayers," offered in secret, and
thy alms and good works coming up as a memorial before
God? How is it, O once holy place, that "the land
mourneth, for the corn is wasted, the new wine is dried
up, the oil languisheth, . . . because joy is withered
away from the sons of men?" "Alas for the day! . . .
how do the beasts groan! the herds of cattle are perplexed,
because they have no pasture, yea, the flocks of sheep are
made desolate." "Lebanon is ashamed and hewn down;
Sharon is like a wilderness, and Bashan and Carmel
shake off their fruits[1]." O my mother, whence is this
unto thee, that thou hast good things poured upon thee
and canst not keep them, and bearest children, yet darest
not own them? why hast thou not the skill to use their
services, nor the heart to rejoice in their love? how is it
that whatever is generous in purpose, and tender or deep
in devotion, thy flower and thy promise, falls from thy
bosom and finds no home within thine arms? Who hath
put this note upon thee, to have "a miscarrying womb,
and dry breasts," to be strange to thine own flesh, and
thine eye cruel towards thy little ones? Thine own
offspring, the fruit of thy womb, who love thee and

[1] Joel i. 10—18. Isa. xxxiii. 9.

would toil for thee, thou dost gaze upon with fear, as
though a portent, or thou dost loathe as an offence;—at
best thou dost but endure, as if they had no claim but
on thy patience, self-possession, and vigilance, to be rid
of them as easily as thou mayest. Thou makest them
"stand all the day idle," as the very condition of thy
bearing with them; or thou biddest them be gone,
where they will be more welcome; or thou sellest them
for nought to the stranger that passes by. And what
wilt thou do in the end thereof? . . .

Scripture is a refuge in any trouble; only let us be on
our guard against seeming to use it further than is
fitting, or doing more than sheltering ourselves under
its shadow. Let us use it according to our measure.
It is far higher and wider than our need; and its language
veils our feelings while it gives expression to them. It is
sacred and heavenly; and it restrains and purifies, while
it sanctions them.

And now, my brethren, "bless God, praise Him and
magnify Him, and praise Him for the things which He
hath done unto you in the sight of all that live. It is
good to praise God, and exalt His Name, and honourably
to show forth the works of God; therefore be not slack
to praise Him." "All the works of the Lord are good;
and He will give every needful thing in due season; so
that a man cannot say, This is worse than that; for in
time they shall all be well approved. And therefore
praise ye the Lord with the whole heart and mouth, and
bless the Name of the Lord[1]."

[1] Tob. xii. 6.　Ecclus. xxxix. 33—35.

" Leave off from wrath, and let go displeasure; flee from evil, and do the thing that is good." " Do that which is good, and no evil shall touch you." " Go your way; eat your bread with joy, and drink your wine with a merry heart, for God now accepteth your works; let your garments be always white, and let your head lack no ointment[1]."

And, O my brethren, O kind and affectionate hearts, O loving friends, should you know any one whose lot it has been, by writing or by word of mouth, in some degree to help you thus to act; if he has ever told you what you knew about yourselves, or what you did not know; has read to you your wants or feelings, and comforted you by the very reading; has made you feel that there was a higher life than this daily one, and a brighter world than that you see; or encouraged you, or sobered you, or opened a way to the inquiring, or soothed the perplexed; if what he has said or done has ever made you take interest in him, and feel well inclined towards him; remember such a one in time to come, though you hear him not, and pray for him, that in all things he may know God's will, and at all times he may be ready to fulfil it.

[1] Ps. xxxvii. 8. 27. Tob. xii. 7. Eccles. ix. 7. 8.

DATES OF
PAROCHIAL AND PLAIN SERMONS.

	Sermon	When written or first preached.
Vol. II.	I. (re-written) . .	1830, November 30.
Published	II.	1834, December 21.
in 1835.	III.	1834, December 25.
	IV.	1831, July 25.
	V.	1831, December 27.
	VI.	1833, December 28.
	VII.	1831, January 1.
	VIII.	1834, end of year.
	IX.	1831, January 25.
	X.	1831, February 2.
	XI.	1832, February 24.
	XII.	1832, March 25.
	XIII. (re-written) .	1831, April 3.
	XIV.	1835, Jan. or Feb.
	XV.	,, ,,
	XVI.	1831, April 25.
	XVII.	1834, December 27.
	XVIII.	1834, end of year.
	XIX.	,, ,,
	XX.	1835, Jan. or Feb.
	XXI.	,, ,,
	XXII.	1834, end of year.
	XXIII.	,, ,,
	XXIV. (re-written) . .	1831, June 24.
	XXV.	1834, December 14.
	XXVI.	1835, Jan. or Feb.
	XXVII. (enlarged) . .	1831, August 24.
	XXVIII.	1835, February 1.
	XXIX.	1831, September 29.
	XXX.	1831, October 18.
	XXXI.	1834, end of year.
	XXXII.	1831, November 30.

	Sermon	When written or first preached.
VOL. III.	I.	1829, July 19.
Published	II. (re-written)	1830, May 9.
in 1836.	III.	1830, May 16.
	IV.	1830, May 23.
	V.	1830, August 1.
	VI.	1830, February 21.
	VII.	1831, November 20.
	VIII.	1831, December 4.
	IX.	1835, April 5.
	X.	1835, April 12.
	XI.	1835, May 3.
	XII.	1835, March 8.
	XIII.	1834, June 8.
	XIV.	1829, November 29.
	XV.	1835, May 17.
	XVI.	1835, October 25.
	XVII.	1834, September 14.
	XVIII.	1835, November 8.
	XIX.	1835, November 15.
	XX.	1835, May 24.
	XXI.	1834, November 2.
	XXII.	1834, October 26.
	XXIII.	1835, February 8.
	XXIV.	1835, February 22.
	XXV.	1835, November 1.
VOL. IV.	I.	1837, July 9.
Published	II.	1837, April 2.
in 1839.	III.	1836, March 20.
	IV.	1835, March 22.
	V.	1837, April 30.
	VI.	1836, March 27.
	VII.	1837, August 6.
	VIII.	1836, June 12.

Sermon		When written or first preached.
IX.	. . . . .	1836, November 6.
X.	. . . . .	1836, November 20.
XI.	. . . . .	1837, May 14.
XII.	. . . . .	1837, October 22.
XIII.	. . . . .	1837, July 16.
XIV.	. . . . .	1836, October 23.
XV.	. . . . .	1837, December 1(
XVI.	. . . . .	1837, December 25.
XVII.	. . . . .	1837, May 7.
XVIII.	. . . . .	1838, April 22.
XIX.	. . . . .	1836, May 29.
XX.	. . . . .	1836, February 21
XXI.	. . . . .	1838, February 25
XXII.	. . . . .	1837, December 3.
XXIII.	. . . . .	1838, April 15.

Vol. V.	I.	. . . . .	1838, December 2.
Published	II.	. . . . .	1838, November 4.
in 1840.	III.	. . . . .	1839, June 2.
	IV.	. . . . .	1836, December 4.
	V.	. . . .	1839, December 22.
	VI.	. . . . .	1838, September 22.
	VII. (altered)	. . .	1837, March 26.
	VIII.	. . . . .	1838, February 11.
	IX.	. . . . .	1839, February 17.
	X.	. . . . .	1840, January 19.
	XI.	. . . . .	1840, January 12.
	XII.	. . . .	1840, January 26.
	XIII.	. . . . .	1838, March 18.
	XIV.	. . . . .	1838, March 25.
	XV.	. . . . .	1838, April 1.
	XVI.	. . . .	1838, December 16.
	XVII.	. . . . .	1838, December 9.
	XVIII.	. . . . .	1837, September 10.

Sermon		When written or first preached.
XIX.	. . . . .	1839, March 10.
XX.	. . . . .	1839, March 3.
XXI.	. . . . .	1834, October 19.
XXII.	. . . . .	1839, June 9.
XXIII.	. . . . .	1839, February 10.
XXIV.	. . . . .	1840, March 1.

Vol. VI
Published
in 1842

I.	. . . . .	1838, March 4.
II.	. . . . .	1840, March 15.
III.	. . . . .	1841, March 21.
IV.	. . . . .	1840, April 12.
V.	. . . . .	1836, April 26.
VI.	. . . . .	1836, April 1.
VII.	. . . . .	1841, April 9.
VIII.	. . . . .	1839, March 31.
IX.	. . . . .	1837, Nov. 12 and 26.
X.	. . . . .	1838, May 6.
XI.	. . . . .	1838, May 13.
XII.	. . . . .	1841, January 24.
XIII.	. . . . .	1841, February 28.
XIV.	. . . . .	1839, October 5.
XV.	. . . . .	1836 or 1837.
XVI.	. . . . .	1838, May 24.
XVII.	. . . . .	1840, Nov. 29 and Dec. 6.
XVIII.	. . . . .	1840, December 13.
XIX.	. . . . .	1836, November 13.
XX.	. . . . .	1840, September 22.
XXI.	. . . . .	1839, September 23.
XXII.	. . . . .	1837, October 29.
XXIII.	. . . . .	1837, May 21.
XXIV.	. . . . .	Date not known.
XXV.	. . . . .	1839, May 26.

Sermon	When written or first preached
Vol. VII. I.	1832, January 1.
Published II.	1828, July 27.
in 1842-43. III.	1829, March 8.
IV.	1829, March 15.
V. (except pp. 68—70)	1825, January 23.
VI.	1841, January 17.
VII.	1830, March 28.
VIII.	1839, February 24.
IX.	1832, April 15.
X.	1842, March 25.
XI.	1842, January 23.
XII.	1838, May 20 and 27.
XIII.	1840, May 3.
XIV.	1840, May 10.
XV.	1829, December 13.
XVI.	1828, June 15.
XVII.	1829, Nov. 8, 15, and 22
XVIII.	1830, March 21.

These Sermons formed the first half of Vol. V. of Plain Sermons, from Nos. 129 to 146 inclusive.

Vol. VIII. I.	1836, October 30.
Published II.	1839, October 27.
in 1842-43. III.	1841, July 4.
IV.	1837, June 25.
V.	1831, June 26.
VI. (re-written)	1830, May 2.
VII.	1830, September 5.
VIII. (except a sentence in p. 121)	1825, December 18.
IX.	1830, September 12.
X.	1840, March 29.
XI.	1836, November 1.

Sermon	When written or first preached.
XII.	1830, October 28.
XIII.	1830, October 17.
XIV.	1830, October 31.
XV.	1832, January 25.
XVI.	1843, April 30.
XVII. (re-written) .	1825, December 25.
XVIII.	1836, March 13.

These Sermons form the second half of Vol. V. of Plain Sermons from **Nos. 147 to 164** inclusive.

SERMONS ON SUBJECTS OF THE DAY.

Sermon	When written or first preached
I.	1842, January 23.
II.	1842, October 16.
III.	1843, February 26.
IV.	1842, October 30.
V.	1840, December 25.
VI.	1838, November 25.
VII.	1838, November 18.
VIII.	1837, January 1.
IX.	1842, May 1.
X.	1843, June 4.
XI.	1831, May 22.
XII.	1841, June 13.
XIII.	1836, August 14.
XIV.	1842, November 13.
XV.	1842, November 20.
XVI.	1842, November 27.
XVII.	1842, December 4.
XVIII.	1840, May 31.
XIX.	1843, February 5 or 12.
XX.	1843, February 19.
XXI.	1841, November 28.

Sermon		When written or first preached.
XXII.	. . . .	1841, December 5.
XXIII.	. . . .	1841, December 19.
XXIV.	. . . .	1841, December 12.
XXV.	. . . .	1842, September 22.
XXVI.	. . . .	1843, September 25.

PAROCHIAL AND PLAIN SERMONS.

Dates of writing or first preaching.		Volume	Sermon
1825	January 23 (except pp. 68 to 70) . .	VII.	5
	June 12	I.	4
	December 18 (except a sentence in p.121)	VIII.	8
	December 25 (re-written)	VIII.	17
1826	August	I.	1
1828	June 15	VII.	16
	July 27	VII.	2
1829	March 8.	VII.	3
	March 15	VII.	4
	May 24	I.	15
	June 14	I.	16
	July 19	III.	1
	November 8, 15, and 22	VII.	17
	November 29	III.	14
	December 13	VII.	15
	December 20 (expanded into two) . .	{ I.	19
		I.	20
1830	February 21	III.	6
	March 21	VII.	18
	March 28	VII.	7
	May 2 (re-written)	VIII.	6
	May 9 (re-written)	III.	2
	May 16	III.	3
	May 23	III.	4
	August 1	III.	5

Dates of writing or first preaching.	Volume	Sermon
1835 February 22	III.	24
March 8	III.	12
March 22	IV.	4
April 5	III.	9
April 12	III.	10
May 3	III.	11
May 17	III.	15
May 24	III.	20
October 25	III.	16
November 1	III.	25
November 8	III.	18
November 15	III.	19
1836 February 21	IV.	20
March 13	VIII.	18
March 20	IV.	3
March 27	IV.	6
April 1	VI.	6
April 26	VI.	5
May 29	IV.	19
June 12	IV.	8
October 23	IV.	14
October 30	VIII.	1
November 1	VIII.	11
November 6	IV.	9
November 13	VI.	19
November 20	IV.	10
December 4	V.	4
This year or next	VI.	15
1837 March 26 (altered)	V.	7
April 2	IV.	2
April 30	IV.	5
May 7	IV.	17
May 14	IV.	11
May 21	VI.	23
June 25	VIII.	4

SERMONS ON SUBJECTS OF THE DAY.

THE END.

Edinburgh University Press:

T. AND A. CONSTABLE, PRINTERS TO HER MAJESTY.

A
SELECT LIST OF WORKS

PUBLISHED BY

LONGMANS, GREEN, & CO.

LONDON, NEW YORK, AND BOMBAY.

MESSRS. LONGMANS, GREEN, & CO.

Issue the undermentioned Catalogues and Lists of their Publications, any of which may be had post free on application :—

1. MONTHLY LIST OF NEW BOOKS AND NEW EDITIONS.

2. QUARTERLY LIST OF ANNOUNCEMENTS AND NEW BOOKS.

3. NOTES ON BOOKS: BEING AN ANALYSIS OF THE WORKS PUBLISHED BY MESSRS. LONGMANS, GREEN & CO. DURING EACH QUARTER.

4. SCIENTIFIC AND TECHNICAL BOOKS.

5. MEDICAL AND SURGICAL BOOKS.

6. EDUCATIONAL AND SCHOOL BOOKS.

7. EDUCATIONAL BOOKS RECENTLY PUBLISHED.

8. BOOKS FOR ELEMENTARY SCHOOLS AND PUPIL TEACHERS.

9. BOOKS FOR SCHOOL PRIZES.

10. BOOKS FOR CHRISTMAS AND NEW YEAR PRESENTS.

11. THEOLOGICAL BOOKS (CHURCH OF ENGLAND).

12. THEOLOGICAL BOOKS (ROMAN CATHOLIC).

13. BOOKS IN GENERAL LITERATURE AND GENERAL THEOLOGY.

CARDINAL NEWMAN'S WORKS.

Parochial and Plain Sermons. Edited by REV. W. J. COPELAND, B.D., late Rector of Farnham, Essex. 8 vols. Sold separately. Crown 8vo. Cabinet Edition, 5s. each; Popular Edition, 3s. 6d. each.

CONTENTS OF VOL. I.:—Holiness necessary for Future Blessedness—The Immortality of the Soul—Knowledge of God's Will without Obedience—Secret Faults—Self-Denial the Test of Religious Earnestness—The Spiritual Mind—Sins of Ignorance and Weakness—God's Commandments not Grievous—The Religious Use of Excited Feelings—Profession without Practice—Profession without Hypocrisy—Profession without Ostentation—Promising without Doing—Religious Emotion—Religious Faith Rational—The Christian Mysteries—The Self-Wise Inquirer—Obedience the Remedy for Religious Perplexity—Times of Private Prayer—Forms of Private Prayer—The Resurrection of the Body—Witnesses of the Resurrection—Christian Reverence—The Religion of the Day—Scripture a Record of Human Sorrow—Christian Manhood.

CONTENTS OF VOL. II.:—The World's Benefactors—Faith without Sight—The Incarnation—Martyrdom—Love of Relations and Friends—The Mind of Little Children—Ceremonies of the Church—The Glory of the Christian Church—St. Paul's Conversion viewed in Reference to his Office—Secrecy and Suddenness of Divine Visitations—Divine Decrees—The Reverence Due to the Blessed Virgin Mary—Christ, a Quickening Spirit—Saving Knowledge—Self-Contemplation—Religious Cowardice—The Gospel Witnesses—Mysteries in Religion—The Indwelling Spirit—The Kingdom of the Saints—The Gospel, a Trust Committed to us—Tolerance of Religious Error—Rebuking Sin—The Christian Ministry—Human Responsibility—Guilelessness—The Danger of Riches—The Powers of Nature—The Danger of Accomplishments—Christian Zeal—Use of Saints' Days.

CARDINAL NEWMAN'S WORKS.

Parochial and Plain Sermons.—*Continued*.

CONTENTS OF VOL. III.:—Abraham and Lot—Wilfulness of Israel in Rejecting Samuel—Saul—Early Years of David—Jeroboam—Faith and Obedience—Christian Repentance—Contracted Views in Religion—A Particular Providence as revealed in the Gospel—Tears of Christ at the Grave of Lazarus—Bodily Suffering—The Humiliation of the Eternal Son—Jewish Zeal a Pattern to Christians—Submission to Church Authority—Contest between Truth and Falsehood in the Church—The Church Visible and Invisible—The Visible Church and Encouragement to Faith—The Gift of the Spirit—Regenerating Baptism—Infant Baptism—The Daily Service—The Good Part of Mary—Religious Worship a Remedy for Excitements—Intercession—The Intermediate State.

CONTENTS OF VOL IV.:—The Strictness of the Law of Christ—Obedience without Love, as instanced in the Character of Balaam—Moral Consequences of Single Sins—Acceptance of Religious Privileges Compulsory—Reliance on Religious Observances—The Individuality of the Soul—Chastisement amid Mercy—Peace and Joy amid Chastisement—The State of Grace—The Visible Church for the Sake of the Elect—The Communion of Saints—The Church a Home for the Lonely—The Invisible World—The Greatness and Littleness of Human Life—Moral Effects of Communion with God—Christ Hidden from the World—Christ Manifested in Remembrance—The Gainsaying of Korah—The Mysteriousness of our Present Being—The Ventures of Faith—Faith and Love—Watching—Keeping Fast and Festival.

CONTENTS OF VOL. V.:—Worship, a Preparation for Christ's Coming—Reverence, a Belief in God's Presence—Unreal Words—Shrinking from Christ's Coming—Equanimity—Remembrance of Past Mercies—The Mystery of Godliness—The State of Innocence—Christian Sympathy—Righteousness not of us, but in us—The Law of the Spirit—The New Works of the Gospel—The State of Salvation—Transgressions and Infirmities—Sins of Infirmity—Sincerity and Hypocrisy—The Testimony of Conscience—Many called, Few chosen—Present Blessings—Endurance, the Christian's Portion—Affliction, a School of Comfort—The Thought of God, the Stay of the Soul—Love, the One Thing Needful—The Power of the Will.

CONTENTS OF VOL. VI.:—Fasting, a Source of Trial—Life, the Season of Repentance—Apostolic Abstinence, a Pattern for Christians—Christ's Privations, a Meditation for Christians—Christ the Son of God made Man—The Incarnate Son, a Sufferer and Sacrifice—The Cross of Christ the Measure of the World—Difficulty of realising Sacred Privileges—The Gospel Sign Addressed to Faith—The Spiritual Presence of Christ in the Church—The Eucharistic Presence—Faith the Title for Justification—Judaism of the Present Day—The Fellowship of the Apostles—Rising with Christ—Warfare the Condition of Victory—Waiting for Christ—Subjection of the Reason and Feelings to the Revealed Word—The Gospel Palaces—The Visible Temple—Offerings for the Sanctuary—The Weapons of Saints—Faith Without Demonstration—The Mystery of the Holy Trinity—Peace in Believing.

CONTENTS OF VOL. VII.:—The Lapse of Time—Religion, a Weariness to the Natural Man—The World our Enemy—The Praise of Men—Temporal Advantages—The Season of Epiphany—The Duty of Self-Denial—The Yoke of Christ—Moses the Type of Christ—The Crucifixion—Attendance on Holy Communion—The Gospel Feast—Love of Religion, a new Nature—Religion Pleasant to the Religious—Mental Prayer—Infant Baptism—The Unity of the Church—Steadfastness in the Old Paths.

CONTENTS OF VOL. VIII.:—Reverence in Worship—Divine Calls—The Trial of Saul—The Call of David—Curiosity, a Temptation to Sin—Miracles no Remedy for Unbelief—Josiah, a Pattern for the Ignorant—Inward Witness to the Truth of the Gospel—Jeremiah, a Lesson for the Disappointed—Endurance of the World's Censure—Doing Glory to God in Pursuits of the World—Vanity of Human Glory—Truth Hidden when not Sought after—Obedience to God the Way to Faith in Christ—Sudden Conversions—The Shepherd of our Souls—Religious Joy—Ignorance of Evil.

Sermons Preached on Various Occasions. Crown 8vo. Cabinet Edition, 6s.; Popular Edition, 3s. 6d.

CONTENTS:—Intellect the Instrument of Religious Training—The Religion of the Pharisee and the Religion of Mankind—Waiting for Christ—The Secret Power of Divine Grace—Dispositions for Faith—Omnipotence in Bonds—St. Paul's Characteristic Gift—St. Paul's Gift of Sympathy—Christ upon the Waters—The Second Spring—Order, the Witness and Instrument of Unity—The Mission of St. Philip Neri—The Tree beside the Waters—In the World but not of the World—The Pope and the Revolution.

CARDINAL NEWMAN'S WORKS.

Selection, **Adapted to the Seasons of the Ecclesiastical Year**, from the 'Parochial and Plain Sermons.' Edited by the REV. W. J. COPELAND, B.D. Crown 8vo. Cabinet Edition, 5s.; Popular Edition, 3s. 6d.

CONTENTS:—*Advent :* Self-Denial the Test of Religious Earnestness—Divine Calls—The Ventures of Faith—Watching. *Christmas Day* Religious Joy. *New Year's Sunday :* The Lapse of Time. *Epiphany.* Remembrance of Past Mercies—Equanimity—The Immortality of the Soul—Christian Manhood—Sincerity and Hypocrisy—Christian Sympathy. *Septuagesima :* Present Blessings. *Sexagesima :* Endurance, the Christian's Portion. *Quinquagesima :* Love, the One Thing Needful. *Lent :* The Individuality of the Soul—Life, the Season of Repentance—Bodily Suffering—Tears of Christ at the Grave of Lazarus—Christ's Privations, a Meditation for Christians—The Cross of Christ the Measure of the World. *Good Friday :* The Crucifixion. *Easter Day :* Keeping Fast and Festval. *Easter Tide :* Witnesses of the Resurrection—A Particular Providence as revealed in the Gospel—Christ Manifested in Remembrance—The Invisible World—Waiting for Christ. *Ascension :* Warfare the Condition of Victory. *Sunday after Ascension :* Rising with Christ. *Whitsun Day :* The Weapons of Saints. *Trinity Sunday :* The Mysteriousness of our Present Being. *Sundays after Trinity :* Holiness Necessary for|Future Blessedness—The Religious Use of Excited Feelings—The Self-Wise Inquirer—Scripture a Record of Human Sorrow—The Danger of Riches—Obedience without Love, as instanced in the Character of Balaam—Moral Consequences of Single Sins—The Greatness and Littleness of Human Life—Moral Effects of Communion with God—The Thought of God the Stay of the Soul—The Power of the Will—The Gospel Palaces—Religion a Weariness to the Natural Man—The World our Enemy—The Praise of Men—Religion Pleasant to the Religious—Mental Prayer—Curiosity a Temptation to Sin—Miracles no Remedy for Unbelief—Jeremiah, a Lesson for the Disappointed—The Shepherd of our Souls—Doing Glory to God in Pursuits of the World.

Sermons Bearing upon Subjects of the Day. Edited by the REV. W. J. COPELAND, B.D., late Rector of Farnham, Essex. Crown 8vo. Cabinet Edition, 5s.; Popular Edition, 3s. 6d.

CONTENTS:—The Work of the Christian—Saintliness not Forfeited by the Penitent—Our Lord's Last Supper and His First—Dangers to the Penitent—The Three Offices of Christ—Faith and Experience—Faith unto the World—The Church and the World—Indulgence in Religious Privileges—Connection between Personal and Public Improvement—Christian Nobleness—Joshua a Type of Christ and His Followers—Elisha a Type of Christ and His Followers—The Christian Church a Continuation of the Jewish—The Principles of Contiuuity between the Jewish and Christian Churches—The Christian Church an Imperial Power—Sanctity the Token of the Christian Empire—Condition of the Members of the Christian Empire—The Apostolic Christian—Wisdom and Innocence—Invisible Presence of Christ—Outward and Inward Notes of the Church—Grounds for Steadfastness in our Religious Profession—Elijah the Prophet of the Latter Days—Feasting in Captivity—The Parting of Friends.

Fifteen Sermons Preached before the University of Oxford, between A.D. 1826 and 1843. Crown 8vo. Cabinet Edition, 5s.; Popular Edition, 3s. 6d.

CONTENTS:—The Philosophical Temper, first enjoined by the Gospel—The Influence of Natural and Revealed Religion respectively—Evangelical Sanctity the Perfection of Natural Virtue—The Usurpations of Reason—Personal Influence, the Means of Propagating the Truth—On Justice as a Principle of Divine Governance—Contest between Faith and Sight—Human Responsibility, as independent of Circumstances—Wilfulness, the Sin of Saul—Faith and Reason, contrasted as Habits of Mind—The Nature of Faith in Relation to Reason—Love, the Safeguard of Faith against Superstition—Implicit and Explicit Reason—Wisdom, as contrasted with Faith and with Bigotry—The Theory of Developments in Religious Doctrine.

CARDINAL NEWMAN'S WORKS.

Discourses Addressed to Mixed Congregations. Crown 8vo.
Cabinet Edition, 6s.; Popular Edition, 3s. 6d.

CONTENTS:—The Salvation of the Hearer the Motive of the Preacher—Neglect of Divine Calls and Warnings—Men not Angels—The Priests of the Gospel—Purity and Love—Saintliness the Standard of Christian Principle—God's Will the End of Life—Perseverance in Grace—Nature and Grace—Illuminating Grace—Faith and Private Judgment—Faith and Doubt—Prospects of the Catholic Missioner—Mysteries of Nature and of Grace—The Mystery of Divine Condescension—The Infinitude of Divine Attributes—Mental Sufferings of our Lord in His Passion—The Glories of Mary for the Sake of Her Son—On the Fitness of the Glories of Mary.

Lectures on the Doctrine of Justification. Crown 8vo. Cabinet
Edition, 5s.; Popular Edition, 3s. 6d.

CONTENTS:—Faith considered as the Instrumental Cause of Justification—Love considered as the Formal Cause of Justification—Primary Sense of the term 'Justification'—Secondary Senses of the term 'Justification'—Misuse of the term 'Just' or 'Righteous'—The Gift of Righteousness—The Characteristics of the Gift of Righteousness—Righteousness viewed as a Gift and as a Quality—Righteousness the Fruit of our Lord's Resurrection—The Office of Justifying Faith—The Nature of Justifying Faith—Faith viewed relatively to Rites and Works—On Preaching the Gospel—Appendix.

On the Development of Christian Doctrine. Crown 8vo. Cabinet
Edition, 6s.; Popular Edition, 3s. 6d.

On the Idea of a University. Crown 8vo. Cabinet Edition, 7s.;
Popular Edition, 3s. 6d.

An Essay in Aid of a Grammar of Assent. Crown 8vo. Cabinet
Edition, 7s. 6d.; Popular Edition, 3s. 6d.

Two Essays on Miracles. 1. Of Scripture. 2. Of Ecclesiastical
History. Crown 8vo. Cabinet Edition, 6s.; Popular Edition, 3s. 6d.

Discussions and Arguments. Crown 8vo. Cabinet Edition, 6s.;
Popular Edition, 3s. 6d.

1. How to accomplish it. 2. The Antichrist of the Fathers. 3. Scripture and the Creed. 4. Tamworth Reading-room. 5. Who's to Blame? 6. An Argument for Christianity.

Essays, Critical and Historical. 2 vols. Crown 8vo. Cabinet
Edition, 12s.; Popular Edition, 7s.

1. Poetry. 2. Rationalism. 3. Apostolic Tradition. 4. De la Mennais. 5. Palmer on Faith and Unity. 6. St. Ignatius. 7. Prospects of the Anglican Church. 8. The Anglo-American Church. 9. Countess of Huntingdon. 10. Catholicity of the Anglican Church. 11. The Antichrist of Protestants. 12. Milman's Christianity. 13. Reformation of the XI. Century. 14. Private Judgment. 15. Davison. 16. Keble.

Apologia pro Vita Sua. Crown 8vo. Cabinet Edition, 6s.; Popular
Edition, 3s. 6d.

Verses on Various Occasions. Crown 8vo. Cabinet Edition, 6s.;
Popular Edition, 3s. 6d.

CARDINAL NEWMAN'S WORKS.

Historical Sketches. 3 vols. Crown 8vo. Cabinet Edition, 6s. each; Popular Edition, 3s. 6d.

1. The Turks. 2. Cicero. 3. Apollonius. 4. Primitive Christianity. 5. Church of the Fathers. 6. St. Chrysostom. 7. Theodoret. 8. St. Benedict. 9. Benedictine Schools. 10. Universities. 11. Northmen and Normans. 12. Mediæval Oxford. 13. Convocation of Canterbury.

The Arians of the Fourth Century. Crown 8vo. Cabinet Edition, 6s.; Popular Edition, 3s. 6d.

Select Treatises of St. Athanasius in Controversy with the Arians. Freely translated. 2 vols. Crown 8vo. Cabinet Edition, 15s.; Popular Edition, 7s.

Theological Tracts. Crown 8vo. Cabinet Edition, 8s.; Popular Edition, 3s. 6d.

1. Dissertatiunculæ. 2. On the Text of the Seven Epistles of St. Ignatius. 3. Doctrinal Causes of Arianism. 4. Apollinarianism. 5. St. Cyril's Formula. 6. Ordo de Tempore. 7. Douay Version of Scriptures.

The Via Media of the Anglican Church. 2 Vols. Crown 8vo. Cabinet Edition, 6s. each; Popular Edition, 3s. 6d. each.

Vol. I. Prophetical Office of the Church.

Vol. II. Occasional Letters and Tracts.

Certain Difficulties felt by Anglicans in Catholic Teaching Considered. 2 vols.

Vol. I. Twelve Lectures. Crown 8vo. Cabinet Edition, 7s. 6d.; Popular Edition, 3s. 6d.

Vol. II. Letters to Dr. Pusey concerning the Blessed Virgin, and to the Duke of Norfolk in defence of the Pope and Council. Crown 8vo. Cabinet Edition, 5s. 6d.; Popular Edition, 3s. 6d.

Present Position of Catholics in England. Crown 8vo. Cabinet Edition, 7s. 6d.; Popular Edition, 3s. 6d.

Loss and Gain. The Story of a Convert. Crown 8vo. Cabinet Edition, 6s.; Popular Edition, 3s. 6d.

Callista. A Tale of the Third Century. Crown 8vo. Cabinet Edition, 6s.; Popular Edition, 3s. 6d.

The Dream of Gerontius. 16mo, sewed, 6d.; cloth, 1s.

Meditations and Devotions. Part I. Meditations for the Month of May. Novena of St. Philip. Part II. The Stations of the Cross. Meditations and Intercessions for Good Friday. Litanies, etc. Part III. Meditations on Christian Doctrine. Conclusion. Oblong Crown 8vo. 5s. *net.*

1923

FOUARD.--Th. Christr, The Son of God. A . . s of Our Lord
and Saviour Jesus Christ. By the ABBÉ CONSTANT FOUARD,
Honorary Cathedral Canon, Professor of the Faculty of Theology
at Rouen, etc., etc. Translated from the Fifth Edition with the
Author's sanction. By GEORGE F. X. GRIFFITH. With an
Introduction by CARDINAL MANNING. Third Edition. With
3 Maps. 2 vols. Crown 8vo. 14s.

"In erudition the author is to the full up to the level of any writers, Catholic or
Protestant, who have as yet attempted the same task, while his reliableness in matters
of dogma gives him an enormous scientific advantage over non-Catholics."—*Dublin Review.*

Saint Peter and the First Years of Christianity. By the
ABBÉ CONSTANT FOUARD. Translated by GEORGE F. X. GRIFFITH.
Crown 8vo. 9s.

St. Paul and His Missions. By the ABBÉ CONSTANT FOUARD.
Translated, with the Author's sanction and co-operation, by GEORGE
F. X. GRIFFITH. With 2 Maps. Crown 8vo. 9s.

[A newspaper clipping is pasted over part of the page, obscuring some text.]

A 16TH CENTURY PETITION.

TO THE EDITOR OF THE TIMES.

Sir,—The extraordinary coincidence of the words of a prayer—ascribed to the 16th century —used at the funeral of Lord Grenfell, as described in your issue of the 2nd inst., and the closing passage of Cardinal Newman's sermon, preached by him as vicar of St. Mary's, Oxford, and first published in 1843, must strike every one. What is the history of the prayer? The following is an extract from the published book of Sermons, the first edition of which lies open in front of me :—

Sermons Bearing on Subjects of the Day. Sermon XX. WISDOM AND INNOCENCE. p. 307. Let us beg Him to stand by us in trouble, and guide us on our dangerous way. May He, as of old, choose " the foolish things of the world to confound the wise, and the weak things of the world to confound the things which are mighty!" May He support us all the day long, till the shades lengthen, and the evening comes, and the busy world is hushed, and the fever of life is over, and our work is done! Then in His mercy may He give us a safe lodging and a holy rest, and peace at the last!

Your obedient servant,
G. AMBROSE LEE.
Heralds' College, Feb. 5. 1925

[Partially visible text from the underlying page, right side:]

. By H. L.

being the Life Crown 8vo.

SIDNEY LEAR.

l Sketch. By

the Rev. Père SIDNEY LEAR.

of Louis XV., n. By H. L.

1 Century in 1 Cardinal de Jacques Olier.

eneva. By H.

., Professeur de l'Académie H. L. SIDNEY

LEAR. With Portrait. Crown 8vo. 3s. 6d.

DRANE—A Memoir of Mother Francis Raphael O.S.D. (Augusta Theodosia Drane), some time Prioress Provincial of the Congregation of Dominican Sisters of S. Catherine of Siena, Stone. With some of her Spiritual Notes and Letters. Edited by Rev. Father BERTRAND WILBERFORCE, O.P. With Portrait. Crown 8vo. 7s. 6d.

The History of St. Dominic, Founder of the Friar Preachers. By AUGUSTA THEODORA DRANE, author of "The History of St. Catherine of Siena and her Companions." With 32 Illustrations. 8vo. 15s.

FÉNELON.—Spiritual Letters to Men. By ARCHBISHOP FÉNELON. Translated by H. L. SIDNEY LEAR, author of "Life of Fénelon," "Life of S. Francis de Sales," etc. etc. 16mo. 2s. 6d.

Spiritual Letters to Women. By ARCHBISHOP FÉNELON. Translated by H. L. SIDNEY LEAR, author of "Life of Fenelon," "Life of S. Francis de Sales," etc. etc. 16mo. 2s. 6d.

GIBSON.—The Abbé de Lamennais and the Liberal Catholic Movement in France. By the Hon. W. GIBSON. With Portrait. 8vo. 12s. 6d.

JAMESON—Works by MRS. JAMESON:

Sacred and Legendary Art. With 19 Etchings and 197 Woodcuts. 2 vols. Cloth, gilt top. 20s. *net.*

Legends of the Madonna: The Virgin Mary as Represented in Sacred and Legendary Art. With 27 Etchings and 165 Woodcuts. 1 vol. Cloth, gilt top. 10s. *net.* .

Legends of the Monastic Orders. With 11 Etchings and 88 Woodcuts. 1 vol. Cloth, gilt top. 10s. *net.*

History of the Saviour, His Types and Precursors. Completed by LADY EASTLAKE. With 13 Etchings and 281 Woodcuts. 2 vols. Cloth, gilt top. 20s. *net.*

LYONS.—Christianity or Infallibility—Both or Neither. By the Rev. DANIEL LYONS. Crown 8vo. 5s.

RIVINGTON.—The Primitive Church and the See of Peter. By the Rev. LUKE RIVINGTON, D.D. With an Introduction by the CARDINAL ARCHBISHOP OF WESTMINSTER. 8vo. 16s.

SODERINI.—Socialism and Catholicism. From the Italian of COUNT EDWARD SODERINI. By RICHARD JENERY-SHEE of the Inner Temple. With a Preface by CARDINAL VAUGHAN. Crown 8vo. 6s.

TYRRELL.—Nova et Vetera: Informal Meditations for Times of Spiritual Dryness. By GEORGE TYRRELL, S.J. Crown 8vo. 6s.

MANUALS OF CATHOLIC PHILOSOPHY.
(Stonyhurst Series.)
EDITED BY RICHARD F. CLARKE, S.J.

Logic. By RICHARD F. CLARKE, S.J., D.D. Crown 8vo. 5s.

First Principles of Knowledge. By JOHN RICKABY, S.J. Crown 8vo. 5s.

Moral Philosophy (Ethics and Natural Law). By JOSEPH RICKABY, S.J. Crown 8vo. 5s.

General Metaphysics. By JOHN RICKABY, S.J. Crown 8vo. 5s.

Psychology. By MICHAEL MAHER, S.J. Crown 8vo. 6s. 6d.

Natural Theology. By BERNARD BOEDDER, S.J. Crown 8vo. 6s. 6d.

Political Economy. By CHARLES S. DEVAS. Crown 8vo. 6s. 6d.

ENGLISH MANUALS OF CATHOLIC THEOLOGY.

Outlines of Dogmatic Theology. By SYLVESTER JOSEPH HUNTER, of the Society of Jesus. Crown 8vo. 3 vols., 6s. 6d. each.

LONDON, NEW YORK, AND BOMBAY:
LONGMANS, GREEN, & CO.

5000/8/97